MW01487813

Oracle R12 Applications DBA Field Guide

Elke Phelps

with

Contributing Authors, Paul Jackson and Norman Leach

Technical Reviewer, Srini Chavali

Foreword, Steven Chan

Oracle R12 Applications DBA Field Guide

Copyright © 2010 Elke Phelps

ISBN 1-45374-273-5

EAN-13 978-1-45374-273-0

Lead Author: Elke Phelps

Contributing Authors: Paul Jackson and Norman Leach

Technical Reviewer: Srini Chavali

Foreword Author: Steven Chan

Project Manager: Elke Phelps

Chief Editor: Elke Phelps

Lead Copy Editor: Norman Leach

Cover Designer: Elke Phelps and Richard L. Benton, Ph.D.

Publisher: Coqui Tech and Press, LLC (www.coquitechandpress.com)

Partner: Oracle Applications User Group (www.oaug.org)

Elke's Photographer: Jay May Photography (www.jaymayphoto.com)

Contents

Detailed Table of Contents v
About the Author xiii
About the Contributors xv
About the Partnership xvii
About the Publisher... xix
Acknowledgments... xxi
Foreword xxiii
Introduction... xxv

Chapter 1 ▪ Services and Architecture... 1
Chapter 2 ▪ Configuration.. 17
Chapter 3 ▪ Installation and Cloning 63
Chapter 4 ▪ Toolkit 85
Chapter 5 ▪ Patching and Upgrading.. 139
Chapter 6 ▪ Monitoring and Troubleshooting............................... 179
Chapter 7 ▪ Performance Tuning 203
Chapter 8 ▪ Resources.. 237

Appendix... 257
Index 277

Detailed Table of Contents

Chapter 1 ▪ Services and Architecture............................…..……….…....1

Servicing User Requests 2
   Client Tier 3
   Application Tier 3
      Web and Forms Services 4
      Concurrent Processing 5
   Database Tier 5
Oracle Applications Architecture 6
   Fundamental Architecture.. 6
   Advanced Architecture 7
      Load Balancing Web and Forms Services 8
      Parallel Concurrent Processing 9
      Unified APPL_TOP 9
      Shared Application Tier Filesystem............................. 10
      Distributed AD.. 11
      Oracle Data Guard 11
      Oracle Real Application Clusters................................. 11
      Mixed Platform Architecture 11
      Providing Internet Access.. 12
      Oracle Application Server Web Cache...........................13
      Secure Sockets Layer..13
Architecture Best Practices...14

Chapter 2 ▪ Configuration...17

Context Files 18
Application Tier Filesystems and Environment 19
   Defining APPS_BASE 20
   Defining APPL_TOP 20
   Defining COMMON_TOP 21
   Defining INST_TOP.. 22
   Applications Technology Stack 23
      Java Tech Stack...24
      Tools Tech Stack..24
   Additional Environment Files.................................. 25
   Administering the Database Connection File 25
   Web and Forms Services Configuration 26
   Concurrent Processing Configuration........................ 29
   Review of Key Application Tier Filesystem Concepts.... 31
Database Tier Filesystems and Configuration 33
   Database Tier Technology Stack 33
   Database Data 34
   Review of Key Database Tier Filesystem Concepts...... 35
   Database Initialization Parameters........................... 36
   Reviewing Database Initialization Parameters 40
   APPS Schema 40
Port Numbering.. 41
   Oracle Port Pools 41
   Developing a Port Standard 41
   Testing Port Availability....................................... 44
Context Files and AutoConfig 44
   Locating and Creating the Applications Context File..... 44
   Locating and Creating the Database Context File 45
   Using OAM... 46
   Using AutoConfig... 47
   Executing AutoConfig 48
   Location of AutoConfig Log Files............................. 52
   Location of AutoConfig Backup Files........................ 52
   Reviewing AutoConfig Execution Changes 53
   Using AutoConfig Performance Profiler 54
   Deploying Customizations with AutoConfig................ 55

Customizing Template Files 55
Adding Customizations Using Oracle Applications Manager 55
Securing Oracle Applications 58
Applications Password Verification 58
Database Password Verification 59
Configuration Best Practices.. 60

Chapter 3 ▪ Installation and Cloning...................................63

Oracle Applications Installations.. 63
Rapid Install 64
Types of Installations.. 65
Rapid Install Log Files.. 78
Installation Documentation.. 79
Rapid Clone 79
Using Rapid Clone to Clone an Oracle Applications Instance 80
Post Cloning Steps 82
Installation and Cloning Best Practices 83

Chapter 4 ▪ Toolkit...85

Oracle Applications Utilities and Commands.................................. 86
Startup and Shutdown Scripts.. 86
Performing Admin Tasks with AD Administration...................... 91
Relinking Applications Executables 94
Regenerating Forms, Libraries and Menus 96
Recompiling JavaServer Pages 97
Adding Products with AD Splicer 100
Licensing products with License Manager 100
Creating a system report with adutconf.sql................................ 101
Changing Application, Oracle and System Passwords.................. 102
Determining Component Versions 105
Identifying Applications File Versions.................................... 106
Identifying Applications Component Versions 106
Oracle HTTP Server Version.................................... 108
Oracle Forms Version.. 109
Java Class File Version.. 109
Database Version 110

UNIX Tips and Commands 112
  Understanding and Setting the Environment 112
  Understanding and Using X Windows 113
  Getting Help for UNIX Commands 113
  Using Common UNIX Commands 114
  Finding and Removing Memory Segments and Semaphores 121
  Finding and Removing Print Jobs 123
  Removing Database Sessions 124
  User Related UNIX Commands 125
  Server Related UNIX Commands 125
Preventative Maintenance 126
  Gathering Statistics 126
  Recompiling Invalid Objects 129
  Stopping and Restarting the Oracle HTTP Server 130
  Performing Routine Purging 130
Scheduling Scripts 135
Toolkit Best Practices 138

Chapter 5 ▪ Patching and Upgrading 139

Oracle Critical Patch Updates 140
Oracle Applications Patching 140
  Types of Applications Patches 141
  Preparing to Patch 142
  Description of Patch Drivers 144
  Documenting the Patching Process 144
  Applying Applications Patches 146
  Patching Related Features in OAM 163
Technology Stack Components Patching and Upgrades 171
  Oracle Application Server Patching and Upgrades 172
  Oracle Database Patching and Upgrades 172
  Additional Components to Upgrade 175
    Upgrading JDK 176
    Upgrading the Sun JRE Plug-in 176
Patching and Upgrading Best Practices 176

Chapter 6 ▪ Monitoring and Troubleshooting...........................179

Server Monitoring and Troubleshooting... 180
    Monitoring availability 180
    Monitoring resource consumption 181
    Monitoring setup... 182
Application Tier Monitoring and Troubleshooting........................... 183
    Web and Forms Services 183
    Concurrent Manager 187
    Using Oracle Applications Manager (OAM) Features 190
    Using Oracle Applications Diagnostics.. 190
    Using EM Grid Control 190
Database Tier 192
    Database Log Files.. 192
    Database Availability.. 193
    Database Session Monitoring 193
    Additional Database Monitoring... 194
    Using Oracle11g Diagnostic Features 195
    Using EM Grid Control 195
Additional Monitoring and Troubleshooting 196
    Client Java Cache Location and Removal 196
    Monitoring Changes to the Environment...................................... 196
    Turning off Debugging Options.. 198
    Network Monitoring 198
Monitoring and Troubleshotting Best Practices 200

Chapter 7 ▪ Performance and Tuning...203

Performance Tuning Process 204
    Identifying Performance Issues.. 204
    Developing an Action Plan 206
Tools for Identifying and Resolving Performance Issues................. 207
    Server Tuning.. 207
    Application Tier Tuning 213
        Apache Tuning... 214
        JVM Tuning... 214
        Forms Tuning... 215
        Concurrent Manager Configuration Recommendations 217

Concurrent Manager Tuning.. 218
Database Tier Tuning... 219
Using Automatic Workload Repository...................................... 219
Using Automatic Database Diagnostics Monitoring 224
Using Active Session History 226
Analyzing the AWR Report.. 227
Analyzing SQL Statements in Oracle11g................................... 227
Using EM Grid Control 229
Client Tuning 229
Resource Utilization... 229
Generating Trace Files 230
Exiting Client Sessions Properly 230
Using the Client System Analyser 230
Manually Analyzing the Client.. 231
Network Latency.. 232
Additional Tuning Considerations 233
Performance Tuning Best Practices....................................... 235

Chapter 8 ▪ Resources..237

Working with Oracle Support.. 238
My Oracle Support.. 238
Dashboard 238
Knowledge Home 239
Search Knowledge Base 241
Advanced Searches 241
Certification Matrix 242
Locating and Downloading Patches.. 243
Oracle Support Service Requests... 245
Details for an SR.. 245
SR Severity Level 246
Creating an SR.. 246
Managing an SR.. 247
My Oracle Support Training Center 250
User Communities and Conferences... 250
User Groups 250
Conferences.. 251

Online Resources 252
   Oracle Web Sites.. 252
   Additional Community Resources.............................. 253
Books and Periodicals.. 254
   Books 254
   Periodicals.. 254
Resources Best Practices.. 255

Appendix.. 257
Index 277

About the Author

Elke Phelps

 is an Oracle Certified Professional and Technical Architect focusing on Oracle Applications deployments. Elke's experience with Oracle Technology began in 1993. Her primary areas of expertise include Oracle Database and E-Business Suite deployments and upgrades, platform migrations and infrastructure design. She has an MBA with concentration in Finance and B.Sc. in Computer Science.

Elke's professional experience includes working for government agencies, small startup firms, as well as Fortune 500 and Fortune 100 companies. She has experience deploying technical solutions to support various lines of business including technical publications, financial services, software engineering, wholesale distribution and healthcare. She is a proven team leader with experience managing a diverse team of employees, contractors and consultants.

Elke's advocacy of Oracle Technology through the publication of the first edition of the Oracle Applications DBA Field Guide (Apress, 2006), the publication of white papers, leadership of the Oracle E-Business Applications Technology Special Interest Group (SIG) and presentations at Oracle conferences since 2004 has earned her the designation of Oracle ACE in 2007 and Oracle ACE Director in 2009. Elke is passionate about teaching people how to adopt and deploy Oracle technology in order to provide strategic business solutions. She is a contributor to the blog hosted at http://www.fieldappsdba.com.

In her spare time, Elke enjoys spending time with her husband, Richard, her cats, Thelonious and Ella and her family and friends. Elke and Richard enjoy traveling especially to Europe, Puerto Rico and the amazing US National Parks. Elke also enjoys hiking, antiquing, gardening and cooking.

About the Contributors

Contributing Authors

Paul Jackson

is an Oracle Applications DBA with over 9 years experience administering Human Resources and Financial modules. He has been actively involved in the user community, including serving as Program Director of the Oracle E-Business Applications Technology SIG with the Oracle Applications User Group. He has presented at multiple conferences and coauthored the first edition of Oracle Applications DBA Field Guide. Prior to working with Oracle Applications, Paul worked as an Oracle DBA and software developer. Paul lives in Louisville, KY with his wife Sarah. Outside of work he enjoys reading, watching movies, exercising and playing poker.

Norman Leach

is an Oracle Certified Professional whose Oracle development experience began in 2001. He has worked in an Oracle Applications DBA role since 2004. He is an active member of the OAUG, speaking at various conferences and serving as the Web master for the OAUG the Oracle E-Business Applications Technology SIG.

Technical Reviewer

Srini Chavali

 has over 25 years of experience in the IT industry during which he has held various IT roles, from consultant to developer to DBA to Apps DBA to manager, and is currently employed by Cummins Inc. as an IT Director.

Srini was introduced to Oracle while employed by Toys"R"Us in 1993 where Oracle 7.1 was being rolled out. After joining Cummins in 1998, Srini started working with Oracle Applications versions 10.4 and 10.7. He was the DBA lead of the implementations of Financial and HR systems (versions 11.5.5 through 11.5.10) at Cummins. In his current role, he leads a team of Apps DBAs that provide all facets of support for the many installations of E-Business Suite in Cummins worldwide.

Srini is also the Vice President of the Oracle E-Business Applications Technology SIG (http://mwsig.oaug.org). He has been a presenter and panel member at COLLABORATE and North Central OAUG GEO (http://www.ncoaug.org) conferences. He is also a contributor to the Field Apps DBA blog (http://www.fieldappsdba.com).

About the Partnership

In keeping with its mission to provide a global forum for sharing information and experience, the Oracle Applications Users Group (OAUG) has partnered with Elke Phelps on the release of the *Oracle R12 Applications DBA Field Guide*. It is through partnerships such as this that the OAUG continues to foster an environment of collaboration and learning.

Formed in 1990, the OAUG is one of the software industry's most successful users groups, serving to increase knowledge, productivity and return on investment for users of Oracle Applications. Visit the OAUG website at http://www.oaug.org for more information.

About the Publisher

Coqui Tech & Press specializes in providing Oracle Applications services, training and publications. Visit the company's website at http://www.coquitechandpress.com for additional details.

XX

Acknowledgments

By Elke

Much time, energy and commitment are required to undertake a book project. My thanks to my husband, Richard, who even with the understanding of an author's required time obligation encouraged me to write the second edition of the guide. Without his support, you would not be reading this book today. Richard - *thank you* for your continued support, patience and love.

All too often we forget about the people who molded our young minds and challenged us to do great things. It is with much appreciation that I thank my former teachers, coaches and mentors, especially Mrs. Cruce, Jim S., and Mr. A., who taught me not only text book lessons, but life lessons. A special thank you to Jenni from OHS Class of '89; it has been fun getting reconnected. Thank you for continuing to be my cheerleader.

Through my engagement in the Oracle user community, I have had the privilege to meet a number of great Oracle Technologists who also happen to be exceptional people. To Nadia, Steven, Sandra, Mike, Debra, Floyd, Ron, Basheer and James, thanks for making the conferences such special experiences. The conference *high* is only as high as it is because of you. It is because of you that I challenge myself to be a better technologist, presenter and listener.

This book is dedicated to Jerry and Gerda, two people from two very different worlds, who along with my mom taught me the importance of values and strength of character. It is because of them that I strive to be a better person. They are greatly missed.

Special thanks to the book contributors, Paul, Norm and Srini. I thank you for your effort, dedication and commitment to this project. The content and quality of the guide is all the better because of you.

By Paul

I have been fortunate to have had many positive influences in my life. These people have encouraged me to be a better person. My parents, Paul and Mary Ann, have always been great examples for me. Ultimately, my successes are due to their influence. In school, Kevin Barnes taught me it was fun to be smart. Early in my career, David Skelton and Jason Driver demonstrated commitment to a successful work life. Currently, Elke, Norman, Srini and Sandra continue to provide examples of how to behave in a professional manner. Many thanks to all of these people. Lastly, I have also been fortunate to find a true partner in my life. My wife, Sarah, acts as an inspiration on how to behave outside of work. I thank her for her assistance with all other aspects of my life. Her patience and understanding were great assets in completing this book.

By Norm

Thanks to Elke, for seeing the value I could add by switching from developer to DBA, for giving me opportunities to grow in my role and for involving me in the latest edition of this book. You make my job challenging, but possible.

Paul, it would be hard to find a better co-worker; your dedication to quality work, and ability to have fun while doing it, has been refreshing. I've learned a lot working with you.

To Sydney, I love our Daddy/Daughter times together. Thank you for the laughter you bring to Mommy and me.

To Jenn, life is great with you. I love you and am thankful for our years together. Thank you for your encouragement, commitment and love.

Foreword

By Steven Chan

I consider myself lucky to be a regular speaker at conferences such as Oracle OpenWorld and OAUG/COLLABORATE. These are very special events where members of the E-Business Suite community share their latest experiences with each other. As part of the E-Business Suite development division, I like to drop in on sessions presented by EBS system administrators to get insights into our users' experiences with our products.

After her session many years ago, Elke pressed a slim book into my hands. "You might find this interesting," she said. "It's hot off the presses." It was the first edition of the book that you're reading now.

I consider it rude to refuse a gift, so I thanked her and slipped it into my laptop bag. Looking back, I don't think I ever really intended to read it. In my ever-changing set of responsibilities at Oracle, I find myself spending more time than I'd like sifting through our own formal documentation and manuals. Reading a third-party version of our documentation didn't seem like something that I would ever find the time to do.

As it turns out, the book was slim enough to stay in my bag for my flight home. Having exhausted the entertainment potential of the latest SkyMall catalog, I started flipping through this book. That's when I realized that I was reading something unusual.

Before I continue, I have a confession to make. A common complaint about software is that it's poorly-documented. I confess that I think that this complaint is unwarranted in the case of the E-Business Suite's technology stack. If anything, I think that we have too much documentation spread over too many manuals, a situation that is further complicated by the plethora of Knowledge Base Notes that seems to expand on a daily-basis.

So, back to the plane and my first reading of this book...As I quickly paged through it, I realized that Elke, Paul, and their first edition reviewers Sandra and Srini, had somehow managed to distill hundreds -- if not thousands -- of pages of the relevant Oracle manuals, release notes, ReadMes, Knowledge Base documents, and their own hard-won expertise, into a dense but remarkably-compact volume.

It wasn't comprehensive by any means, and didn't claim to be. That was its strength. It was able to see the forest for the trees. It touched on nearly everything important that a DBA would really need to know about administering an Oracle E-Business Suite environment without drowning the reader in unnecessary details...

...and it was small enough to fit into a laptop bag.

I've gotten a chance to know Elke, Paul, Norman, and Srini better over the years. As a group, they are often the first to adopt new technologies in their EBS environments. I've grown to respect and value their expertise highly, and admire their ongoing efforts to share that with the rest of the EBS community.

They have done an excellent job with this second edition, which has been refreshed and expanded without losing its concise and practical focus. You hold the product of many years of experience in your hands, one that I expect will save you countless hours of arduous research and painful experimentation.

Enjoy!

Steven Chan
Oracle E-Business Suite Development

Steven Chan is a Senior Director in the Oracle Applications Technology Group (ATG). The Applications Technology Group is responsible for the Oracle E-Business Suite technology stack. Steven manages EBS technology stack certifications, ATG product management, ATG documentation and curriculum teams, and ATG Quality Assurance in the E-Business Suite Development division. You can email Steven directly at: steven.chan@oracle.com

Introduction

The *Oracle R12 Applications DBA Field Guide* includes the necessary information to administer Oracle E-Business Suite Release 12 and the underlying technology stack based upon Oracle 10gAS and Oracle Database 11g. Included in this guide are topics ranging from architecture, configuration, installation, cloning, patching, monitoring, troubleshooting to performance tuning.

Incorporated in this guide are time-proven best practices for administering the highly complex Oracle E-Business Suite. In addition, best practices for administering and deploying the Oracle E-Business Suite are provided. Also included are proven tips and techniques for Oracle Applications DBAs. Many of the tips that are contained in this guide are unpublished essentials that will benefit every Oracle Applications DBA.

It is impossible to provide in-depth details for this complex system in a small reference manual; however, the objective of this guide is to provide the most critical information required to provide a stable, proactively managed system. As such, it will serve as a useful supplement to the exiting documentation for the Oracle E-Business Suite. All of the information provided is presented in a format that is easy to read and quick to navigate. This, the second edition of the Oracle Applications DBA Field Guide, continues to focus on its niche market of being an inexpensive, concise guide for Oracle Applications DBAs.

Chapter 1

Services and Architecture

The Oracle E-Business Suite, also known as Oracle Applications, is a complex Enterprise Resource Planning (ERP) program that consists of many service components. The components that support the Oracle Applications Architecture are deployed on a logical three tier architecture that consists of the client, application and database tiers.

This chapter will focus on describing services and functions for each of the three tiers as well as the deployments of simple architectures to advanced architectures and configurations. This chapter will focus on the following topics:

* **Oracle Applications tiers:** An in-depth look at each tier and the services that comprise the Oracle Applications Logical Architecture. The logical architecture includes the client tier, the application tier, and the database tier.

* **Oracle Applications architecture:** A look at the physical architecture of the E-Business Suite from basic to advanced, complex configurations. This includes describing a multi-node application tier deployed with a Unified **APPL_TOP** and Shared Application Tier Filesystem. This section will also discuss multi-node database tier deployments using Oracle Data Guard and Oracle Real Application Clusters (RAC). Additional advanced architecture topics include information regarding a Mixed Platform Architecture, proxy servers, external application servers, Secure Socket Layer (SSL) Encryption, and Oracle Application Server Web Cache.

In addition to the primary components identified so far, there are many other components of the E-Business Suite architecture, including networking infrastructure, servers, routers, and load balancing devices, to mention only a few.

> ▶ **Note**   Many of the complex, advanced architecture configurations require in depth knowledge of the environment for deployment; as such, the details of how to implement one are beyond the scope of this guide.

Servicing User Requests

In order to understand the primary components of the Oracle E-Business Suite, it is important to know how the user accesses the application. As the first step to accessing Oracle Applications, a user will launch a web browser and enter the URL that is the *web entry point* for the application. The Web service then services the access request.

The first page that is displayed is a login screen. Once logged in, the user picks a responsibility, such as *System Administrator*, and then a menu option, such as *Security→ User →Define*, to begin his or her work. The menu option will direct the user to an HTML or JavaServer Pages (JSP) page also known as *Oracle HTML Applications*, or to a *Forms* screen. The Web service will continue to service HTML or Java servlet requests; however, if a Forms application is launched, a Forms servlet or the Forms Server will service it to the client via the Native Sun JRE Plug-in in the browser. Throughout this process, the user is retrieving data and executing packages from within the Oracle Database.

Now that you have a very high level overview of how users access the application, we can look at some specifics of the components that Service Requests. The following components will be described:

* **Client tier:** This section will describe the requirements and processes on the user workstation.

* **Application tier:** This section will provide information regarding the Web services, Forms services, and Concurrent Processing that comprise the application tier. These services provide the client access to the application via HTML pages and Oracle Forms as well as a mechanism for scheduling jobs.

* **Database tier:** This section will describe the Oracle Database services. These services include the Oracle Database Listener and Oracle Database Server which is the repository of all Oracle Applications data and database code.

▶ *Note*   Each service runs on a node. A node is a physical server comprised of processing power (CPU) and memory. Multiple nodes servicing different functions may be hosted on the same server. For example, a Web Node, Forms Node, and Concurrent Processing Node may all run on the same physical server.

Client Tier

Oracle Applications are served as either HTML Applications or Oracle Forms Applications which are accessed via the client's browser. A user's first interaction with the application is a login screen that is presented in the web browser, and from there the user can either continue to access HTML pages or access Forms applications. Oracle Forms run as Java applets on the client; this is achieved by utilizing the native Sun JRE Plug-in. A list of Oracle certified browsers for R12 can be found in *My Oracle Support Article ID 389422.1.* In addition to certified browsers, this document contains a list of recommended browser settings, certified Java Runtime Environment (JRE) requirements, and Applications patch requirements. Additional information regarding the native Sun JRE Plug-in can be found in *My Oracle Support Article ID 393931.1.*

▶ *Tip R12 Lingo*   R11i Self Service Applications are referred to as Oracle HTML Applications in R12.

Application Tier

The application tier is a logical grouping of services that is comprised of the various Applications components. This section will provide information regarding the following Applications components:

* **Web and Forms services:** This section will provide an overview of the Web and Forms service components of the application tier.

* **Concurrent Processing:** This section will describe the Concurrent Processing service provided in the application tier.

▶ *Tip R12 Concepts*   Once categorized as a node in and of itself, the concept of an Admin Node, a node used for administrative purposes in R11i, is no longer applicable for R12. In R12, each Applications node, which includes Web, Forms, and Concurrent Processing Nodes, can serve as an Admin Node.

Web and Forms Services   *IMP*

Web and Forms services are key components of the application tier. Web and Forms services are provided by the Oracle Application Server. All R12 installations include two installations of the Oracle Application Server in two separate ORACLE_HOMEs. One ORACLE_HOME is used for Web services and is referred to as the Java Tech Stack. The other ORACLE_HOME is used to service Forms and is referred to as the Tools Tech Stack. Additional details regarding the ORACLE_HOMEs used for Web and Forms services are provided in Chapter 2 of this guide.

The Oracle Process Manager (OPMN) is the controlling mechanism for starting and stopping all of the Oracle Application Server components. Additional details for starting and stopping services will be provided in Chapter 4 of this guide. The Java Tech Stack of the Oracle Application Server includes the HTTP Server and Oracle Container for Java (OC4J) components. The OC4J components include OC4J-oacore, OC4J-Forms, and OC4J-oafm.

The Oracle HTTP Server is based upon Apache technology. The Oracle HTTP Server listens for incoming requests on a specific port. It then services the requests by serving up HTML pages. If a call for Java is received, the HTTP Server passes the service call to the OC4J-oacore component. The OC4J-oafm service is used to provide Web services required by some modules in R12.

▶ *Tip R12 Concepts*   The R11i Oracle Application Server utilized JServs. In R12, JServs are replaced with the Oracle Container for Java (OC4J).

By default, Forms services are configured to use Forms servlets in R12. The following is a description of how requests are serviced using the default Forms servlet configuration. If a call for Oracle Forms is received, the HTTP Server passes the service call to OC4J-Forms that in turn calls the Tools Tech Stack in the second ORACLE_HOME for the request to be processed by the frmweb and formsapp.ear services. Web and Forms services typically run on the same node, referred to as the Web and Forms Node.

▶ *Tip R12 Concepts*   In R12, Forms servlets are the default configuration for servicing Forms requests. A Forms Socket Server may also be utilized; however, Forms servlets are recommended. Additional information regarding Forms Socket Server deployment in R12 may be found in *My Oracle Support Article ID 384241.1.*

Concurrent Processing

Concurrent Processing is a special feature of Oracle Applications. It allows the user to execute jobs, which are called *concurrent requests*. The node that runs the Concurrent Manager processes is called the Concurrent Processing Node. Concurrent requests may be scheduled as a one time request or on a repeating schedule, and they can be submitted to execute immediately or at a specific time.

Out of the box, Oracle Applications comes with the *Standard Manager*. This manager is the default scheduler for concurrent requests. Custom managers with custom names may also be created. Concurrent Processing may also service special transactions that are triggered by activity in the application. These types of requests are serviced by the *Transaction Manager*. Additional details regarding Concurrent Manager processing will be provided in Chapter 2 of this guide.

▶ *Tip*   Traditionally, Oracle recommended that the Concurrent Processing Node run on the same tier as the Database Node. However, with the availability of fast network connectivity between the Concurrent Processing Node and the Database Node, it is now recommended that the Concurrent Processing Node run on the application tier.

Database Tier

The heart and soul of the E-Business Suite is the database. The database not only stores the data in tables under various schemas, but also stores many other objects (such as procedures, packages, database triggers, functions, indexes, and sequences) that are required for the application to function. The Oracle Database also has a Database Listener that services incoming requests to connect to the database. The Database Node is where the Oracle Database instance and Database Listener run.

Oracle Applications Architecture

Some implementations of Oracle Applications are deployed with a basic architecture. Others require advanced configuration for specific features. We will start with an overview of the basic architecture and then move into advanced configuration options.

Fundamental Architecture

When a system is deployed with a basic approach to architecture, it typically does not have large transactional processing requirements, a large number of concurrent users, or special requirements for availability. For this type of environment, there are typically no advanced configuration requirements. These implementations may run on one node, meaning that the application and database services are running on one physical server. This is a quite inefficient deployment method. Not only can performance of the system suffer due to contention of resources, this deployment also contains a single point of failure.

Some implementations run the Applications components on one server, while the Database Node runs on a separate server. Multi-node environments do not require special configuration or design effort unless multiple nodes for the same component are required. Additional details regarding this type of configuration will be described in greater detail in the *Advanced Architecture* section in this chapter. A simple, three tier physical Oracle Applications environment is displayed in Figure 1-1.

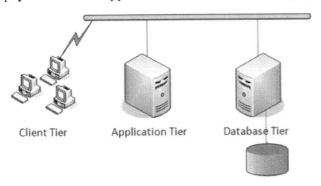

Client Tier   Application Tier   Database Tier

Figure 1-1. *Oracle Applications: A Basic, Three tier Physical Architecture*

▶ *Tip*   A two node implementation with one application server for Web, Forms, and Concurrent Processing services and one Database Node for the database service is the minimum number of nodes recommended to run Oracle Applications. An implementation with all services running on one node may cause contention between application and database processing, which will result in performance degradation.

Advanced Architecture

When the application and database tier provide services using multiple nodes, or when there are additional deployment considerations, we begin to enter into advanced configuration topics and design. Advanced configurations for Oracle Applications include having multiple Web and Forms Nodes, Concurrent Processing Nodes, and Database Nodes. The number of nodes required is dependent upon your environmental requirements for concurrent user support, transactional processing, availability, security, and location of users.

This section will not provide the details required for implementing a complex architecture, but it will give you an understanding of the advanced concepts so you can begin research into which advanced configuration topologies might be required by the organization you service. The following topics will be covered:

* **Load Balancing Web and Forms services:** A description and overview of how to load balance Web and Forms services is provided.

* **Parallel Concurrent Processing:** A description and overview of load balanced Concurrent Processing is described.

* **Unified APPL_TOP:** The R12 concept of supporting all services on all nodes regardless of node type is discussed.

* **Shared Application Tier Filesystem:** The support of a shared Applications layer and the advantages of using this feature is described.

* **Oracle Data Guard:** The usage and deployment considerations of a standby database are given.

* **Oracle Real Application Clusters (RAC):** A description of a multi-node implementation of the Oracle Database which is used to increase performance and improve availability is provided.

* **Mixed Platform Architecture:** The concept of a multi-node environment with the application tier deployed on a different operating system than the database tier is presented.

* **Providing Internet access:** A description of the use of reverse proxy servers and external application servers to support Internet connections to your company's intranet deployed Oracle Applications is provided.

* **Oracle Application Server Web Cache:** An overview of the use of Oracle Application Server Web Cache to assist with application performance is described.

* **Secure Sockets Layer (SSL) Encryption:** An overview of SSL and its implementation requirements for Oracle Applications is described.

Load Balancing Web and Forms Services

When a large number of users need to access your environment or high availability is critical, it may be necessary to create multiple nodes that service the same function. For example, if your business or customer requires the ability to support 5,000 concurrent HTML Applications users, servicing these requests with one Web Node may cause contention in the system. This would result in users being unable to access the application. In order to resolve this problem, multiple Web Nodes would need to be placed into operation.

Load balancing is the term used to describe how users or transactions are distributed to multiple nodes that service the same function. When more than one node is used, the nodes that service the same function are called a *farm*. For example, if you determine that your environment requires multiple Web Nodes, the multiple Web Nodes are collectively referred to as a *Web farm*. The Web services may be further load balanced by implementing multiple OC4Js. If your environment requires a large amount of Java processing, configuring additional OC4Js will reduce contention for its resources.

▶ *Note*   Oracle has not certified and does not support load balancing of the same types of nodes on the same physical server.

Web Node load balancing may be achieved by employing a hardware load balancing device or with DNS load balancing. Forms load balancing is implemented with the Web services utilizing Forms servlets. Information regarding load balancing for the Oracle E-Business Suite R12 can be found in *My Oracle Support Article ID 380489.1.*

▶ *Tip R12 Concept*   In R11i, Forms load balancing could be implemented with either the Forms Metric Server or with the HTTP Server configured with Forms servlets. In R12, the only mechanism supported for Forms load balancing is the deployment of Forms servlets.

Parallel Concurrent Processing

Depending upon your Concurrent Processing transactional requirements or high availability requirements, you may require implementing multiple Concurrent Processing Nodes. When the Concurrent Processing Nodes are load balanced, this configuration is referred to as *Parallel Concurrent Processing.* Parallel Concurrent Processing is load balanced by the Internal Concurrent Manager. If Parallel Concurrent Processing is required, then a shared filesystem implemented with either Network File System (NFS) or a shared disk array is required to share Concurrent Manager log and output files.

Unified APPL_TOP

When deploying a multi-node environment for Oracle R12, all services are available for use with each node in the implementation. This feature is called *Unified* APPL_TOP. This simply means that if a node is designated as a Concurrent Processing Node, for example, the node also contains all of the files and executables necessary to provide the services of a Web Node. Additional configuration may be necessary to start the services, but no additional software installation or deployment is required.

▶ *Tip R12 Concept*   In R11i, services were only deployed to a node per the node type that was set in the configuration. R12 departs from this concept and by default deploys a Unified APPL_TOP. A Unified APPL_TOP makes it easier to enable additional services if needed.

Shared Application Tier Filesystem

Each installation of Oracle Applications contains two ORACLE_HOMEs for the Oracle 10g Application Servers; one for the Java Tech Stack, the other for the Tools Tech Stack. In addition to this, each installation is comprised of an APPL_TOP and COMMON_TOP. By default, if deploying a multi-node environment, a Unified APPL_TOP is utilized.

The APPL_TOP directory comprises all product files and directories, all core technology files and directories, and the Applications context file and environment files. The COMMON_TOP directory contains files and directories that are used by all application products. Additional details regarding the Oracle Applications filesystem structures are provided in Chapter 2 of this guide.

Disk space is required for each copy of the installation on each node. In addition to the additional disk space, maintenance windows are also increased. As you perform upgrades or apply patches, you will need to upgrade and/or patch each of the copies of the 10gAS ORACLE_HOMEs, APPL_TOP, and COMMON_TOP on each node in the multi-node deployment. To reduce disk space requirements and reduce maintenance windows, Oracle has developed the concept of a *Shared Application Tier Filesystem*.

In a Shared Application Tier Filesystem implementation, a shared filesystem (either NFS or a disk array) is used to store the Oracle 10gAS ORACLE_HOMEs, APPL_TOP and COMMON_TOP structures. Because the APPL_TOP and COMMON_TOP directories contain Applications code and binaries, placing them on a shareable filesystem will reduce maintenance downtime during Applications patching. Placing the ORACLE_HOMEs for the multiple Oracle 10gAS on a shareable filesystem will reduce maintenance downtime during Technology Stack patching. Implementing a Shared Application Tier Filesystem provides even greater manageability of the Applications environment. Additional details regarding a Shared Application Tier Filesystem deployment can be found in *My Oracle Support Article ID 384248.1*.

▶ *Tip*   When deploying a Shared Application Tier Filesystem that utilizes a Network Attached Storage (NAS) device, consider the features and functions of the device during implementation. Many NAS devices have features that can assist with the maintenance, backup, cloning, and replication requirements needed for your environment.

Distributed AD

Distributed AD is yet another advanced configuration feature of Oracle Applications. With this configuration, you can use one or more of the servers in your implementation to perform administrative functions. With Distributed AD, an administrative task will distribute workers on multiple servers that are configured as Admin Nodes. This feature may assist in reducing downtime by expediting administrative functions, such as when a patching session spawns multiple workers across multiple nodes.

Oracle Data Guard

Oracle Data Guard is an Oracle Database feature that allows you to create a standby database. The standby database is a copy of your production environment. Oracle Data Guard utilizes standard functionality of the Oracle Database architecture to keep the standby instance synchronized with changes in data that are made to the primary database.

There are multiple reasons to consider implementing Oracle Data Guard. Standby databases created using Oracle Data Guard can be used to create a highly available database environment when the standby is deployed to a different node than the primary database. Standby databases may be used to perform point in time backups of production. Standby databases may also be opened and used as a point in time reporting database.

Oracle Real Application Clusters (RAC)

Another advanced database feature is called *Oracle Real Application Clusters (RAC)*. This feature provides a multi-node implementation for the database tier. In a RAC environment, multiple Database Nodes function as one database instance, accessing the same physical database. Oracle RAC implementations are typically deployed to provide additional transactional processing power as well as a highly available environment.

Mixed Platform Architecture

Oracle provides support and certification for the deployment of a multi-node environment where the application tier is running on an operating system or platform that is different from the database tier; this is called a *Mixed Platform Architecture*. An example of this is an application tier running Red Hat Linux and a database tier that runs on Sun Solaris. A

Mixed Platform Architecture may be deployed if a specific platform is not certified for the application or database tier. Another reason to deploy a Mixed Platform Architecture is to deploy cheaper commodity servers for the application tier in order to lower your total cost of ownership. Information regarding certified Mixed Platform Architectures can be found in the certification matrix on My Oracle Support. Additional details for how to use My Oracle Support are provided in Chapter 8 of this guide.

▶ *TIP R12 Lingo*   In R11i an application tier, with one Operating System (OS) and a database tier with a different OS was referred to as Split Tier Configuration. In R12, the term is Mixed Platform Architecture.

Providing Internet Access to an Oracle Applications Deployment

Companies typically deploy their Oracle Applications environment local to the company's Intranet. There are several advanced configuration options for implementing a secure Internet deployment of your Oracle Applications environment. One method is to deploy a proxy or reverse proxy server in your *Demilitarized Zone* (DMZ). Another method is to deploy an external Oracle Applications Server. Additional information regarding these deployments is provided in the following section. Details regarding Oracle R12 DMZ deployments may be found in *My Oracle Support Article ID 380490.1*.

Reverse Proxy Servers

A *reverse proxy server* is a server that resides in a DMZ and allows for an Internet user to access the Oracle Applications environment located behind the company's firewall. The reverse proxy server routes all traffic from the Internet client to the Oracle Application environment and back to the Internet client. Direct communication from the Internet client to the Oracle Applications servers never occurs with this configuration.

External Web Servers

Another method for providing access to Oracle Applications for Internet users is the deployment of *External Web Servers*. External Web Servers are configured with standard Oracle R12 configuration utilities and provide protected access to your Oracle Applications environment. The External Web Server sits in your DMZ and allows for Internet users to access Applications that have been configured to run on the External Server. Not all Oracle modules are certified to run in an External Web Server configuration. A complete list of modules certified with an External Web Server deployment may be found in *My Oracle Support Article ID 380490.1, Appendix A*.

▶ *Tip*   Reverse proxy and External Web Servers may also be load balanced to meet scalability and availability requirements.

Oracle Application Server Web Cache

Oracle Application Server Web Cache is an Oracle product that can assist in enhancing application performance. Oracle Application Server Web Cache increases performance by caching and compressing both static and dynamic information from the environment. Additional details regarding implementing Oracle Application Server Web Cache may be found in *My Oracle Support Article ID 380486.1*.

▶ *Tip*   Oracle Application Server Web Cache may also be deployed as a load balancer and reverse proxy server.

Secure Sockets Layer Encryption

Secure Sockets Layer (SSL) is a method of encrypting transactions and data over a network. Securing transactional data is often a requirement when said transactions contain sensitive data or information, such as credit card data.

If encryption is required, it may be implemented with Oracle Applications. SSL can be deployed for the Oracle Application Server and Database Server. Software SSL solutions or hardware encryption devices known as SSL accelerators may be used. Details for implementing SSL are given in *My Oracle Support Article ID 376700.1*.

▶ *Tip R12 Concepts*   If SSL is a requirement for your R12 environment, then Forms servlets must be deployed. In R12, SSL is not supported with Forms Server.

Architecture Best Practices

When designing the architecture of your Oracle E-Business Suite implementation, it is important to understand the various features you will be expected to deliver for the environment. Key requirements include the following:

- **Determine scalability requirements for your environment.** To assess this requirement, estimate the number of concurrent users and concurrent transactions both batch and real time for your environment. As you collect this information, make certain that you have an understanding of performance requirements. Based upon the information you collect you may need to consider implementing a multi-node environment for your Web and Forms services, Parallel Concurrent Processing for your Concurrent Processing Node and Oracle RAC for the database tier. You may also need to consider implementing Oracle Application Server Web Cache to meet performance requirements.

- **Determine the location of your users.** To assess this requirement, determine if your users will be Intranet only users, Internet only users, or a mix of Intranet and Internet users. Determine which modules will be used by the Internet users. Based upon the information you collect, you may need to consider a deployment of a reverse proxy server or an External Web Server.

- **Determine the security configuration needed to protect your environment.** To assess this requirement, discuss with your company's or customer's security department the need for data encryption. Determine if access to the Applications from the Internet is necessary. The information you collect will help you decide if SSL for the application and database tier is a requirement. It will also help determine if a DMZ reverse proxy server or External Web Server is a needed for your deployment.

- **Determine your service level agreement (SLA) with your customers.** To assess this requirement, setup discussions with your customers. Determine how much downtime, both planned and unplanned, is acceptable. Based upon the information you collect, architect an environment that supports these requirements. The architecture may include a number of high availability solutions including load balancing Web and Forms services, Parallel Concurrent Processing, RAC, and Oracle Data Guard. You may also need to consider spanning services across multiple data centers to protect against a catastrophic data center outage. Periodically review your SLA with your customers to make certain that you are continuing to meet their requirements.

If you are considering implementing multiple nodes for load balancing, it is recommended that you consider implementing the additional nodes on commodity servers utilizing a Mixed Platform Architecture if necessary. Commodity servers are cheaper servers generally based on the Intel architecture running Linux. Implementing commodity servers will allow you to transition to a load balanced, multi-node configuration with a lower total cost of ownership. An example of an advanced multi-node Oracle Applications environment is displayed in Figure 1-2.

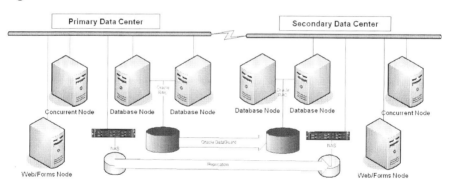

Figure 1-2. *Oracle Applications: An Advanced Multi-node Physical Architecture*

Infrastructure upgrade requirements, including client workstation, server, networking, and hardware firmware upgrades, to mention a few, should be implemented with caution. A "minor" upgrade to one of these components may cause outages for your Oracle Applications environment. Be certain to sufficiently test all such upgrades or modifications to the supporting Oracle E-Business Suite infrastructure, and have a plan to roll back changes if necessary.

Chapter 2

Configuration

There are numerous services and components that need to be configured in order to deploy the Oracle Applications environment. Oracle has made several improvements that assist in simplifying the management of the complex configuration of the environment. Multiple logical filesystems exist in R12 to ease the management of the filesystem structures and contents. In addition to this, beginning with R11i, Oracle has provided a configuration management utility called AutoConfig. AutoConfig simplifies the management of all configuration files for the environment. Even with the improved manageability features, it is still important for an Oracle Applications DBA to be familiar with files and settings of the application. It is the detailed knowledge of the environment that will assist the Oracle Applications DBA in monitoring, troubleshooting, performance tuning and advanced configurations that are commonplace for every deployment. This chapter will discuss key aspects of configuring the application and the tools used to do so. This chapter will cover the following topics:

* **Context files:** In this section, a description of the context file for the application tier and the database tier will be given. The context files will be discussed in more detail in the context files and AutoConfig section.

* **Application tier filesystems and environment:** This section will cover the primary environment settings and filesystems for the application tier including <APPS_BASE>, APPL_TOP, COMMON_TOP, INST_TOP and the ORACLE_HOMEs for the Java and Tools Tech Stack. In this section, additional key environment files and environment variables will also be reviewed.

* **Database tier filesystems and environment:** This section will cover the primary environment settings and filesystems for the database tier. The recommended settings for database version 11g initialization parameters for optimum performance with Oracle R12 Applications will be given. This section also includes an overview of the Oracle Applications Tablespace Model (OATM) and the APPS schema.

* **Port numbering:** This section will cover the methods by which ports can be assigned to the Oracle Applications environment. An overview of Oracle's port pooling and manual port assignments will be covered.

* **Context files and AutoConfig:** The context files contain settings that allow for centralized configuration and configuration management for the Oracle E-Business Suite. This section will cover how to define, locate, create, and maintain the Applications and database context files. Context files are used by the AutoConfig utility to automate configuration of the application and database tiers. A description of how template files are utilized by AutoConfig, how to review and compare the execution of AutoConfig and how to locate the AutoConfig execution log files and backup files will be provided.

* **Securing Oracle Applications:** This section will provide guidance for setting password verification complexity in the Applications and database.

Context Files

Before beginning the discussions regarding the Oracle R12 Applications environment, filesystems and configuration, the core concept of *context files* need to be described. There are two Oracle E-Business Suite files used for centralized configuration management, the *Applications context file* and *database context file*.

The Applications context file is an XML file that is the central configuration file for the application tier. In this file are configuration parameters necessary to configure all components of the application tier. The database context file is an XML file that is the central configuration file for the database tier. In this file are many of the configuration parameters necessary to manage the database tier. Additional details regarding the Applications context files and database context files will be covered in the multiple sections in this chapter.

> ▶ *Tip*   The CONTEXT_NAME of an environment is defined by appending the instance name and the name of the host server. As such, the CONTEXT_NAME is as follows: <INSTANCE_NAME>_<HOST_NAME>.

Application Tier Filesystems and Environment

In order to effectively manage the Oracle Applications Technology Stack, you should become knowledgeable of the filesystems, environment files, environment variables and configuration files of the primary components and services of the application tier. This section will focus on providing you the information needed to understand the architecture of the application tier. The following are the key topics that will be covered:

* **Defining <APPS_BASE>:** This section will describe the concept of <APPS_BASE>.

* **Defining APPL_TOP:** This section will describe the content, location and environment files for APPL_TOP.

* **Defining COMMON_TOP:** This section will describe the content, location and environment files for COMMON_TOP.

* **Defining INST_TOP:** This section will describe the content, location and environment files for INST_TOP.

* **Applications Technology Stack:** This section will describe the two ORACLE_HOMEs that comprise the Applications Technology Stack. The Applications Technology Stack includes the content, location and environment files for Java Tech Stack and the Tools Tech Stack.

* **Additional environment (ENV) files:** This section will cover additional ENV files that are important for the Oracle Applications deployment.

* **Overview of key application tier environment files and environment variables:** This section provides an overview of the key environment files as well as the definition of key environment variables.

*   **Web and Forms services configuration:** This section will cover the key configuration files and their most important parameters for managing the Oracle Application Server for both the Java and Tools Tech Stack. Key configuration files such as opmn.xml, httpd.conf and appsweb.cfg will be reviewed.

*   **Concurrent Processing configuration:** In this section, we'll discuss the key configuration settings and parameters for Concurrent Processing.

*   **Review of key application tier filesystem concepts:** This section provides a graphical presentation of the key filesystem concepts presented in this section.

Defining <APPS_BASE>

<APPS_BASE> is the base directory for your Oracle Applications installation. <APPS_BASE> can be a directory or you can leave it undefined. If you leave it undefined then all underlying filesystem structures will be off of the base directory "/". The application tier includes the Applications files and the Applications Technology Stack. Both are located in the following base directory:

/<APPS_BASE>/apps

The Applications files are located in the following directory:

/<APPS_BASE>/apps/apps_st

The Applications Technology Stack is located in the following directory:

/<APPS_BASE>/apps/tech_st

▶ *R12 Implementation Tip*   It is important to define <APPS_BASE> prior to performing an installation. Installation topics will be covered in Chapter 3 of this guide.

Defining APPL_TOP

Oracle Applications are comprised of a deployment of a wide range of Applications modules. The filesystem structure that contains the Applications files is called APPL_TOP. When applying Applications patches or upgrading the Oracle Applications environment that include product specific updates, it is the contents of APPL_TOP that are updated or upgraded. Additional information regarding Applications patching is covered in Chapter 5 of this guide. APPL_TOP is defined as follows:

APPL_TOP= /<APPS_BASE>/apps/apps_st/appl

Under the APPL_TOP directory is the installation of every product for Oracle Applications. Each product has its own corresponding product top or [PRODUCT_SHORT_NAME]_TOP directory structure. For example, the short name for accounts payable is AP. AP's product top is AP_TOP. AP_TOP is defined as follows:

AP_TOP=/<APPS_BASE>/apps/apps_st/appl/ap/12.0.0

Located in the APPL_TOP directory is a key Applications environment file for R12. The name and location of the environment file is as follows:

$APPL_TOP/$CONTEXT_NAME.env

Also located in the APPL_TOP directory is the consolidated environment file for R12. The consolidated ENV file sets the environment for the Applications as well as the Java and Tools Tech Stack. The name and location of the consolidated environment file is as follows:

$APPL_TOP/APPS$CONTEXT_NAME.env

APPS$CONTEXT_NAME.env files should be sourced in the profile of the instance owner on the application tier. Sourcing this file in the instance owner's .profile will call all other necessary environment files in the appropriate order to set the application tier environment.

▶ *Tip*   APPL_TOP and all [PRODUCT_SHORT_NAME]_TOPs have corresponding environment variables for ease of location and maffnagement. For example: APPL_TOP= /<APPS_BASE>/apps/apps_st/appl. To go to the APPL_TOP directory, simply execute the following command: $UNIX>cd $APPL_TOP. To get a full list of all [PRODUCT_SHORT_NAME]_TOPs, execute the following command: $UNIX>env | grep TOP.

Defining COMMON_TOP

While APPL_TOP contains all product specific files, COMMON_TOP contains all common files for all products. Some examples of what is included in COMMON_TOP are the Java class files, Java libraries and other files common to the applications. When applying Applications patches or upgrading the Oracle Applications environment, the contents

of COMMON_TOP may also be updated or upgraded. Additional
information regarding Applications patching is covered in Chapter 5 of
this guide. COMMON_TOP is located as follows:

/<APPS_BASE>/apps/apps_st/comn

▶ *Tip*   COMMON_TOP has a corresponding environment variable for ease of
location and management. The environment variable COMMON_TOP is set as follows:
COMMON_TOP=/<APPS_BASE>/apps/apps_st/comn To navigate to the
COMMON_TOP directory, simply execute the following command: $UNIX>cd
$COMMON_TOP.

Defining INST_TOP

Oracle R12 Applications provides a new filesystem concept called
INST_TOP, also known as the *Instance Home* or *Instance Top*. INST_TOP
is a centralized location for all Applications configuration and log files.
Each server in the environment has an INST_TOP that contains the
required files specific to its configuration as well as log files. Prior to
INST_TOP, configuration and log files were located under various
directories on the server. The centralization of configuration and log files
makes it easier to administer and troubleshoot the R12 environment.

It is recommended to locate INST_TOP in a base directory other than
<APPS_BASE>. Locating it in another directory structure will allow you to
provide additional security to the environment by making the APPL_TOP
and the Java and Tools Tech Stack directories read only during normal
business activities. Making these directories read only is possible as all
activities that require writes will occur in INST_TOP. The write activities
include the writing of log files by the various service components. The
only write activities that occur to the APPL_TOP and Java and Tools Tech
Stack directories are during maintenance or patching activities.
Additional details regarding AutoConfig and the location of log files are
covered in a later section in this chapter.

The base directory for INST_TOP will be referred to as
<INST_TOP_BASE>. The location of INST_TOP is as follows:

INST_TOP=/<INST_TOP_BASE>/apps/$CONTEXT_NAME

▶ *R12 Implementation Tip*   INST_TOP should be created as a filesystem on local disk for each application server in your environment.

The Applications context file is located in INST_TOP. The location of the Applications context file is as follows:

$INST_TOP/appl/admin/$CONTEXT_NAME.xml

Configuration files may be located by referencing the environment variable ORA_CONFIG_HOME. The central location of the configuration files in INST_TOP is as follows:

ORA_CONFIG_HOME = $INST_TOP/ora

Log files can be located by referencing the LOG_HOME environment variable. The central location of the configuration files in INST_TOP is as follows:

LOG_HOME=$INST_TOP/logs

▶ *R12 Implementation Tip*   If you have a multi-node Applications deployment, the use of INST_TOP assists in the deployment of a Shared Application Tier Filesystem. The concept of a Shared Application Tier Filesystem is described in Chapter 1 of this guide. If using a Shared Application Tier Filesystem deployed on a NAS device, you may be able to utilize the features of the device to make the specific filesystems read only during normal business hours. During maintenance windows, the filesystems need to be set to read-write mode to allow for updates.

Applications Technology Stack

The Applications Technology Stack is comprised of two Oracle 10gAS installations, or two ORACLE_HOMEs. One ORACLE_HOME is the Java Tech Stack, the other ORACLE_HOME is the Tools Tech Stack. Additional details regarding each of the ORACLE_HOMEs is provided in the following sections. The base location of the Applications Technology Stack is as follows:

/<APPS_BASE>/apps/tech_st

Java Tech Stack

The Java Tech Stack is the ORACLE_HOME or Oracle 10gAS installation that includes the Web services for Oracle R12 Applications. The Web services include the HTTP Server and Java components or OC4J. For R12.1, this installation is Oracle 10gAS version 10.1.3. The Oracle Process Manager (OPMN) uses this installation for managing the other components of the Oracle 10gAS. Additional information regarding OPMN will be covered in Chapter 4 of this guide. The following is the location of the Java Tech Stack:

/<APPS_BASE>/apps/tech_st/10.1.3

The following is the environment file for the Java Tech Stack:

$INST_TOP/ora/10.1.3/$CONTEXT_NAME.env

▶ *Tip*   The location of the Java Tech Stack is referenced by the environment variable $IAS_ORACLE_HOME. To quickly navigate to the Java Tech Stack directory, simply execute the following command: $UNIX>cd $IAS_ORACLE_HOME.

Tools Tech Stack

The Tools Tech Stack is the ORACLE_HOME or Oracle 10gAS installation that includes the Forms services for Oracle R12 Applications. For R12.1, this installation is Oracle 10gAS 10.1.2. The following is the location of the Tools Tech Stack:

/<APPS_BASE>/apps/tech_st/10.1.2

The following is the environment file for the Tools Tech Stack:

$INST_TOP/ora/10.1.2/$CONTEXT_NAME.env

▶ *Tip*   The location of the Tools Tech Stack is referenced by the environment variable $ORACLE_HOME. To quickly navigate to the Tools Tech Stack directory, simply execute the following command: $UNIX>cd $ORACLE_HOME.

Additional Environment Files

There are several additional key ENV files that need to be discussed as part of the R12 application tier. The adovars.env file contains information regarding the location of Java, HTML and JRE files. This environment file is called by the main environment file. The following is the location of the adovars.env file:

/<APPS_BASE>/apps/apps_st/appl/admin/adovars.env

The fndenv.env file is the Applications Object Library environment setup file. The following is the location of the fndenv.env file:

$FND_TOP/fndenv.env

The devenv.env file is the Applications Object Library developer's setup file. It can be used to compile and link custom code with Oracle Applications. The following is the location of the devenv.env file:

$FND_TOP/usrxit/devenv.env

Administering the Database Connection File

The database connection (DBC) file is used by the application to establish JDBC thin client connections to the database. JDBC thin client connections are used by the Web and Forms services to connect to the database. As with other configuration files, the file is automatically created when the system is installed and maintained by AutoConfig. The DBC file contains information regarding the guest account as well as configuration items for JDBC connectivity including connection pooling.

▶ *R12 Implementation Tip*   Due to the contents of the DBC file, it is important to restrict access to its directory and contents.

The name and location of the DBC file is as follows:

$INST_TOP/appl/fnd/12.0.0/secure/[SID].dbc

Key configuration parameters that are contained in the DBC file are provided in Table 2-1.

Table 2-1. *Key Parameters in the DBC File*

Context File Parameter	Parameter in DBC File	Description
s_guest_user/s_guest _pass	GUEST_USER_PWD	Guest account.
s_dbhost	DB_HOST	Database hostname.
s_dbport	DB_PORT	Port number for database listener.
s_fnd_jdbc_buffermi n	FND_JDBC_BUFFER_M IN	Minimum number of connections the pool maintains.
s_fnd_jdbc_bufferma x	FND_JDBC_BUFFER_M AX	Maximum number of connections the pool allows.
s_fnd_jdbc_buffer_de cay_interval	FND_JDBC_BUFFER_D ECAY_INTERVAL	Specifies how often the connection pool checks buffer size.
s_fnd_jdbc_buffer_de cay_size	FND_JDBC_BUFFER_D ECAY_SIZE	Maximum number of connections removed during a cycle.

▶ *Tip*   Modifications to environment files and the DBC file should be performed utilizing appropriate mechanisms for updating configuration files. This information is provided in the context files and AutoConfig Section of this chapter.

Web and Forms Services Configuration

Although configuration management is handled by AutoConfig, it is important to be knowledgeable of the key configuration files for the Web and Forms services. For example, at times it may be necessary to change log levels and debug levels in the configuration files during troubleshooting. This can be done within the configuration files without running AutoConfig given you know the location and parameters within the configuration files that need to be changed. Additional information regarding debugging configuration will be provided in Chapter 6 of this guide.

The Web services include the HTTP Server and Java components or OC4J. By default in R12, Forms services are configured to use Forms servlets. With R12, Web and Forms services are managed by OPMN. The OPMN configuration file is as follows:

$ORA_CONFIG_HOME/10.1.3/opmn/conf/opmn.xml

Additional configuration files for Web and Forms services which identify port definitions, memory settings, logging levels, log file locations and other configuration options are located in the following directories:

$ORA_CONFIG_HOME/10.1.3/config
$ORA_CONFIG_HOME/10.1.3/Apache/Apache/conf
$ORA_CONFIG_HOME/10.1.3/j2ee/oacore/config
$ORA_CONFIG_HOME/10.1.3/j2ee/oafm/config
$ORA_CONFIG_HOME/10.1.3/j2ee/forms/config
$ORA_CONFIG_HOME/10.1.2/forms/server

Key parameter settings for the HTTP Server located in the httpd.conf file are shown in Table 2-2. Key parameter settings for the Forms services located in the appsweb.cfg file are shown in Table 2-3.

Table 2-2. *Key Parameters in the httpd.conf File*

Context File Parameter	Parameter	Example Value	Description
s_web_pid_file	PidFile	$INST_TOP/pids/10.1.3/Apache/httpd.pid	Location of file containing process ID for the HTTP Server.
s_minspare_servers	MinSpareServers	5	Minimum number of idle processes required.
s_maxspare_servers	MaxSpareServers	10	Maximum number of idle processes allowed.
s_webport	Port	19010	Port the server is listening on.
s_webhost	ServerName	webserver.domain.com	Location of web server.

Table 2-2. *Continued*

Context File Parameter	Parameter	Example Value	Description
s_apache_loglevel	LogLevel	Error	Level at which log messages are written.
s_maxclients	MaxClients	1024	Number of concurrent client requests allowed.

Table 2-3. *Key Parameters in the appsweb.cfg File*

Context File Parameter	Parameter	Example Value	Description
s_formshost	serverName	fs1	Name of Forms Server.
s_formsdomain	domainName	domain.com	Name of domain for Forms Server.
s_frmConnectMode	connectMode	servlet	Mode of connecting to Forms Server.
sun_plugin_ver	sun_plugin_version	1.6.0_07	Version of the client JRE.

Use of load balanced Web and Forms services for the application tier requires additional advanced configuration settings for the environment, the details of which are out of scope for this guide. Information regarding configuration requirements for a load balanced deployment can be found in *My Oracle Support Article ID 380489.1.*

As previously stated, log files are centrally located on each server under INST_TOP. The location of all log files starts with the base directory location as identified by the environment variable $LOG_HOME. The log files for OPMN and the Web and Forms services are located in the following directories:

$LOG_HOME/ora/10.1.3/opmn
$LOG_HOME/ora/10.1.3/Apache

$LOG_HOME/ora/10.1.2/forms

where

LOG_HOME=/<INST_TOP_BASE>/apps/$CONTEXT_NAME/logs

Concurrent Processing Configuration

Concurrent processing configuration is achieved by setting parameters in the Applications context file as well as settings that are defined by accessing the Concurrent Manager definition screens in the application. This section will cover the following:

* **Concurrent Manager definition:** This section will cover Concurrent Manager configuration as well as cover key concepts for defining custom Concurrent Managers. The configuration provided in this section is performed when accessing the Concurrent Manager Definition screen in the application.

* **Concurrent Manager log and output file location:** This section will cover the key configuration parameters in the Applications context file for defining the location of the Concurrent Manager log and output files.

Concurrent Manager Definition

The *Internal Concurrent Manager* (ICM) and the *Standard Manager* are defined in the system by default. The ICM controls all other Concurrent Managers. The Standard Manager is available to execute concurrent requests. In addition to the Standard Manager, you may define additional custom managers.

Each Concurrent Manager can be defined to run a number of processes. The number of processes specifies the number of requests or threads of requests that can be run by the manager. The number of processes that you configure for a manager is dependent on the number of requests that you need to process concurrently, which in turn determines the hardware requirements for your Concurrent Node. In addition to the number of processes, the sleep time of the manager determines the frequency by which the manager looks to determine if there is a new request that needs to be executed.

Work Shifts can be defined to enable a manager or increase manager processing during specified times. *Specialization Rules* can also be enabled that define include and/or exclude lists. Include lists may be used to define what types of requests are executed by the manager. You may also define exclude lists which define what types of requests are not executed by the manager. Parallel Concurrent Processing is automatically enabled along with Generic Service Management (GSM). The concept of Parallel Concurrent Processing is described in Chapter 1 of this guide. Primary and secondary concurrent nodes need not be defined; however, they can be explicitly defined within the definition of the manager. The *Concurrent Manager Definition* screen is displayed in Figure 2-1.

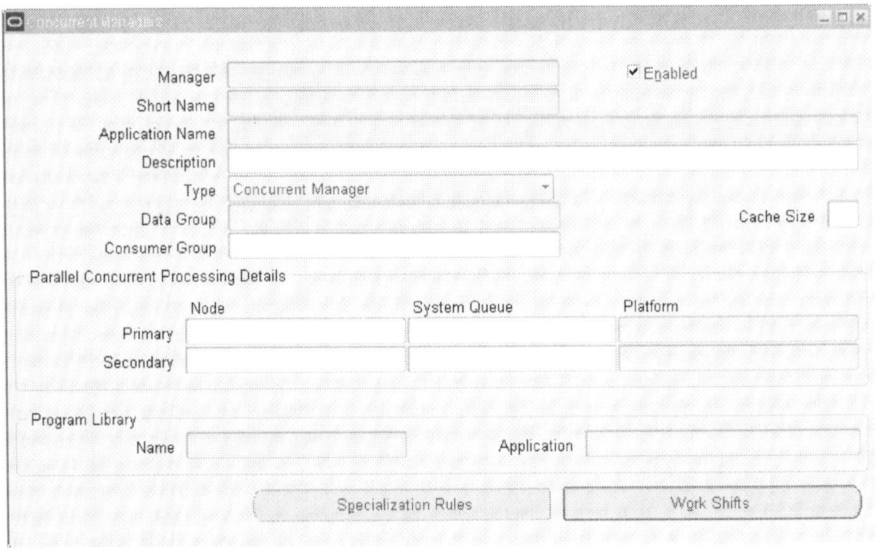

Figure 2-1. *Concurrent Manager Definition Screen*

Concurrent Manager Log and Output File Location

When a concurrent request is executed, it creates a log and an output file. The log file contains logging information for the request that is executed. The output file contains output for the execution of the request. Concurrent Manager log and output file parameters are located in the Applications context file. Changes to the parameters would be added to the CONTEXT_NAME.env file by executions of AutoConfig. A list of the Concurrent Manager configuration variables in the context file are provided in Table 2-4.

Table 2-4. *Key Parameters in the CONTEXT_NAME.env File*

Context File Parameter	Parameter	Example Value	Description
s_applcsf	APPLCSF	$INST_TOP/logs/appl/conc	Location of Concurrent Manager log and output directories.
s_appllog	APPLLOG	log	Directory for log files located under $APPLCSF.
s_applout	APPLOUT	out	Directory for output files located under $APPLCSF.

▶ *Tip*   When deploying a multi-node configuration, you should consider locating the Concurrent Manager log and output files on a shared filesystem drive. This will facilitate the availability of the log and output files in the event of a node failure.

Review of Key Application Tier Filesystem Concepts

Key filesystem concepts were presented in this section. The key filesystem concepts have root starting points of <APPS_BASE> and <INST_TOP_BASE>.

<APPS_BASE> may be located on a network attached storage device and shared among all application servers in the environment. This is called a *Shared Application Tier Filesystem.* A graphical depiction of the contents of the <APPS_BASE> filesystem is provided in Figure 2-2.

<INST_TOP_BASE> should be located on a local filesystem on each server in the environment. Critical components of this filesystem include INST_TOP, ORA_CONFIG_HOME, LOG_HOME, APPLLOG and APPLOUT. The environment files for the Java Tech Stack and Tools Tech Stack are located in this filesystem. Ease of navigation to contents in this filesystem can be achieved utilizing $INST_TOP, $ORA_CONFIG_HOME, $LOG_HOME, $APPLLOG and $APPLOUT. A graphical depiction of the contents of the <INST_TOP_BASE> filesystem is provided in Figure 2-3.

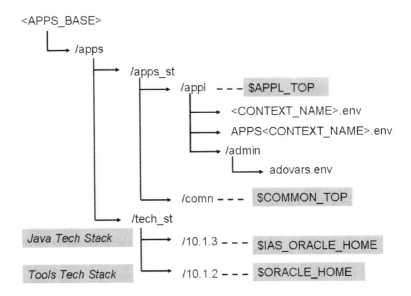

Figure 2-2. *<APPS_BASE> Application Tier Filesystem Layout*

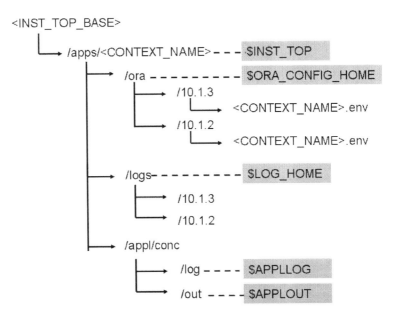

Figure 2-3. *<INST_TOP_BASE> Application Tier Filesystem Layout*

Database Tier Filesystems and Configuration

* **Database Technology Stack:** This section will describe the ORACLE_HOME for the Database Tech Stack. The Database Tech Stack includes the content, location and environment files for database tier. It also includes the configuration files for the database listener.

* **Database data:** This section will describe the default location of the database data files as well as provide details regarding the Oracle Applications Tablespace Model (OATM), the logical tablespace model used by Oracle Applications.

* **Review of key database tier filesystem concepts:** This section provides a graphical presentation of the key filesystem concepts presented in this section.

* **Database initialization parameters:** This section will cover recommended Oracle11g initialization parameters when using Oracle R12 Applications.

* **APPS Schema:** In this section, the relevance and use of the APPS schema will be provided.

Database Tier Technology Stack

The database tier includes the Database Technology Stack. The Database Technology Stack is located in the following directory:

/<APPS_BASE>/db/tech_st/11.1.0

It is the location of the Database Technology Stack that sets the location of the ORACLE_HOME for the database tier where:

ORACLE_HOME=/<APPS_BASE>/db/tech_st/11.1.0

The Database Technology Stack environment file is located as follows:

$ORACLE_HOME/$CONTEXT_NAME.env

Custom variables are defined and located in the database custom environment file. The custom environment file for the database is located as follows:

$ORACLE_HOME/custom$CONTEXT_NAME.env

The database listener configuration is located in the TNS_ADMIN location. The location of TNS_ADMIN is as follows:

$ORACLE_HOME/network/admin/$CONTEXT_NAME

Database Data

With a default installation of R12, the database data files will be located in one directory and logically in the database it will be organized according to the *Oracle Applications Tablespace Model* (OATM). When installing R12, the default location of the database data files is as follows:

/<APPS_BASE>/db/apps_st/data

To simplify the management of the Oracle Applications Database, Oracle created the Oracle Applications Tablespace Model (OATM). This model helps to reduce management overhead by limiting the number of tablespaces used by the application. Additional details regarding OATM may be found in *My Oracle Support Article ID 269293.1*. With OATM, Oracle has reduced the number of tablespaces required for the Applications to twelve as shown in Table 2-5.

Table 2-5. *OATM Tablespaces*

Tablespace Name	Description
APPS_TS_TX_DATA	Contains transactional data.
APPS_TS_TX_IDX	Contains indexes for transactional tables.
APPS_TS_SEED	Contains reference and setup data and indexes.
APPS_TS_INTERFACE	Contains interface and temporary data and indexes.
APPS_TS_SUMMARY	Contains summary objects, such as materialized views.
APPS_TS_NOLOGGING	Contains materialized views not used for summary management.
APPS_TS_QUEUES	Contains Advanced Queuing dependent tables and indexes.
APPS_TS_MEDIA	Contains multimedia objects, such as video, sound and spatial data.

Table 2-5. *Continued*

Tablespace Name	Description
APPS_TS_ARCHIVE	Contains purge related objects.
UNDO	Automatic Undo Management tablespace.
TEMP	Temporary tablespace, used for sorting and temporary tables.
SYSTEM	System tablespace.

▶ *Tip*   You should consider creating additional tablespaces to hold custom objects to create a logical separation between seeded EBS functionality and custom object data.

Review of Key Database Tier Filesystem Concepts

Key database tier filesystem concepts were presented in this section. The key filesystem concepts have root starting points of <APPS_BASE>. Critical components of this filesystem include the Database Tech Stack, database data files and TNS_ADMIN. Ease of navigation to contents in this filesystem can be achieved utilizing $ORACLE_HOME and $TNS_ADMIN. The environment files that are located here include $CONTEXT_NAME.env and custom$CONTEXT_NAME.env A graphical depiction of the filesystems is provided in Figure 2-4.

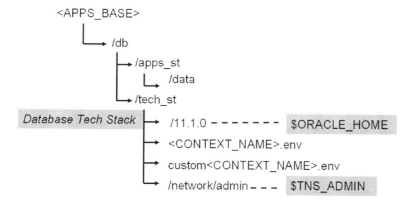

Figure 2-4. *<APPS_BASE> Database Tier Filesystem Layout*

Database Initialization Parameters

Database initialization parameters define the configuration settings, including memory settings, that will be used when the database is started or running. The database initialization file or spfile is a binary file stored on the database server. When using an spfile, initialization parameters can be modified with alter system statements while you are connected to the database. Here's an example:

SQL> alter system set processes =2000 scope=spfile;

▶ *Tip*   Initialization parameters are sometimes deprecated with new versions of the database. Be sure to review new and deprecated initialization parameters when upgrading to a new version of the database.

When initialization parameters are changed, it is possible to add comments to the new value. This is a useful documentation step which will help the Oracle Applications DBA to track why a parameter was set to a particular value. This can be done with the following SQL syntax:

alter system set parameter = [value] comment='comment text';

Oracle provides some recommended and mandatory settings for the database initialization parameters of the E-Business Suite. Please refer to *My Oracle Support Article ID 396009.1* for a detailed listing of the database initialization parameters. It is important to match the recommended settings where possible; however, due to environment specific naming conventions or bugs, this is not always possible. A list of common Oracle database initialization parameters for Oracle R12 Applications is shown in Table 2-6.

▶ *Tip*   If your environment requires different settings than recommended by Oracle documented standards, the changes should be performed under the guidance of Oracle Support. Be sure to open a Service Request (SR) with Oracle Support to review the issue and requirements. All differences from recommended settings should be clearly documented. Additional details regarding opening a SR with Oracle are provided in Chapter 8 of this guide.

Table 2-6. *Common Oracle Database Initialization Parameters for R12*

Initialization Parameter	Recommended Value	Description
db_name	*Environment dependent*	Name of the database. This value is environment dependent.
control_files	*Environment dependent*	Location and name of database controlfiles. It is preferable to create three controlfiles on different disk volumes in case of a hardware failure. This value is environment dependent.
db_block_size	8192	Database block size. For Oracle Applications this must be set to 8192.
_system_trig_enabled	TRUE	Enables system triggers.
O7_dictionary_accessibility	*Version dependent*	This parameter enables data dictionary querying. For Oracle Applications 11.5.10 and higher it can be set to FALSE. For versions 11.5.9 and lower, this parameter must be set to TRUE.
nls_date_format	DD-MON-RR	Default date format.
nls_sort	BINARY	When set to BINARY, the collating sequence for the ORDER BY clause is based on the numeric values of characters.
nls_comp	BINARY	When set to BINARY, comparisons in the WHERE clause and in PL/SQL blocks are binary.
nls_length_semantics	BYTE	Required for NLS and character sets.

Table 2-6. *Continued*

Initialization Parameter	Recommended Value	Description
cursor_sharing	EXACT	Determines which types of SQL statements can share cursors.
aq_tm_processes	1	Determines the number of background processes to monitor queue messages.
job_queue_processes	2	Maximum number of processes created for execution of jobs.
log_archive_start	TRUE	Enables automatic archive logging.
_sort_elimination_cost_ratio	5	Affects cost based optimizer.
_like_with_bind_as_equality	TRUE	Affects cost based optimizer.
_fast_full_scan_enabled	FALSE	Affects cost based optimizer.
_b_tree_bitmap_plans	FALSE	Affects cost based optimizer.
optimizer_secure_view_merging	FALSE	Affects cost based optimizer.
_sqlexec_progression_cost	2147483647	Affects cost based optimizer.
undo_management	AUTO	Enables system managed undo.
undo_tablespace	*Environment dependent*	Name of the undo tablespace.
workarea_size_policy	AUTO	Allows system to automatically size PGA based upon pga_aggregate_target.
olap_page_pool_size	4193404	Specifies the size (in bytes) of the OLAP pool.
compatible	*Environment dependent*	The version of the database. For example, 11.1.0 or 11.2.0.

Table 2-6. *Continued*

Initialization Parameter	Recommended Value	Description
diagnostic_dest	*Environment dependent*	Location of the diagnostics for the database
_optimizer_autostats_job	FALSE	Turn off automatic statistics
sec_case_sensitive_logon	FALSE	Not currently supported with Oracle Applications

A list of recommended settings for Oracle11gR1 and 11gR2 database initialization parameters for use with Oracle R12 Applications is shown in Table 2-7.

Table 2-7. *Recommended Settings for Oracle11gR1 and 11gR2 Database Initialization Parameters for R12*

Parameter Name	Dev/Test Instance	Production Instance			
		Max Users *			
		100		500		1000		2000
processes	200	200		800		1200		2500
sessions	400	400		1600		2400		5000
sga_target	1G	1G		2G		3G		14G
shared_pool_size	400M	600M	800M	1000M	2000M
shared_pool_reserved_size	40M	60M		80M		100M		200M
pga_aggregate_target	1G	2G		4G		10G		20G

* Max Users is not a parameter. It is the number of concurrent users which provides guidelines for production level settings for the parameters in the table

▶ *Tip*   With 11g, Oracle has introduced the concept of a diagnostic destination. It is this location that defines the location of the alert log, user dump files and core dump files. Each of the dump locations is a subdirectory under the path defined by diagnostic_dest.

Reviewing Database Initialization Parameters

You can query the v$parameter view in order to get a listing of all the current initialization settings. The results can be spooled to a file that can be stored for later reference:

```
SQL> spool db_parameters.log
SQL> select name, value
SQL> from v$parameter order by name;
SQL> spool off
```

To retrieve the value for one setting, the show parameter [name or partial parameter name] command can be used within SQL*Plus. This is the fastest way to check a small number of values:

```
SQL> show parameter processes
```

NAME	TYPE	VALUE
aq_tm_processes	integer	5
db_writer_processes	integer	1
job_queue_processes	integer	10
log_archive_max_processes	integer	2
processes	integer	1000

Rather than manually checking all initialization settings, Oracle provides a script called bde_chk_cbo.sql to help verify the values. Details regarding the bde_chk_cbo.sql script can be found in *My Oracle Support Article ID 174605.1*. When this script is executed, a report containing the database initialization parameters will be generated. You may review this report in order to validate recommended database initialization settings.

▶ *Tip*　　The initialization parameters are recommendations from Oracle. Some of the parameters may need to be tweaked per requirements in your environment.

APPS Schema

The APPS schema is one of the most important schemas in the database. The APPS account is the one that is used by an Oracle Applications DBA to perform the majority of the Applications maintenance including patching. For overall system security it is recommended that access to the

APPS password, particularly in production, be limited to only the necessary members of the Oracle Applications DBA team.

▶ *Tip*   Schedule changes of the APPS password in production on a regular basis.

Port Numbering

Configuration values in the context files include numerous port numbers. Managing more than one instance can become quite cumbersome. There are two common methods that can be utilized to configure ports. You can use Oracle's port pooling mechanism or assign ports manually per a standard port configuration for your environment. This section describes the two methods for assigning ports.

Oracle Port Pools

Oracle provides a mechanism by which all port assignments for the environment are handled automatically. The mechanism is called port pooling. Port pooling will assign all ports for an environment according to the port pool assignment. There are 100 port pools available, numbered uniquely from 0-99. You must assign a different port pool for each environment running on the same servers; otherwise, you will encounter port conflicts. The context file entry, s_port_pool, defines the port pool that is used by an environment.

▶ *Tip*   Testing port availability should be performed prior to assigning ports for an installation of Oracle Applications. Additional details for checking port availability are provided in the *Testing Port Availability* section of this chapter.

Developing a Port Standard

Rather than using port pools, you can create a customized port numbering scheme. For example, you could place all ports for one instance within a range of 500 possible values, such as 19000–19500. For the next instance, all values could be incremented by 500. Table 2-8 shows an example port numbering convention for two test instances.

Table 2-8. *Example Port Numbering Scheme*

Port Description	Context File Parameter	Port Pool 0	Test 1 Port	Test 2 Port
Database	s_dbport	1521	19000	19500
RPC	s_rpcport	1626	19005	19505
Web SSL	s_webssl_port	4443	19443	19943
ONS Local	s_ons_localport	6100	19010	19510
ONS Remote	s_ons_remoteport	6200	19020	19520
ONS Request	s_ons_requestport	6500	19030	19530
Web Listener	s_webport	8000	19040	19540
Forms Listener	s_formsport	9000	19050	19550
Metric Server Data	s_metdataport	9100	19065	19565
Metric Server Request	s_metreqport	9200	19070	19570
JTF Fulfillment	s_jtfuf_port	9300	19080	19580
MSCA Server	s_mwaPortNo	10200-10205	19090-19095	19590-19595
MSCA Telnet Server	s_mwaTelnetPortNo	10200, 10202, 10204	19100-19102	19600-19602
MSCA Dispatcher	s_mwaDispatcherPort	10800	19110	19610
Java Object Cache	s_java_object_cache_port	12345	19120	19620
OC4J JMS Port Range for OaCore	s_oacore_jms_portrange	23000-23004	19130-19134	19630-19634
OC4J JMS Port Range for Forms	s_forms_jms_portrange	23500-23504	19150-19154	19650-19654

Table 2-8 *Continued*

Port Description	Context File Parameter	Port Pool 0	Test 1 Port	Test 2 Port
OC4J JMS Port Range for Home	s_home_jms_portrange	24000-24004	19170-19174	19670-19674
OC4J JMS Port Range for Oafm	s_oafm_jms_portrange	24500-24504	19190-19194	19690-19694
OC4J AJP Port Range for Oacore	s_home_ajp_portrange	21500-21504	19210-19214	19710-19714
OC4J AJP Port Range for Forms	s_forms_ajp_portrange	22000-22004	19230-19234	19730-19734
OC4J AJP Port Range for Home	s_home_ajp_portrange	22500-22504	19250-19254	19750-19754
OC4J AJP Port Range for Oafm	s_oafm_ajp_portrange	25000-25004	19270-19274	19770-19774
OC4J RMI Port Range for Oacore	s_oacore_ajp_portrange	20000-20004	19290-19294	19790-19794
OC4J RMI Port Range for Forms	s_forms_rmi_portrange	20500-20504	19310-19314	19810-19814
OC4J RMI Port Range for Home	s_home_rmi_portrange	21000-21004	19330-19334	19830-19834
OC4J RMI Port Range for Oafm	s_oafm_rmi_portrange	25500-25504	19350-19354	19850-19854
Oracle Connection Manager	s_cmanport	1521	19001	19501

Testing Port Availability

The UNIX netstat and grep commands can be used to check if a port is in use on the server. If netstat returns rows for the port, then the port is in use. The following example tests whether or not port 19000 is being used:

$UNIX>netstat –a | grep 19000

```
tcp4 0 0 *.19000 *.* LISTEN
tcp4 0 0 dbserver.19000 client.55555 ESTABLISHED
```

In this case, port 19000 is already in use. The LISTEN section of the output shows that a service is listening on port 19000, while the ESTABLISHED section indicates that a connection has been established to port 19000 by a client.

▶ *Tip*   It is good practice to update the /etc/services file on the server with all services that require ports. This assists in documenting port allocation for the server. Alternatively, you could create a file called /etc/oraservices to list all ports used by your Oracle Applications installation.

Context Files and AutoConfig

As previously stated, the nodes that comprise Oracle Applications have numerous configuration files and settings and administering these files can be quite cumbersome. In order to improve the management of the configuration files, Oracle has created AutoConfig, an automated tool that manages the files as well as some values in the database, such as Applications profiles. Values that are used for many of the configuration settings in E-Business Suite are stored in a common repository in the form of an XML file. On the application tier, this global configuration file is called the *Applications context file*. On the database tier, the configuration file is called the *database context file*.

Locating and Creating the Applications Context File

The Applications context file is an XML file named $CONTEXT_NAME.xml. The CONTEXT_NAME variable is set to

$ORACLE_SID_[hostname] by default. The Applications context file is located in the following directory:

$INST_TOP/appl/admin

The Applications context file may also be referenced using the environment variable $CONTEXT_FILE which is defined as follows:

$CONTEXT_FILE=$INST_TOP/appl/admin/CONTEXT_NAME.xml

    If the Applications context file is accidentally removed or lost, it can be recreated by using configuration information in INST_TOP or the database. The Applications context file is recreated using the retrieve option of adclonectx.pl.

    If the Applications context file is accidentally removed or lost and INST_TOP is still intact, the context file can be rebuilt or retrieved by executing the following on the Applications node:

$UNIX>perl $COMMON_TOP/clone/bin/adclonectx.pl retrieve

Upon executing this command, you will need to select the option to retrieve the appropriate context file. If INST_TOP has been lost as well, you can still retrieve the context file by running the following on the Database Node:

$UNIX>perl $ORACLE_HOME/appsutil/clone/bin/adclonectx.pl retrieve

Upon executing this command, you will need to select the option to retrieve the appropriate context file and a location where a file can be written. You will then need to move the context file to its proper location on the application tier.

Locating and Creating the Database Context File

The database context file is an XML file named CONTEXT_NAME.xml. The CONTEXT_NAME variable is set to $ORACLE_SID_[hostname] by default. The Database context file is located in the $ORACLE_HOME/appsutil directory.

    If the database context file does not exist, it can be created by executing the adbldxml.sh script as follows:

$UNIX>$ORACLE_HOME/appsutil/bin/adbldxml.sh

If the database context file is accidentally removed or lost, it can retrieved by executing the following on the Database Node:

$UNIX>perl $ORACLE_HOME/appsutil/clone/bin/adclonectx.pl retrieve

Upon executing this command, you will need to select the option to
retrieve the database context file.

▶ *R12 Implementation Tip*   In R12, using adbldxml.sh to build the context file is
supported only on the database tier.

Using OAM to Modify the Applications and Database Context File

The recommended method for editing the context files is to use Oracle
Applications Manager (OAM). OAM offers a user friendly, searchable
interface for modifying the context files. OAM also offers the ability to
save and recover context file versions as well as display differences
between versions of context files. Additionally, with OAM you can add
comments to the variables for documentation purposes.

To edit the context files in OAM, click on *Sitemap* → *AutoConfig*,
and then click on the *Edit Parameters* icon next to the appropriate context
file. The parameters on the *Context File Parameters* screen are ordered by
tabs that categorize the parameters in the file. The tabs are *Global*,
System, *Local*, *Install*, *Environments*, *Processes*, and *Custom* as shown in
Figure 2-5. To edit the values, simply click on the text entry field and
make changes to the text.

Figure 2-5. *Using OAM to edit the Applications context file*

Using AutoConfig

When modifications have been made to the context file, or when post patch step requirements dictate, AutoConfig needs be executed on all nodes in order to implement the configuration changes. Executing AutoConfig will propagate the changes made to the context files to the database and to configuration files on each of the nodes as needed.

How AutoConfig Operates

AutoConfig makes use of driver files, template files and context variable values to manage the configuration for the EBS system. When AutoConfig runs, it uses driver files to tell it the actions to perform and uses the template files and context variables to create configuration files. Context variables are also used to perform profile updates in the database.

Transparent to you, AutoConfig uses a process called Context Value Management (CVM) to manage and update the variables in the context files. It is used to add new variables, update the values of existing variables, apply new versions of context file templates and run some pre steps required for AutoConfig. CVM supports updates to context files on both application and database tiers.

AutoConfig Template and Driver Files

AutoConfig uses a driver file to direct its actions for each product that it supports. The driver file lists out each template file and the action to perform with each template file. The template files are used to create the configuration files. Each configuration file has either one generic template that is applicable for all operating systems, or multiple OS specific templates. The template files are a mixture of static text and variables that are replaced by values from the context files. For example, the adstpall_ux.sh template file contains the following line:

FND_TOP=%s_fndtop%

In this example, FND_TOP= is static text that will appear as is in the resulting configuration file. %s_fndtop% is a replacement variable that will be replaced by the value of that variable in the context file.

Using the AutoConfig Search Utility

The AutoConfig Search Utility, also known as the TXK Context Variable Information Utility, will provide information about context variables and the templates where they are used based on all or part of the context variable name provide by the user. The utility will generate an html report with the results of the run. The AutoConfig Search Utility can be executed with the following command:

$FND_TOP/bin/txkrun.pl –script=GenCtxInfRep – keyword=<search string> - outfile=<filename>.html

An example of executing the AutoConfig Search Utility to find information on the webentryhost is as follows:

$UNIX>$FND_TOP/bin/txkrun.pl –script=GenCtxInfRep \ –keyword=webentryhost –outfile=webentryhost.html

The output generated by executing this command is displayed in Figure 2-6.

Technology Stack (TXK) Context Variable Information Report

Report Header

Date	Sat, 20 Mar 2010 18:50:50
Search Keyword	webentryhost
Context Type	Apps Context
Context File	/home/r12vis/inst_top/apps/VIS_erlinux01/appl/admin/VIS_erlinux01.xml
Output File	/inst_top/apps/VIS_erlinux01/appltmp/TXK/webentryhost.html
Report Type	html

Matched Context Variables

Show All/Hide All

s_login_page s_webentryhost s_unicodeURL s_endUserMonitoringURL s_external_url

Template Files Matched in Product Tops

AD_TOP

Source Files	Target Files	Matched Context Variables
/admin/template/index.html	/inst_top/apps/VIS_erlinux01/portal/index.html	s_login_page

Figure 2-6. *Example output from the AutoConfig Search Utility*

Executing AutoConfig

AutoConfig can be executed against all nodes of Oracle Applications, including the Database Node, using the scripts listed in the next section. The scripts can request different inputs as well as perform slightly different functions. All Applications processes should be shut down prior to executing AutoConfig. However, the database and database listener must be up and available for updates when AutoConfig is run.

Scripts used to Execute AutoConfig

There are three scripts available to execute AutoConfig. These scripts accept different parameters for the execution. The following sections will describe the adconfig.pl, adconfig.sh and adautocfg.sh scripts used to execute AutoConfig.

adconfig.pl

The base Perl script for AutoConfig is adconfig.pl. Although adconfig.pl can be called directly, it is generally more convenient to call one of the wrapper scripts below. The location of adconfig.pl on the application tier is as follows:

$AD_TOP/bin/adconfig.pl

The location of adconfig.pl on the database tier is located as follows:

$ORACLE_HOME/appsutil/bin/adconfig.pl

The adconfig.pl script can be called using the following code:

$UNIX>perl adconfig.pl contextfile=$CONTEXT_FILE

Parameters such as parallel can be passed to adconfig.pl in the following manner:

$UNIX>perl adconfig.pl contextfile=$CONTEXT_FILE –parallel

adconfig.sh

The wrapper script that calls adconfig.pl is adconfig.sh. This script does some checks such as determining if a valid version of Perl is available for use, and asks for only the context file and the apps password as inputs. This is the wrapper to run if you want to use any of the non-default options. The location of adconfig.sh on the application tier is located as follows:

$AD_TOP/bin/adconfig.sh

The location of adconfig.sh on the database tier is located as follows:

$ORACLE_HOME/appsutil/bin/adconfig.sh

The script adconfig.sh can be executed using the following code:

$UNIX>adconfig.sh contextfile=$CONTEXT_FILE

Parameters such as parallel can be passed to adconfig.sh in the following manner:

$UNIX>adconfig.sh contextfile=$CONTEXT_FILE –parallel

adautocfg.sh

The wrapper script that calls adconfig.sh is adautocfg.sh. This sets all the parameters, except for the apps password, to the default. As such, this script can't be used to run AutoConfig with other options such as –parallel or –profile. If the default parameters are acceptable, this is the most convenient wrapper to run. The adautocfg.sh script on the application tier is located as follows:

$ADMIN_SCRIPTS_HOME/adautocfg.sh

The adautocfg.sh script on the database tier is located as follows:

$ORACLE_HOME/appsutil/scripts/$CONTEXT_NAME/adautocfg.sh

The adautocfg.sh script can be called using the following statement:

$UNIX>adautocfg.sh

AutoConfig Screen Output

Each time you run AutoConfig, output will be displayed on the screen showing pertinent information. Below is an example of the screen output from a successful AutoConfig run on an Applications node:

```
r12vis@erlinux01:/r12vis/apps/apps_st/appl/ad/12.0.0/bin$ ./adconfig.pl
contextfile=/home/r12vis/inst_top/apps/VIS_erlinux01/appl/admin/VIS_erlinux01.
xml
Enter the APPS user password:

The log file for this session is located at:
/inst_top/apps/VIS_erlinux01/admin/log/03312104/adconfig.log

AutoConfig is configuring the Applications environment...

AutoConfig will consider the custom templates if present.
   Using CONFIG_HOME location    : /inst_top/apps/VIS_erlinux01
   Classpath              :
/r12vis/apps/apps_st/comn/java/lib/appsborg2.zip:/r12vis/apps/apps_st/comn/java/c
lasses

   Using Context file    :
/home/r12vis/inst_top/apps/VIS_erlinux01/appl/admin/VIS_erlinux01.xml
```

Context Value Management will now update the Context file

Updating Context file...COMPLETED

Attempting upload of Context file and templates to database...COMPLETED

Configuring templates from all of the product tops...
Configuring AD_TOP........COMPLETED
Configuring FND_TOP.......COMPLETED

      .
      .
      .

Configuring IGC_TOP.......COMPLETED

AutoConfig completed successfully.

▶ *Tip*   The statement "AutoConfig completed successfully" is the default statement at the end of AutoConfig execution log file. You need to review the entire log file to determine if there were errors during the execution of AutoConfig.

Executing AutoConfig in Parallel

AutoConfig may be executed across multiple nodes at the same time by using the parallel option. This can dramatically reduce the time required for running AutoConfig across a multi-node installation. When running in parallel mode, AutoConfig uses a locking mechanism to insure there are no conflicting updates against the database or the filesystem. The following is the syntax for running AutoConfig in parallel:

perl adconfig.pl contextfile=$CONTEXT_FILE [product=<product_top>] –parallel

The optional parameter, product_top is the short name of the product to be configured. If this optional parameter is not passed in, AutoConfig will configure all products. If you wanted to run AutoConfig in parallel mode but only against the Applications Object Library, whose short name is FND, you would execute the following:

perl adconfig.pl contextfile=$CONTEXT_FILE [product=FND] –parallel

> ▶ *Tip*   The AutoConfig parallel option MUST be specified on each node in order to prevent potential conflicts.

Location of AutoConfig Log Files

The execution of AutoConfig generates a log file. You should review the log file for any errors that may exist and work to resolve them. The log file for the execution of AutoConfig on the application tier is located as follows:

$INST_TOP/admin/log/[MMDDHHMI]/adconfig.log

The log file for the execution of AutoConfig on the database tier is located as follows:

$ORACLE_HOME/appsutil/log/$CONTEXT_NAME/[MMDDHHMI]/adconfig.log

where MM is the month, DD is the day, HH is the hour and MI is the minute when AutoConfig was executed.

> ▶ *Tip*   A successful AutoConfig run will display the following line at the bottom of the log file as well as at the bottom of the screen output: AutoConfig is exiting with status 0

Location of AutoConfig Backup Files

The execution of AutoConfig also generates backup files and a restore script. The backup files for the execution of AutoConfig on the application tier are located in the following directory:

$INST_TOP/admin/out/[MMDDHHMI]

The backup files for the execution of AutoConfig on the database tier are located in the following directory:

$ORACLE_HOME/appsutil/log/$CONTEXT_NAME/out/[MMDDHHMI]

where MM is the month, DD is the day, HH is the hour and MI is the minute when AutoConfig was executed

Reviewing AutoConfig Execution Changes

To review configuration changes that will be made by executing AutoConfig, you can execute the adchkcfg.sh script, known as the *Check Config* utility. This Check Config utility generates an HTML file named cfgcheck.html that displays the changes that will be made in the configuration. The adchkcfg.sh script for the application tier is in the following location:

$AD_TOP/bin

The adchkcfg.sh script for the database tier is in the following location:

$ORACLE_HOME/appsutil/bin

The HTML output file for the application tier is located as follows:

$INST_TOP/admin/out/[MMDDHHMI]

The HTML output file for the database tier is located as follows:

$ORACLE_HOME/appsutil/out/$CONTEXT_NAME/[MMDDHHMI]

where MM is the month, DD is the day, HH is the hour and MI is the minute when adchkcfg.sh was executed.

The output file has a tab for *File System* changes and a tab for *Database* changes. Each tab is broken up into different sections that can be expanded or contracted to view details. A screenshot of the HTML file generated by executing the Check Config utility is shown in Figure 2-7.

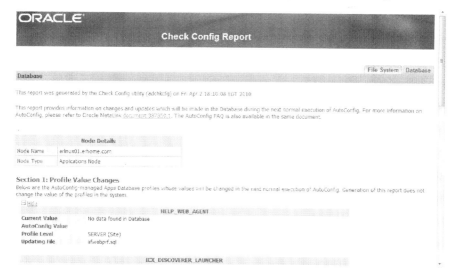

Figure 2-7. *Example output from an AutoConfig Check Config Report*

▶ *Tip*   If you want to restore configuration files from the backup of an AutoConfig run on an Applications node or the Database Node, you can execute the restore.sh script. The location of the script is as follows for the Applications and database tier, respectively:
$INST_TOP/admin/out/[MMDDHHMI]/restore.sh
$ORACLE_HOME/appsutil/out/$CONTEXT_NAME/[MMDDHHMI]/restore.sh

Using AutoConfig Performance Profiler

The *AutoConfig Performance Profiler* can be used to gather information on timings in an AutoConfig run. The profiler outputs an HTML file that lists all the product tops and the time taken to process each template within the product top. You can use this report to identify bottlenecks in the AutoConfig run by examining the run times and comparing with previous runs where appropriate. This can be particularly useful if you see an increase in your AutoConfig run time after making customizations or applying patches. The AutoConfig Performance Profiler on the application tier is executed as follows:

$AD_TOP/bin/adconfig.pl contextfile=$CONTEXT_FILE \
[product=<product_top>] -profile

▶ *Note*   The optional parameter, product_top is the short name of the product to be configured. If no product is passed in, AutoConfig will configure all products.

The AutoConfig Performance Profiler on the database tier is executed as follows:

$UNIX>$ORACLE_HOME/appsutil/bin/adconfig.pl
contextfile=$CONTEXT_FILE -profile

An excerpt of the output generated by executing the Performance Profiler is displayed in Figure 2-8.

AutoConfig Performance Profile Report

AutoConfig Summary

Start Time	End Time	Total Time (sec)
2010-07-18 15:07:51	2010-07-18 15:16:36	525.00

Context Value Management

Scripts	Instantiation Time (sec)	Execution Time (sec)	Total Time (sec)	Time (%)	Status
cvm	-	41.50	41.50	9.54	Passed

Product Summary Report

Product Top	Instantiation Time (sec)	Execution Time (sec)	Total Time (sec)	Time (%)	Status
ad/fnd	38.35	313.36	351.71	80.85	Passed
icx	0.25	0.80	1.05	0.24	Passed
ieo	2.08	-	2.08	0.48	Passed
bis	0.46	7.65	8.11	1.86	Passed
ams	0.25	1.10	1.35	0.31	Passed
cct	0.44	-	0.44	0.10	Passed
wsh	0.22	0.61	0.83	0.19	Passed
cln	0.21	0.60	0.81	0.19	Passed
okl	0.42	0.82	1.21	0.29	Passed

Figure 2-8. *Example output from an AutoConfig Performance Profile Report*

Deploying Customizations with AutoConfig

At times, it is necessary to add custom parameters and environment variables to the configuration that are not stored within the parameters of the Applications or database context files. This section will describe the following methods for adding customizations to the configuration:

* Customizing Template Files
* Using OAM to add customizations

Customizing Template Files

The need may arise to customize Oracle's seeded templates. However, Oracle does not support direct modifications to their templates. Therefore, you will need to set up a custom template file. This is done by copying the seeded template from its directory to a subdirectory named custom and making any required changes to the template in the custom location. During the next execution, AutoConfig will pick up the custom template and use it to create the configuration file.

If you need to find the location for a template of a file that you want to modify, you can run adtmplreport.sh. The following is an example of executing adtmplreport.sh on the application tier:

$AD_TOP/bin/adtmplreport.sh \
contextfile=<CtxFile> target=<configurationfile>

The adtmplreport.sh can be executed on the database tier as follows:

$ORACLE_HOME/appsutil/bin/adtmplreport.sh contextfile=<CtxFile>
target=<configurationfile>

Executing the adtmplreport.sh script creates a log file containing the name and location of the template file that is used for the creation of the configuration file. You can also specify the –verbose parameter when executing adtmplreport.sh to display the output on the screen. The following is an example of executing adtmplreport.sh:

$UNIX>adtmplreport.sh contextfile=$CONTEXT_FILE \
target=$INST_TOP/ora/10.1.3/Apache/Apache/conf/httpd.conf \
–verbose

```
##################################################
        Generating Report .....
##################################################
[FND_TOP]
TEMPLATE FILE   :
/r12vis/apps/apps_st/appl/fnd/12.0.0/admin/template/httpd_conf_1013.tmp
TARGET FILE     :
/inst_top/apps/VIS_erlinux01/ora/10.1.3/Apache/Apache/conf/httpd.conf

For details check log file: /inst_top/apps/VIS_erlinux01/admin/log/03242120.log
```

▶ **Tip**   Certain template files cannot be customized. If the template file's entry in the driver file has the word LOCK, any custom template files will be ignored.

AutoConfig performs a version check between all seeded templates and their custom counterparts and will abort if it detects any differences. This ensures that you are aware of new versions of templates as they are released via patches. If AutoConfig aborts due to a template version conflict, the following will be displayed on the screen during the run:

Version Conflicts among development maintained and customized templates encountered; aborting AutoConfig run.

AutoConfig will write detailed information about incompatibilities in the adconfig.log; however, it is up to you to reconcile any differences.

▶ *Tip*   If you apply a patch that updates an Oracle seeded AutoConfig template, you will need to recopy and redeploy any related custom templates. Failure to do this will result in a failure during the next execution of AutoConfig.

Adding Customizations Using Oracle Applications Manager

Oracle Applications Manager (OAM) may also be used to create new custom parameters. This feature can be accessed by clicking *Site Map* → *AutoConfig* → *Manage Custom Parameters*. Clicking the *Add* button will allow you to create a custom parameter. Figure 2-9 shows the options for creating a new custom parameter using OAM.

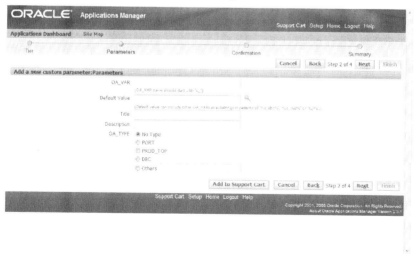

Figure 2-9. *OAM screen for adding custom parameters*

Securing Oracle Applications

Improving Oracle Applications Security can be accomplished at the application or database levels. Password validation can be maintained by both the Applications and database. User access can be controlled via Applications responsibilities and database roles. This section will provide configuration options for securing Applications and database logins.

▶ *Tip*   Be certain to schedule the change of the system passwords as necessary when key personnel changes occur.

Applications Password Verification

At the Applications level, profile settings can be used to add security to the Applications user passwords. These profile options assist in enforcing standards on Applications passwords. Table 2-9 outlines the profile options used to provide password security for Applications users.

Table 2-9. *Profile Options Available for Applications Password Security*

Profile Option	Description
Signon Password Hard to Guess	When set to YES, the password must contain at least one letter or number. It may not contain the username or repeating characters.
Signon Password Length	When set to a nonnegative integer, the password will be required to be the specific length.
Signon Password Failure Limit	When set to a nonnegative integer, the user will not be able to log in again after the number of unsuccessful logins equal to the set value.

Table 2-9. *Continued*

Profile Option	Description
Signon Password No Reuse	When set to a nonnegative integer, the user will not be able to reuse his or her password for the number of days equal to the set value.
Signon Password Custom	You may create your own custom validation Java class for password verification. The details are outside the scope of this guide, but the option is available for your use.

Database Password Verification

The Oracle Applications DBA can define additional password security for users defined in the database. This may be accomplished through password verification functions and database profiles. Password verification functions, once defined, may be assigned to the database profile, which is then assigned to the database user.

The database profile feature has several standard options, such as the ability to lock the account after a set number of failed login attempts. Additionally, the profile allows for the creation of a customized password verification function to enforce password complexity. Password verification functions define specific requirements for the content of a password, including length, characters and special characters, to name a few.

The following is an example password function that checks all passwords for a special character, such as "#" or "_":

```
CREATE OR REPLACE FUNCTION
"SYS"."PASSWORD_VERIFY_FUNCTION" (
username varchar2,
password varchar2,
old_password varchar2)
RETURN boolean IS
n boolean;
m integer;
isspecial boolean;
specialarray varchar2(25);
```

```
BEGIN
specialarray:='#_';

-- Check for required special character
isspecial:=FALSE;
FOR i IN 1..length(specialarray) LOOP
FOR j IN 1..m LOOP
IF substr(password,j,1) = substr(specialarray,i,1) THEN
isspecial:=TRUE;
END IF;
END LOOP;
END LOOP;
IF isspecial = FALSE THEN
raise_application_error(-20001, 'The password should contain one of the following
special characters # or _ ');
END IF;

-- Everything is fine, return TRUE ;
RETURN(TRUE);
END;
```

▶ *Tip*   As of 11g, Oracle provides the ability to use case sensitivity for database passwords. This can be configured by setting the database initialization parameter sec_case_sensitive_logon. This functionality; however, is NOT currently supported by Oracle Applications deployments.

Configuration Best Practices

Configuration changes should always be implemented in a sandbox or test environment prior to promoting to production. Documenting your configuration decisions and standards is a critical component in successfully managing the environment. When changes are made to configuration, create a change log in your standards documentation. Be sure to also update process documents to reflect changes in processes as they relate to changes in configuration.

When upgrades are performed or patches are applied, remember to update the configuration documentation with any new configuration or changes in configuration. If configuration changes involve memory or performance related changes, be certain to load test the environment before promoting the change to production.

We recommend sizing a development or test instance to match production if it will be used to simulate production load levels. If no such requirement exists, then reducing sizing parameters in a test or development instance can save CPU and memory resources. Additional tips regarding resizing resources for development and test instances are provided in the cloning section in Chapter 3 of this guide.

Chapter 3

Installation and Cloning

Building upon the knowledge of the architecture and services content from Chapter 1 and configuration content from Chapter 2, this chapter will focus on installing and cloning Oracle Applications. This chapter is not meant to serve as a step by step installation or cloning guide, but will provide you the basics of understanding the installation and cloning process. How to upgrade to Oracle Applications Release 12.1.1 is out of scope for this guide.

*   **Oracle Applications installations:** This section will cover the tool used to perform installations, types of installations and a high level overview of the various installation options.

*   **Oracle Applications cloning:** This section will cover the tool used to perform clones as well as recommendations for post cloning steps.

Oracle Applications Installations

This section will cover topics regarding Oracle Applications installations. The following sections will be covered:

*   **Rapid Install:** This section will cover Rapid Install, the tool used for installing Oracle Applications.

*   **Types of Installations**: This section will define the types of installations available with the Oracle Applications Release 12.1.1 Rapid Install Wizard.

*   **Rapid Install Log Files**: This section will identify the locations of the application and database tier log files associated with Rapid Install.

*   **Installation documentation:** This section will describe the importance of documenting the installation decisions.

Rapid Install

Rapid Install, also known as rapidwiz, is the utility that is used to perform Oracle Applications installations. To use Rapid Install, you must have downloaded and staged the Oracle Applications installation media on the server. Prior to running Rapid Install, you must also set your DISPLAY to a system that has the ability to run X Windows. Additional details regarding X Windows are provided in Chapter 4 of this guide. Once this is complete, you can execute Rapid Install with the following command from the rapidwiz directory where the installation media has been staged:

$UNIX>./rapidwiz

To see a complete listing of options for running Rapid Install, you run rapidwiz with the help option. The results of running rapidwiz with the help option are displayed in Figure 3-1. The execution of the command to yield the help is as follows:

$UNIX>./rapidwiz –help

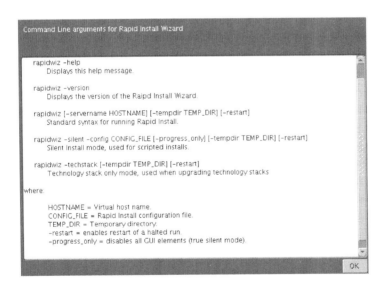

Figure 3-1. *Display of rapidwiz help option*

▶ *Tip*   You may use adautostg.pl to stage the media from the shipped DVDs or download directory. The adautostg.pl script will unbundle the media in preparation for installation.

Types of Installations

Rapid Install can be used to perform multiple types of installations. The following are the most common installations that can be performed with Oracle Applications Release 12.1.1 Rapid Install Wizard:

* **Oracle Applications Release 12.1.1 Technology Stack**

* **Oracle Applications Release 12.1.1**

Additional details regarding the installation types are covered in the following sections.

▶ *Note*   The concepts in Chapters 1 and 2 provide the foundation required for making appropriate decisions during the installation process.

Oracle Applications Release 12.1.1 Technology Stack

Installing the Technology Stack is typically performed if you are upgrading an existing environment to R12.1.1 or performing a new installation of the enviornment. You may also choose this option if you are upgrading or installing the Technology Stack components of the database or application tier.

In order to select one of the Technology Stack installation options, you must run Rapid Install with the Technology Stack installation option. To execute a Technology Stack installation, run the following command:

$UNIX>./rapidwiz –techstack

The following are the choices when executing a Rapid Install Technology Stack installation:

* **Database Technology Stack (11gR1 RDBMS)**

* **Applications Technology Stack (10.1.2.3 AS + 10.1.3.4 AS)**

Additional details regarding the Technology Stack Install options are covered in the next sections.

Installing the Database Technology Stack

When choosing to install the Technology Stack, you may install the Database Technology Stack. To pick this option, you must select the

Database Technology Stack (11gR1 RDBMS) radio button on the installation screen as shown in Figure 3-2.

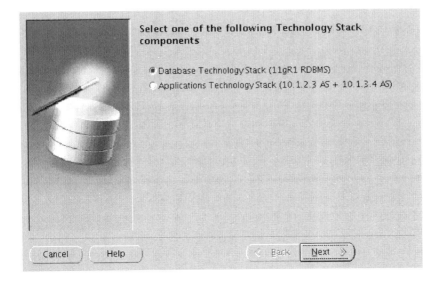

Figure 3-2. *Rapid Install: Installing the Database Technology Stack*

Selecting the Database Technology Stack will install the 11gR1 database binaries. After you choose this option, and click *Next*, you will be required to enter information regarding the Database Node as depicted in the *RDBMS Inputs Page* in Figure 3-3.

▶ *Note*   To cancel an installation, you may be required to click the *Cancel* button multiple times with one final confirmation to cancel.

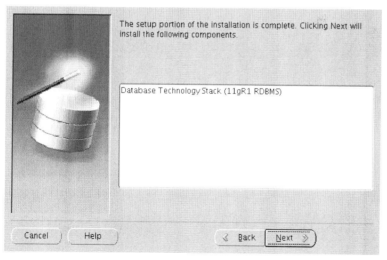

Figure 3-3. *Database Technology Stack Install: RDBMS Inputs Page*

On this screen you may change information regarding the Database Node configuration. Once the appropriate information for the Database Node has been entered, click *Next*. Now the installation is ready to begin. To confirm and begin the installation click the *Next* button on the *Setup Verification Install* to start the installation of the *Database Technology Stack* as displayed in Figure 3-4.

Figure 3-4. *Database Technology Stack Install: Setup Verification Install Screen*

Installing the Applications Technology Stack

When you execute rapidwiz with the techstack option, you may also choose to install the Applications Technology Stack. You may select this option by clicking the *Applications Technology Stack (10.1.2.3 AS + 10.1.3.4 AS)* radio button as show in Figure 3-5.

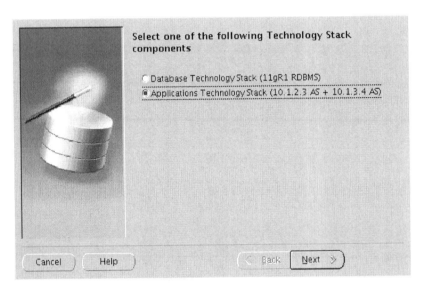

Figure 3-5. *Rapid Install: Installing the Applications Technology Stack*

▶ *Tip*   Selecting the *Applications Technology Stack* will install the Java Tech Stack and the Tools Tech Stack. For additional details regarding the Java and Tools Tech Stack refer to Chapter 2 of this guide.

After selecting to install the *Applications Technology Stack* and clicking the *Next* button, you will need to enter the location of the Applications context file as depicted in Figure 3-6.

Figure 3-6. *Applications Technology Stack Install: Enter the Applications Context File*

Next, you will be prompted to enter the location of the *Web Oracle Home* and the *Tools Oracle Home* as shown in Figure 3-7. The *Web Oracle Home* is synonymous with the Java Tech Stack. The *Tools Oracle Home* is synonymous with the Tools Tech Stack. Please enter the appropriate locations for your installation. Once you have entered the information, click the *Next* button.

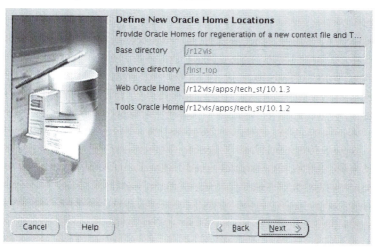

Figure 3-7. *Applications Technology Install: Define New Oracle Home Locations*

Now the installation is ready to begin. You will once again click the *Next* button to start the installation of the *Applications Technology Stack* as displayed in Figure 3-8.

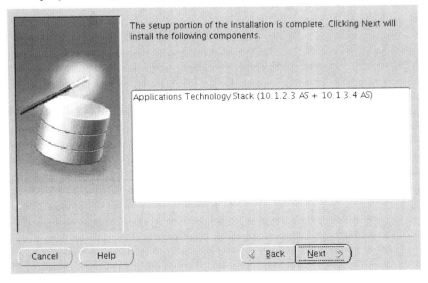

The setup portion of the installation is complete. Clicking Next will install the following components.

Applications Technology Stack (10.1.2.3 AS + 10.1.3.4 AS)

| Cancel | Help | | Back | Next |

Figure 3-8. *Setup Verification Install Screen: Click Next to Continue the Applications Technology Installation*

Install Oracle Applications Release 12.1.1

When executing rapidwiz without any installation options, you have the option to perform a new 12.1.1 installation or upgrade to 12.1.1. This section will cover the *Install Oracle Applications Release 12.1.1* option. Details regarding performing an upgrade to 12.1.1 are out of scope for this guide.

After starting rapidwiz with no options, the first screen that is displayed lists the various components available during the installation. This screen is shown in Figure 3-9. The actual installation that occurs is dependent upon the selections and decisions that are made during the installation process. After clicking the *Next* button on the *Oracle Applications Release 12.1.1 Rapid Install Wizard* screen, you will be taken to the screen shown in Figure 3-10.

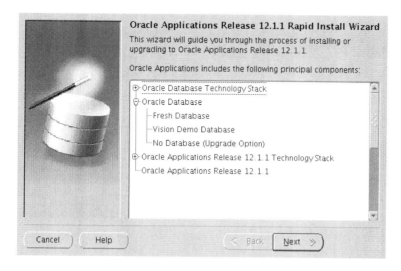

Figure 3-9. *Oracle Applications Release 12.1.1 Rapid Install Wizard*

You have a few choices available in the *Select Wizard Operation* screen as shown in Figure 3-10. You may choose *Install Oracle Applications Release 12.1.1* with or without the *Use Express Install* option or you may *Upgrade to Oracle Applications Release 12.1.1*. Choose the *Install Oracle Applications Release 12.1.1* radio button without selecting the *Use Express Install* option and click the *Next* button.

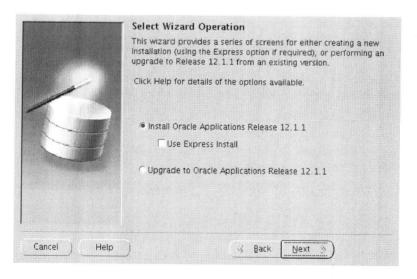

Figure 3-10. *Select Wizard Operation*

▶ *Note* Performing an Express Install eliminates many of the decisions needed to be made during the installation process. If you wish to customize or make choices regarding installation options, you should not choose the *Use Express Install* option.

The next screen that is displayed is the *Configuration Choice* screen as shown in Figure 3-11. One of the first decision points is to determine whether or not you will create a new configuration or load your configuration from an existing database as shown in Figure 3-11.

If you choose to load your configuration, the configuration will be loaded from the database. Loading an existing configuration typically occurs if you are installing a later Technology Stack for an existing environment.

For the purposes of this example, a new configuration file is being created. Click the radio button labeled *Create a new configuration* and click the *Next* button.

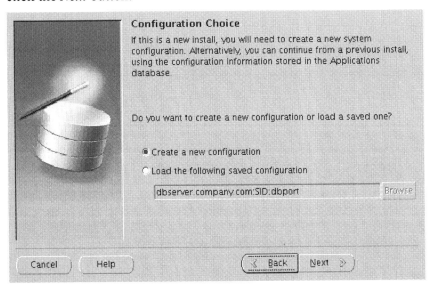

Figure 3-11. *Configuration Choice*

The next screen that is displayed is the *Global System Settings* screen as shown in Figure 3-12. When choosing to create a new configuration, you will need to select a port pool as shown in Figure 3-12. At this point you may also edit the ports by clicking the *Edit Ports* button. When you have completed selecting the port pool and editing the ports, click the *Next* button.

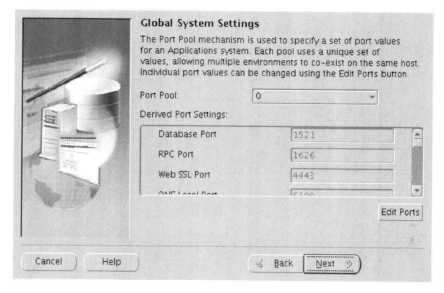

Figure 3-12. *Global System Settings*

The next screen requires that you enter information regarding the Database Node Configuration as shown in Figure 3-13. Here you will decide whether or not to perform a *Vision Demo Database* installation or a *Fresh Database* installation. Selecting *Vision Demo Database* will create a new database with seeded Oracle Vision Data. Selecting a *Fresh Database* install will create a new database for an R12 installation. Select *Fresh Database* install and click the *Next* button.

▶ *Tip*   A *Vision Instance* is not meant to be implemented as a deployable environment. A Vision Instance is a sandbox instance for functional and technical teams. Vision installations are performed and maintained for the purposes of testing configuration and functionality

Figure 3-13. *Database Node Configuration*

The next step in the process is to complete the information required on the *Primary Applications Node Configuration* screen as shown in Figure 3-14. On this screen, you will enter information regarding the primary node configuration. You may also enable or disable services on the primary node by clicking the *Edit Services* button. Clicking the *Edit Services* button will display the services as shown in Figure 3-15.

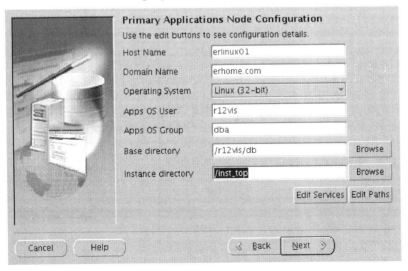

Figure 3-14. *Primary Applications Node Configuration*

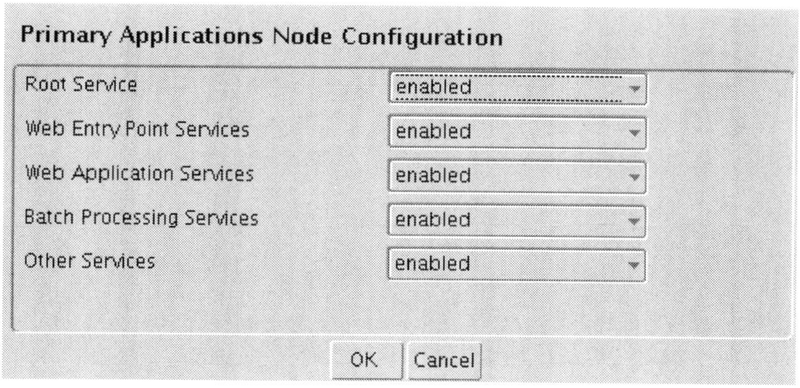

Primary Applications Node Configuration

Root Service	enabled ▾
Web Entry Point Services	enabled ▾
Web Application Services	enabled ▾
Batch Processing Services	enabled ▾
Other Services	enabled ▾

OK   Cancel

Figure 3-15. *Primary Applications Node Configuration: Edit Services*

Once you complete the settings to enable or disable the appropriate services, click the *OK* button. This will take you back to the *Primary Applications Node Configuration* screen. From here you may also choose to edit the paths by clicking the *Edit Paths* button. Clicking the *Edit Paths* button will display the screen shown in Figure 3-16.

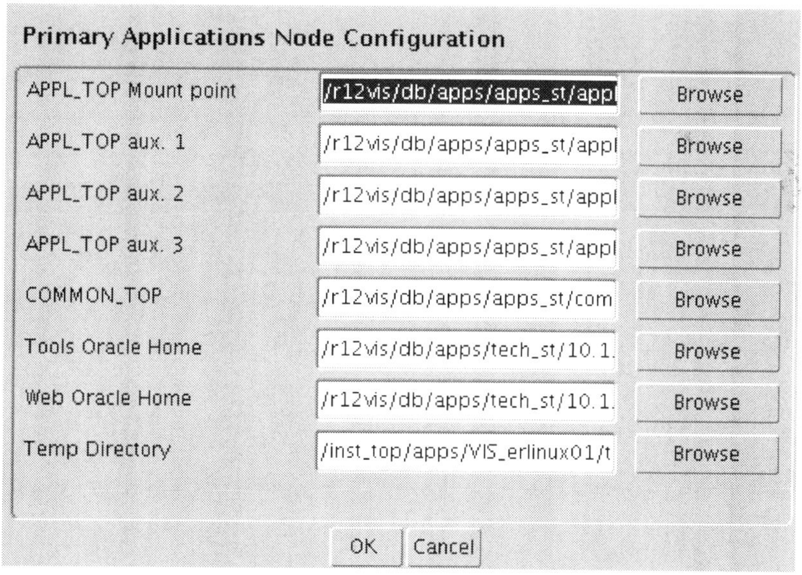

Primary Applications Node Configuration

APPL_TOP Mount point	/r12vis/db/apps/apps_st/appl	Browse
APPL_TOP aux. 1	/r12vis/db/apps/apps_st/appl	Browse
APPL_TOP aux. 2	/r12vis/db/apps/apps_st/appl	Browse
APPL_TOP aux. 3	/r12vis/db/apps/apps_st/appl	Browse
COMMON_TOP	/r12vis/db/apps/apps_st/com	Browse
Tools Oracle Home	/r12vis/db/apps/tech_st/10.1.	Browse
Web Oracle Home	/r12vis/db/apps/tech_st/10.1.	Browse
Temp Directory	/inst_top/apps/VIS_erlinux01/t	Browse

OK   Cancel

Figure 3-16. *Primary Applications Node Configuration: Edit Paths*

Once you have completed editing the paths, click the *OK* button. This will take you back to the *Primary Applications Node Configuration* screen. Once you are complete, click the *Next* button. The next screen is the *Node Information* screen as shown in Figure 3-17.

On the *Node Information* screen you can add additional nodes to your configuration. Once you have finalized adding all required nodes to the environment, then you may click the *Next* button.

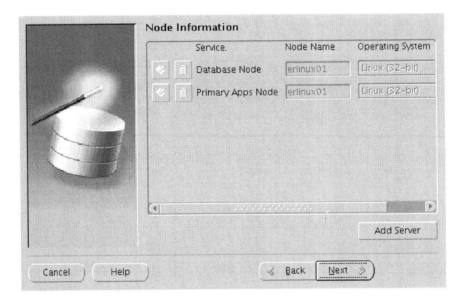

Figure 3-17. *Node Information: Add Server button*

▶ *Tip*   If you are performing a single node implementation, all required services will be enabled for the Primary Applications Node. If you are performing a multi-node implementation, then you can enable and disable services running only those that are provided by the node that is being configured.

When you reach this point, all installation options and decisions have been made and the installation runs through a series of system checks prior to performing the installation. An example of the system checks is shown in Figure 3-18. Once the system checks are finalized, the *Validate System Configuration* screen is displayed as shown in Figure 3-19.

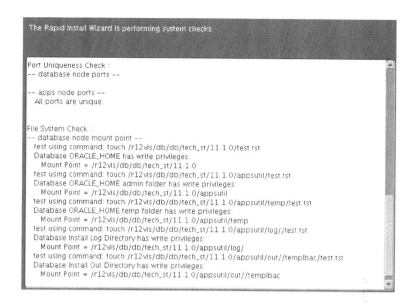

Figure 3-18. *Rapid Install: System Checks Screen*

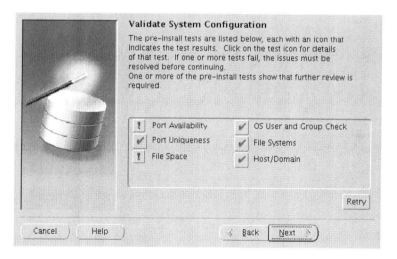

Figure 3-19. *Rapid Install: Validate System Configuration*

Green check marks on the *Validate System Configuration* screen indicate that there are no issues. Red exclamation points on the *Validate System Configuration* screen indicate that there are issues that need to be resolved.

▶ *Note*   The installation, and issues with installation, can be researched by reviewing the installation log files. Additional details regarding installation log files are provided in the *Rapid Install Log Files* section in this chapter.

If any issues are identified, you will need to resolve the issues displayed in the *Validate System Configuration* screen and retry the validation. Once validation is successful, the next step is to perform the installation. To begin the installation, click the *Next* button on the *Validate System Configuration* screen.

▶ *Note*   The software installation may take some time. The speed of the installation is dependent upon the resources available in the environment. Review the installation log files for details regarding installation progress.

Rapid Install Log Files

Log files for rapidwiz installations are helpful to review and document the installation or troubleshoot errors that may occur. Log files for rapidwiz are located in different directories based upon the installation that is occurring. Log files for the application tier are located as follows:

$INST_TOP/logs/[MMDDHHMI].log
$INST_TOP/logs/ora/10.1.2/install/make_[MMDDHHMI].log
$INST_TOP/logs/ora/10.1.3/install/make_[MMDDHHMI].log
$INST_TOP/admin/log/ohclone.log
$INST_TOP/admin/log/ApplyAppsTechStack.log
$APPL_TOP/admin/$CONTEXT_NAME/log/ApplyAppsTechStack.log
$APPL_TOP/admin/$CONTEXT_NAME/log/installAppl.log

Log files for the Database Technology Stack are located as follows:

$ORACLE_HOME/appsutil/log/$CONTEXT_NAME/[MMDDHHMI].log
$ORACLE_HOME/appsutil/log/$CONTEXT_NAME/dbInstall.log
$ORACLE_HOME/appsutil/log/$CONTEXT_NAME/ ohclone.log
$ORACLE_HOME/appsutil/log/$CONTEXT_NAME/ --
make_[MMDDHHMI].log
$ORACLE_HOME/appsutil/log/[CONTEXT_NAME/ --
ApplyDBTechStack_[MMDDHHMI].log
$ORACLE_HOME/appsutil/log/[CONTEXT_NAME/ installdbf.log

$ORACLE_HOME/appsutil/log/$CONTEXT_NAME/ NetServiceHandler.log
$ORACLE_HOME/appsutil/log/$CONTEXT_NAME/ --
applyDatabase_[MMDDHHMI].log

where MM is the month, DD is the day, HH is the hour and MI is the minute when rapidwiz was run.

Installation Documentation

It is important that as you make decisions regarding your installation that the decisions are documented as standards for your environment. This documentation will include all aspects of the installation including the location of <APPS_BASE>, INST_TOP, and the port pool used, to name only a few. While it may seem tedious to document these decisions, administrative and management tasks will be easier when the installation is documented properly.

Rapid Clone

Rapid Clone is Oracle's provided utility for cloning the Oracle EBS environment. Rapid Clone can be used to clone the application and database tiers. The following components will be described in this section:

* **Using Rapid Clone to clone an Oracle Applications instance:** Rapid Clone is Oracle's supplied method of cloning an Oracle Applications instance. It handles the majority of the configuration changes required for the target instance.

* **Post cloning steps:** This section will describe how to handle configuration changes that are not modified by Rapid Clone. These changes include standard Oracle functionality as well as custom changes you may want to consider as part of your post cloning steps.

▶ *Tip*　　When cloning, the system that is being cloned is referred to as the source system or source instance. The instance that is being created by the cloning process is called the target system or target instance.

Using Rapid Clone to Clone an Oracle Applications Instance

Rapid Clone may be used to clone both the Applications and database of an Oracle Applications instance. There are certain prerequisite tasks that need to be performed prior to running Rapid Clone; the required prerequisites are detailed in *My Oracle Support Article ID 406982.1*. Once you have completed and verified all the prerequisites, you are ready to begin the cloning process.

The first thing you must do is prepare the source system for cloning. This is done by running adpreclone.pl on the application and database tiers. This step does not make any configuration changes to the source system, but prepares templates and scripts that will be used to reconfigure the target system. The script, adpreclone.pl, is called with different parameters depending on the tier on which you execute it. The following is an example of the execution of adpreclone.pl on the application tier:

```
$UNIX>cd $INST_TOP/admin/scripts
$UNIX>perl adpreclone.pl appsTier
```

The following is the execution of adpreclone.pl on the database tier:

```
$UNIX>cd $ORACLE_HOME/appsutil/scripts/$CONTEXT_NAME
$UNIX>perl adpreclone.pl dbTier
```

When adpreclone.pl is successfully run, the following output will be displayed:

```
Completed Stage...
Fri Mar 19 21:43:17 2010
```

▶ *Tip*   Before performing your first clone or after any Rapid Clone or AutoConfig updates have been applied to the system, you execute adpreclone.pl. If no updates have been made, adpreclone.pl does not need to be run prior to each clone.

After running adpreclone.pl, shut down the Applications and database and copy the source system filesystem and files to the target system filesystem and files. Different methods for copying the source filesystem to the target may be used; however, when doing so, make sure any symbolic links are preserved. In addition to this, the owner of the files may need to be updated to your appropriate target user. The following is an example of a command that can be used to copy the source filesystem, vis, to the target filesystem vis_clone:

$UNIX>(cd /vis; tar –cf - .)|(cd /vis_clone; tar –xf -)

As some operating systems behave differently, please thoroughly test all commands before using them in a production environment.

▶ **Note**   Performing a clone from a hot backup of the database is supported, but requires some extra steps. See *My Oracle Support Article ID 406982.1* and *My Oracle Support Article ID 760772.1* for more information.

Now that the filesystem structures have been copied, you are ready to configure the target system. This is done by running adcfgclone.pl on the application and database tiers. Running adcfgclone.pl creates a tier appropriate context file and then runs scripts to configure your cloned system. It also automatically starts the database and Applications services.

The following commands are used to execute adcfgclone.pl on the database tier:

$UNIX>cd $ORACLE_HOME/appsutil/clone/bin
$UNIX>perl adcfgclone.pl dbTier

The following commands are used to execute adcfgclone.pl on the application tier:

$UNIX>cd $COMMON_TOP/clone/bin
$UNIX>perl adcfgclone.pl appsTier

▶ *Note*   The Applications clone requires the database to be available, so complete and validate your database clone before starting the Applications clone.

When you run adcfgclone.pl as per the previous example, you will be prompted for information that will be used to configure the target system. The information requested varies depending on the tier currently being configured, but common items include the database SID, filesystem information and port pool information.

This method of cloning may not meet your requirements. For instance, you may not wish to use a port pool for your target instance. In situations such as this, you can prepare a context file and pass the file location in adcfgclone.pl as a parameter. You can preset all of the configuration information in the context file and then run adcfgclone.pl non-interactively. This will skip the part of adcfgclone.pl that creates the context file. To run adcfgclone.pl with a context file passed in as a parameter, execute the following:

perl adcfgclone.pl <tier> <location of context file>

For each execution of Rapid Clone, adcfgclone.pl creates log files. Be sure to carefully review the log files after each run to validate a successful run. The log file for the application tier is located as follows:

$INST_TOP/apps/$CONTEXT_NAME/admin/log/ApplyAppsTier_<timestamp>.log

The log file for the database tier is located as follows:

$ORACLE_HOME/appsutil/log/$CONTEXT_NAME/ApplyDBTier_<timestamp>.log

Post Cloning Steps

As previously stated, Rapid Clone does not update all configuration items that you may want to change in the target system. This section describes changes that you may want to make per requirements for your environment.

Profile Settings

Rapid Clone will update many of your application's site level profile settings. However, you may need to manually update some site level profile settings and you will need to manually update non-site level profiles as needed. Check the fnd_profile_option_values table after clones for any references to the source system that may need to be modified. You may consider creating a custom script that is called after each clone to set these values according to requirements for your environment.

Workflow Cleanup

Rapid Clone does not update any host or instance specific information in the workflow configuration. Review your workflow configuration and identify changes that need to be made. Guidance around changes that may be required can be found in *My Oracle Support Article ID 406982.1.* Consider creating a custom script that you can execute after each clone to consistently deploy the recommended changes to the workflow cleanup.

▶ *Tip*   After performing a clone, set the value of the Outbound Email Account Test Address in the target instance to a test email address. This will redirect all workflow emails in the target instance to a single email address, thus preventing test emails from being sent to active email accounts. Additional details regarding setting the Outbound Email Account Test Address are provided in *My Oracle Support Article ID 459932.1.*

Custom Setup Steps

Depending on your environment, you may have additional custom configuration that you would like to perform after the clone is complete. For instance, you may want to give a select group of EBS users additional permissions within the application. Or, you may want to relax restrictions on your filesystem in development. You may also want to obfuscate sensitive data. Custom steps such as these can be easily added to your cloning steps. Consider creating a custom script that you can execute after each clone to consistently deploy these requirements.

Installation and Cloning Best Practices

Prior to performing an installation, it is important to understand the fundamental concepts of an Oracle E-Business Suite environment. This understanding will assist in making good decisions during the installation process. The concepts provided in Chapters 1 and 2 provide the foundation required to make appropriate decisions during an installation. It is critical to document installation decisions during the install process. Installation decisions will be utilized to appropriately document processes for your environment.

Be sure to thoroughly read release notes prior to performing an installation. There may be specific platform requirements that were not covered in this overview chapter. In addition to release notes, please make certain that your installation meets platform certification requirements. Performing an installation that is not certified means that you will not receive appropriate support from Oracle for your deployment.

Prior to performing an upgrade, review recommended resource requirements for the server CPU, memory and filesystems. Order necessary hardware or hardware upgrades in order to meet resource requirements.

Prior to performing a clone, you should check to make certain that you have adequate space in the target filesystem. The target filesystem should be sized to accommodate all the content that will be copied from the source filesystem. Consider modifying configuration of the target instance including memory settings and number of services to support only what is required for the target environment. Often times, less memory and fewer services are sufficient for non-production environments.

Be certain to perform a test clone of an environment after major upgrades and major patching efforts. Upgrades and patches can alter the outcome of a cloning process. Testing your cloning process will allow you to make appropriate changes if necessary.

Chapter 4

Toolkit

In order to manage Oracle Applications, it is a good idea for every Oracle Applications DBA to develop and maintain a toolkit. An Oracle Applications DBA's toolkit is a source for commands, utilities and scripts that can be executed to find information or implement tasks in a speedy fashion. All of the scripts and tips provided thus far in this guide are part of your toolkit. This chapter will provide additional toolkit information on the following topics:

*   **Oracle Applications utilities and commands**: There are a number of utilities used to administer the environment. This section will cover utilities and commands that are used by the Oracle Applications DBA to perform administration tasks for the Oracle Applications environment.

*   **Applications component versions**: An Oracle Applications DBA is often required to determine versions for the different components of the Oracle E-Business Suite. This information may assist with patching requirements, be provided to Oracle Support, or be used to troubleshoot an issue. This section will outline methods for obtaining Applications component and database version information.

*   **UNIX Tips and Commands**: UNIX commands are key to the administration of a UNIX deployed Oracle Applications environment. This section will describe and outline the syntax of useful UNIX commands.

*   **Preventative maintenance**: Routinely performing certain tasks can make the difference between a system running and performing as expected or running poorly. It is critical for the overall health of Oracle Applications for certain tasks to be executed on a scheduled basis. This section will describe preventative maintenance tasks that should be performed periodically.

*   **Scheduled jobs and scripts**: Performing proactive maintenance is a must for an Oracle Applications DBA. This section will offer tips for scheduling jobs and scripts using crontab and other scheduling tools.

Oracle Applications Utilities and Commands

We have covered numerous Oracle Applications utilities and commands, but there are still a number of them that need to be discussed in order to successfully administer the E-Business Suite:

*   Startup and shutdown scripts

*   Performing admin tasks with AD Administration

*   Relinking Applications executables with adrelink

*   Adding products with adsplice

*   Licensing products with License Manager

*   Creating a system report with adutconf.sql

*   Changing Applications passwords with FNDCPASS

*   Regenerating forms, libraries and menus

*   Recompiling JavaServer Pages (JSPs)

Startup and Shutdown Scripts

Each tier and each component of the Oracle E-Business Suite has a corresponding script that can be used to start, stop and, in some cases, query the status of the component. This section will describe the scripts used to start and stop the various components beginning with the database tier components followed by the application tier components.

Database Tier Component Startup and Shutdown Scripts

The database tier component startup and shutdown scripts are located in the following directory:

/<APPS_BASE>/db/tech_st/11.1.0/appsutil/scripts/$CONTEXT_NAME/

▶ *Tip*   Since the directory where the startup/shutdown scripts are located is navigated to so frequently, an environment variable may be set in order to ease navigation to this directory. For example, set the following environment variable: DB_ADMIN_SCRIPTS_HOME=/r12/db/tech_st/11.1.0/appsutil/scripts/$CONTEXT_NAME; where /r12 is the <APPS_BASE> for the installation.

All log files for the scripts are located in the following directory:

/<APPS_BASE>/db/tech_st/11.1.0/appsutil/log/$CONTEXT_NAME/

▶ *Tip*   Since the directory where the log files are located is navigated to so frequently, an environment variable may be set in order to ease navigation to this directory. For example, set the following environment variable: DB_LOG_HOME=/r12/db/tech_st/11.1.0/appsutil/log/$CONTEXT_NAME; where /r12 is the <APPS_BASE> for the installation. Only the listener writes a startup/shutdown log file. A startup/shutdown log file does not exist for the database.

A complete list of the startup and shutdown scripts for the database tier is located in Table 4-1.

Table 4-1. *Database Tier Component Startup and Shutdown Scripts*

Script	Parameters	Component Description	Log File
addbctl.sh	[start|stop {normal|immediate|abort}]	Database	N/A
adalnctl.sh	[start|stop|status {listener_name}]	Database Listener	adalcntl.txt

Application Tier Component Startup and Shutdown Scripts

The application tier component startup and shutdown scripts are located in the following directory:

/<INST_TOP_BASE>/apps/$CONTEXT_NAME/admin/scripts

The $ADMIN_SCRIPTS_HOME environment variable may be used for ease of navigation to the location of the Applications startup and shutdown scripts. The definition of this environment variable is as follows:

ADMIN_SCRIPTS_HOME=/<INST_TOP_BASE>/apps/$CONTEXT_NAME/ad min/scripts

Most log files for the application tier component startup and shutdown scripts are located in the following directory:

/<INST_TOP_BASE>/apps/$CONTEXT_NAME/logs/appl/admin/log

The log file for the Forms Server, if in use, is in the following directory:

/<INST_TOP_BASE>/apps/$CONTEXT_NAME/logs/ora/10.1.2/forms

The $LOG_HOME environment variable may be used for ease of navigation to the location of the Applications startup and shutdown log files. The following is an example of how to use to use this environment variable to navigate to the log files:

$UNIX>cd $LOG_HOME/appl/admin/log

In addition to the individual scripts for each component, there is a script that can be used to start all application tier components called adstrtal.sh. There is a corresponding script that may be used to stop all application tier components called adstpall.sh. Start and stop scripts must be executed on all nodes where services are enabled. A complete list of the startup and shutdown scripts is located in Table 4-2.

▶ **Tip**　　Prior to executing adstrtal.sh, the database must be running. If the database is not running, then the following error will be displayed upon executing adstrtal.sh: Database connection could not be established.

Table 4-2. *Applications Component Startup and Shutdown Scripts*

Script	Parameters	Component Description	Log File
adstpall.sh	[APPS user] [APPS password]	Stop APPL_TOP Server processes.	adstpall.log
adstrtal.sh	[APPS user] [APPS password]	Start APPL_TOP Server processes.	adstrtal.log
adopmnctl.sh	[start|stop|status]	OPMN Services.	adopmnctl.txt

Table 4-2. *Continued*

Script	Parameters	Component Description	Log File
adalnctl.sh	[start|stop|status] [listener_name]	Applications TNS Listener.	adalcntl.txt
adapcctl.sh	[start|stop|status]	Oracle HTTP Server Listener (Apache Web Server Listener).	adapcctl.txt
adoacorectl.sh	[start|stop|status]	OPMN managed OACORE OC4J services.	adoacorectl.txt
adformsctl.sh	[start|stop|status]	OPMN managed FORMS OC4J services.	adformsctl.txt
adoafmctl.sh	[start|stop|status]	OPMN managed OAFM OC4J services.	adoafmctl.txt
adcmctl.sh	[start|stop|abort|status] [apps user]/[apps password]	Concurrent Manager.	adcmctl.txt
jtffmctl.sh	[start|stop]	Fulfillment Server.	jtffmctl.txt
adformsrvctl.sh	[start|stop|status]	Forms Server Listener.	socket.log

▶ *R12 Implementation Tip*   The services that need to be managed with the startup/shutdown scripts are dependent upon your deployment. Some services may be disabled as they are not required for your environment.

To use the component startup/shutdown scripts, login to the server as the instance owner and execute the command with the parameter to start, stop, or check the status of the component. The following is an example of starting all the Applications services as the VIS instance owner:

```
$UNIX>su – vis
$UNIX>cd $ADMIN_SCRIPTS_HOME
$UNIX>./adstrtal.sh
```

A significant change in the management of the Oracle HTTP Services is the use of Oracle Process Manager (OPMN) to manage the starting and stopping of these services. OPMN must be running in order for it to manage the other services. The controlling script for starting and stopping OPMN and the other managed services is opmnctl. The opmnctl script can be found in the following directory:

$INST_TOP/ora/10.1.3/opmn/bin

In order to use opmnctl, you must first set the environment correctly by executing the following commands:

$UNIX>cd $INST_TOP/ora/10.1.3
$UNIX>. $CONTEXT_NAME.env

A complete list of usage options may be reviewed by executing opmnctl with the help option. The output of opmnctl help options is displayed in Figure 4-1.

```
usage:opmnctl [verbose] [<scope>] <command> [<options>]

verbose: print detailed execution message if available

Permitted <scope>/<command>/<options> combinations are:

  scope     command     options
  -------   ---------   ---------
            start                        - Start opmn
            startall                     - Start opmn & all managed processes
            stopall                      - Stop opmn & all managed processes
            shutdown                     - Shutdown opmn & all managed processes
  [<scope>] startproc   [<attr>=<val> ..] - Start opmn managed processes
  [<scope>] restartproc [<attr>=<val> ..] - Restart opmn managed processes
  [<scope>] stopproc    [<attr>=<val> ..] - Stop opmn managed processes
  [<scope>] reload                       - Trigger opmn to reread opmn.xml
  [<scope>] status      [<options>]      - Get managed process status
  [<scope>] dmsdump     [<attr>=<val> ..] - Get DMS stats
  [<scope>] set         [<attr>=<val> ..] - Set opmn log parameters
  [<scope>] query       [<attr>=<val>]   - Query opmn log parameters
            ping        [<max_retry>]    - Ping local opmn
            validate    [<filename>]     - Validate the given opmn xml file
            config      [<options>]      - Modify the default opmn xml file
            help                         - Print brief usage description
            usage       [<command>]      - Print detailed usage description
```

Figure 4-1. *Usage options for opmnctl*

To start OPMN and all managed services, execute the following:

$UNIX>opmnctl startall

To stop OPMN and all managed services, execute the following:

$UNIX>opmnctl stopall

To check the status of all OPMN managed services, execute the following:

$UNIX>opmnctl status

The output of the opmnctl with the status option is shown in Figure 4-2.

```
Processes in Instance: VIS_erlinux01.erlinux01.erhome.com
--------------------------------+--------------------+--------+---------
ias-component                   | process-type       |   pid  | status
--------------------------------+--------------------+--------+---------
OC4JGroup:default_group         | OC4J:oafm          |   6628 | Alive
OC4JGroup:default_group         | OC4J:forms         |   6559 | Alive
OC4JGroup:default_group         | OC4J:oacore        |   6480 | Alive
HTTP_Server                     | HTTP_Server        |   6428 | Alive
```

Figure 4-2. *Status output for opmnctl*

Performing Admin Tasks with AD Administration

There are numerous administration tasks that an Oracle Applications DBA must perform. The administration tasks are typically for maintenance purposes, to resolve a Service Request, to perform a precursory patching step or post patching step or to perform configuration. Oracle has created an administration tool for the Oracle Applications DBA to ease the administration tasks that must be performed. The tool that is provided is the AD Administration utility, or adadmin. This section will cover the various administrative tasks that can be performed with adadmin.

To execute adadmin, as the Applications software owner, type adadmin from the command line on any of your application tier nodes. The following is an example of executing adadmin:

$UNIX>adadmin

Upon execution of the adadmin utility, you will be prompted with several questions. These include validating the APPL_TOP and database, entering the APPS and SYSTEM passwords, and validating the utility's environment settings, such as log filename.

▶ *Tip*   You can create an input parameter file for the prompted variables to make manual responses to the questions unnecessary. To do this, execute adadmin with the defaultsfile option. This will create a file that will contain information that can be used during the next execution of adadmin.

Upon providing the information for the prompted variables, the adadmin menu is displayed as shown in Figure 4-3.

▶ *Tip*   You should create a standard naming convention for adadmin log files. The default location of the adadmin log files is $APPL_TOP/admin/$SID/log. Reviewing adadmin executions and errors will be easier when utilizing such standards. Additionally, adadmin log files should be added to your filesystem cleanup process. Additional details regarding filesystem cleanup are provided in the *Preventative Maintenance* section in this chapter.

```
              AD Administration Main Menu
         - - - - - - - - - - - - - - - - - - - - - - - - - - - - - - - - - - - - -

         1.    Generate Applications Files menu

         2.    Maintain Applications Files menu

         3.    Compile/Reload Applications Database Entities menu

         4.    Maintain Applications Database Entities menu

         5.    Change Maintenance Mode

         6.    Exit AD Administration




Enter your choice [6] :
```

Figure 4-3. *AD Administration Main Menu*

▶ *Tip*   As with other AD utilities, the menu options for the AD Administration utility may vary depending upon the AD patch level in the instance.

As an Oracle Applications DBA, you should be familiar with the menu options available in the adadmin utility. An overview of the main menu options and submenus for adadmin is provided in Table 4-3.

Table 4-3. *AD Administration Main Menu and Sub Menus*

Menu	Submenu
1. Generate Applications Files menu	1. Generate message files
	2. Generate form files
	3. Generate report files
	4. Generate product JAR files
	5. Return to Main Menu
2. Maintain Applications Files menu	1. Relink Applications programs
	2. Copy files to destinations
	3. Convert character set
	4. Maintain snapshot information
	5. Check for missing files
	6. Return to Main Menu
3. Compile/Reload Applications Database Entities menu	1. Compile APPS schema
	2. Compile menu information
	3. Compile flexfields
	4. Reload JAR files to database
	5. Return to Main Menu
4. Maintain Applications Database Entities menu	1. Validate APPS schema
	2. Recreate grants and synonyms for APPS schemas
	3. Maintain multi-lingual tables
	4. Check DUAL table
	5. Return to Main Menu
5. Change Maintenance Mode	1. Enable Maintenance Mode
	2. Disable Maintenance Mode
	3. Return to Main Menu
6. Exit AD administration	

▶ *Tip*   If your previous run of adadmin ended in failure, the next execution of adadmin will be prompt you to decide to continue with your failed session or start a new session. To start a new session, you must answer the questions appropriately.

Relinking Applications Executables

At times, it is necessary to relink executables for the applications. This requirement occurs for many reasons including post patching steps and resolving Applications execution issues. The AD Admin utility may be used to relink all Applications executables. Additionally, the AD Relink utility may be used to relink AD executable programs with the Oracle product libraries. This section will cover both these topics.

Using AD Admin to Relink Applications Executables

AD Admin also provides the ability to relink Applications executables. From the *Maintain Applications Files* menu, select the option to *Relink Applications Programs*. This program will require you to respond to the following questions:

Question: Do you wish to proceed with the relink [Yes]?

Recommended response: Press the Enter key or type **Yes** to proceed with the relink; otherwise, type **No**.

Question: Enter the name of your Oracle Applications environment file below.

Recommended response: $CONTEXT_NAME.env

Question: Enter list of products to link [all]

Recommended response: This option gives you the opportunity to narrow the scope of the relink; for example, you may want to limit the relink to a specific category of products. An example of this would be to enter **AP**. Press Enter or type **all** if you want to generate all products; otherwise type the products to relink.

Question: Relink with debug information [no]

Recommended response: Press Enter or type **No** if you do not want to relink with debugging information; otherwise, type **Yes**. It is helpful to relink with debugging information if you are experiencing errors during the relink process.

Using AD Relink to Relink AD Executables

The AD Relink utility may be used to relink AD executable programs. The syntax of the adrelink.sh command is as follows:

adrelink.sh force={y|n} [<optional args>] "<targets>"

or

adrelink.sh force={y|n} [<optional args>] filelist=<file>

In both cases, "<targets>" is "<product> <module name>", and <file> is the name of a file that contains a list of files to relink. Valid <optional args> values for adrelink.sh are listed in Table 4-4.

Table 4-4. *Description and Values for <optional_args> with adrelink.sh*

<optional args>	Values	Description
force	[y|n]	This option specifies whether the relink should be forced, meaning relink is not optional.
envfile	[adsetenv.sh]	This option is only used by the adsetup script.
link_debug	[y|n]	This option specifies whether the relink is done with or without debugging. The default value is n.
backup_mode	[none|all|file]	This option specifies whether a backup should be made when executing a forced relink; none means no files will be backed up, all means all files will be backed up, and file means files listed in the $APPL_TOP/admin/adlinkbk.txt file will be backed up. The default value is file.

The following is an example of using adrelink.sh to force relink the adadmin module:

$UNIX>adrelink.sh force=y "ad adadmin'"

The following is an example of using adrelink.sh to force relink the adadmin and adpatch modules:

$UNIX>adrelink.sh force=y "ad adadmin" "ad adpatch"

The following is an example of using adrelink.sh to force relink all AD executables:

$UNIX>adrelink.sh force=y "ad all"

▶ *Tip*   To list additional examples of using adrelink.sh, execute the following:
$UNIX>adrelink.sh examples

Regenerating Forms, Libraries and Menus

At times it is necessary to regenerate forms, libraries, or menus to fix issues with them, to synchronize the generated object with the underlying database object, or as a post patching step. This section will cover regenerating forms, libraries and menus by using AD Admin.

AD Admin provides a menu for regenerating forms, libraries and menus. There are many options associated with this menu selection, so only an overview of using the menu will be provided here.

To regenerate forms, you should start an AD Admin session and select the following menu options: *Generate Applications Files Menu*, then *Generate Forms Files*. With this option, you can regenerate Forms PL/SQL Library Files, Forms menu files and Forms executable files. The following is an example of some of the options you have when using AD Admin to regenerate forms:

Question: Do you want to regenerate Oracle Forms PL/SQL library files [Yes]?

Recommended response: Press the Enter key or type **Yes** to regenerate Forms PL/SQL libraries; otherwise, type **No**.

Question: Do you want to regenerate Oracle Forms menu files [Yes]?

Recommended response: Press the Enter key or type **Yes** to regenerate Forms menu files; otherwise, type **No**.

Question: Do you want to regenerate Oracle Forms executable files [Yes]?

Recommended response: Press the Enter key or type **Yes** to regenerate Forms executable files; otherwise, type **No**.

Question: Enter list of products ('all' for all products) [all]

Recommended response: This option gives you the opportunity to narrow the scope of the recompile; for example, you may want to limit the recompile to GL products. Press Enter or type **all** if you want to generate all products; otherwise, type the product module, such as **GL**, **AP**, or **BEN**.

Question: Generate specific Forms objects for each selected product [No]?

Recommended response: This option gives you the opportunity to further reduce the scope of the regeneration, by limiting the form, library, or menu to be regenerated. Press Enter or type **No** if you want to generate all forms, libraries and menus for a specific product; otherwise type **Yes**, and a list of forms, libraries and menus will be displayed. You will then be able to choose from this list of objects.

Recompiling JavaServer Pages (JSPs)

By default with R12, JavaServer Pages (JSPs) are no longer automatically recompiled upon access. Removing the automatic recompilation of JSPs by default was done to improve performance. There may be a need to recompile JSP pages if changes were made to the underlying JSP. Recompiling JSPs can be achieved manually or by modifying the default configuration of the Applications. This section will cover both options.

Manually Recompiling JSPs

Recompiling JSPs is accomplished by using the JSP precompiler. The JSP precompiler is invoked using the ojspCompile.pl Perl script. Prerequisites and requirements for using the JSP precompiler are outlined in *My Oracle Support Article ID 215268.1*. The syntax of using the precompiler is as follows:

```
ojspCompile.pl [COMMAND] [ARGS]
```

Key options for the [COMMAND] parameter are outlined in Table 4-5. Key options for the [ARGS] parameter are outlined in Table 4-6.

Table 4-5. *[COMMAND] Parameter Options for ojspCompile.pl*

[COMMAND]	Parameter	Description
--compile		Update the dependency and compile the delta.
-out	<file>	Update the dependency and output the delta to the file.

Table 4-6. *[ARGS] Parameter Options for ojspCompile.pl*

[ARGS]	Parameter	Description
-s	<regex>	Search for condition in JSP filename; for example: -s 'jtf%'.
-p	<procs>	Specify the number of parallel executions.
-log	<file>	Specify the name of the log file.
--flush		Force all parent JSP pages to be recompiled.

The following is an example of force compiling all JSP pages with parallel execution of 10:

$UNIX>ojspCompile.pl --compile --flush -p 10

The following is an example of compiling all delta JSP pages:

$UNIX>ojspCompile.pl --compile -log /oracle/admin/vis/log/compile_jsps.log

The following is an example of compiling all JSPs that start with the string jtf:

$UNIX>ojspCompile.pl --compile -s 'jtf%'

Automatically Recompiling JSPs

As previously stated, the default behavior of R12 is to not recompile JSPs upon access. To alter the default, you must change the main mode setting from justrun to recompile. This can be achieved by logging into OAM, then selecting *Site Map→AutoConfig*. From this screen, you must edit each configuration file for all application tier nodes. Click the *Edit Parameters* pencil next to each application tier node as shown in Figure 4-4. This will display the screen shown in Figure 4-5.

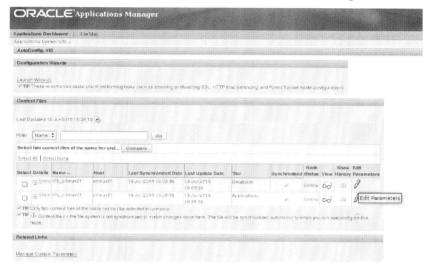

Figure 4-4. *OAM: Edit parameters*

Figure 4-5. *Modify configuration parameters for JSP recompliation*

On the *Edit Parameters* screen, search for the OA_VAR value s_jsp_main_mode. Modify the value of this setting from justrun to recompile and click the *Save* button as shown in Figure 4-5. Continue this process of editing the s_jsp_main_mode parameter for all Applications nodes in your environment. Once you have changed the parameter for all Applications nodes, you must run AutoConfig. Additional details regarding executing AutoConfig are described in Chapter 2 of this guide.

Adding Products with AD Splicer

At times it is necessary to add new products that were not originally deployed with your environment. This is necessary if an existing product upgrade requires a new dependent product or when deploying new modules that were not included in the maintenance pack deployed in your environment. The utility used to add or *splice* in new products is called AD Splicer or adsplice.

The adsplice utility is like many of the AD Utilities. Upon executing adsplice, you will be asked a series of questions including log file name, SYSTEM and APPS passwords. The following is an example of how to execute the AD Splicer utility:

$UNIX>adsplice

Upon execution, you will also be asked to enter the name of the AD Splicer control file, also known as the newprods.txt file. This file is typically delivered with a patch.

Licensing products with License Manager

When deploying an Oracle Applications environment, it is necessary to *license* the products for use. Licensing is accomplished by using the *License Manager* feature in OAM. To access *License Manager*, first login to OAM and go to the *Site Map*. From the *Site Map*, click *License Manager*. The *License Manager Home Page* is divided into two sections: *License* and *Reports* as shown in Figure 4-6.

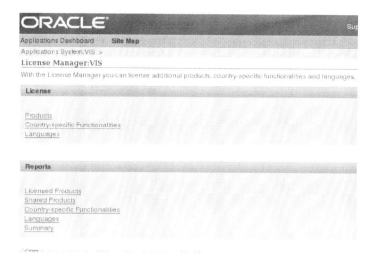

Figure 4-6. *License Manager Home Page: License and Reports*

To license additional products, click *Products*. From here you can select to *License E-Business Suite*, *License Component Applications*, or *License Applications Product*.

▶ *Caution*   Use care when licensing products. Once a product is licensed it cannot be "unlicensed".

You may also run reports to show the products that are licensed for your installation. A comprehensive report of the environment can be displayed by clicking the *Summary* link under the *Reports* section on the *License Manager Home Page*.

▶ *Note*   Prior to licensing the product with License Manager, check with your Oracle Sales Representative to ensure that you have the appropriate licensing agreements to use the required products.

Creating a system report with adutconf.sql

An Oracle Applications Database Configuration Report may be created by executing the adutconf.sql SQL. To create this report, execute the following in a SQL*Plus session when logged into the database as APPS:

SQL>@$AD_TOP/sql/adutconf.sql

Executing adutconf.sql will generate a report called adutconf.lst in the directory where you started the SQL*Plus session. The report includes information regarding your installation and environment. Key information included in the report includes the following: database tablespaces, product information, multi-org enabled, existing operating units, registered applications, registered Oracle schemas, product installation status, version info and patch level, product database configuration, registered data groups, base language and other installed languages and NLS Settings.

Changing Application, Oracle and System Passwords

An *Applications user* is a user that is defined in the E-Business Suite. For example, an HR Specialist named Lori Smith using Oracle HRMS is defined as an Applications user. An *Oracle user* is a database user only and is a schema owner of modules that are used in the application; for example, AP, GL and BEN. At times it is necessary to change passwords for Applications users and Oracle users. In addition to the Applications user and Oracle accounts, there are system accounts that need password management. The system accounts that will be covered in this section are APPS and APPLSYS. The primary utility used to change passwords is called FNDCPASS. FNDCPASS will be covered in the next three sections.

▶ *Note*   When changing the different types of user passwords with FNDCPASS, the primary difference is the use of the USER, ORACLE, or SYSTEM parameter. The USER parameter is for Applications users. The ORACLE parameter is used for Oracle schema owners. The SYSTEM parameter is for changing the APPLSYS and APPS passwords. Additional details regarding FNDCPASS can be found in *My Oracle Support Article ID 437260.1*

Changing an Applications User's Password

An Applications user's password can be changed via the Applications or with the FNDCPASS utility. To change a user's password in the application, login to the application. After logging in, select a responsibility that has the *Define User* privilege. By default, this privilege is assigned to the *System Administrator* responsibility. Once logged in, navigate to the *Define User* screen by selecting *Security* → *User* →*Define*. Query for the user in question, type in a new password twice, and save the form. The Define User screen is shown if Figure 4-7.

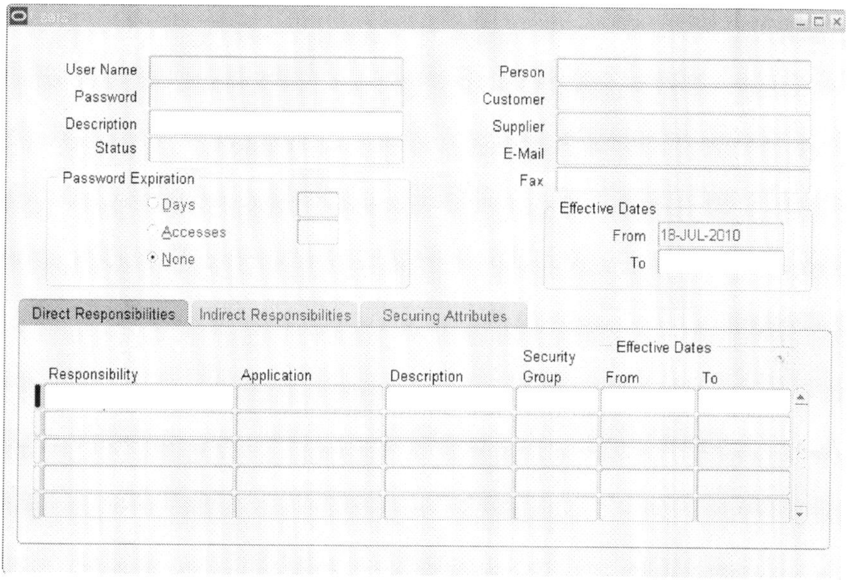

Figure 4-7. *Resetting an Applications user's password with the Define User functionality*

Another method for changing an Applications user's password is to use the command line utility FNDCPASS from any Applications node. To change the password of a user in the application, the following parameters are used with FNDCPASS:

```
FNDCPASS [apps_user]/[apps_password] 0 Y system/[system_password] \
USER [user_name] [new_user_password]
```

For example, the following command will change user grudd's password to passwd#1:

```
$UNIX>FNDCPASS APPS/APPS 0 Y system/manager USER grudd passwd#1
```

▶ **Tip**   When performing password changes, the new passwords must adhere to rules that are set with Applications profile options for password integrity as well as database profile options for password integrity. Applications password integrity rules are set in the ICX:Sign% profile options. Database password integrity is defined with database profiles. Additional details regarding password integrity is covered in Chapter 2 of this guide.

Changing an Oracle User's Password

To change the password of an Oracle user, the following parameters are used with FNDCPASS:

FNDCPASS [apps_user]/[apps_password] 0 Y system/[system_password] \
ORACLE [user_name] [new_oracle_password]

For example, the following command will change Applications schema AP's password to passwd#1:

$UNIX>FNDCPASS APPS/APPS 0 Y system/manager ORACLE AP passwd#1

Changing the APPLSYS and APPS Password

The primary system accounts for the environment that require password changes are the APPLSYS and APPS accounts. The APPLSYS and APPS passwords must be kept in sync.

▶ **Tip**   You should change Oracle account passwords and system account passwords on a regular basis. Create a standard interval for these changes in your environment and define this as a policy for your installation.

The FNDCPASS utility changes both APPLSYS and APPS when it is executed with the following parameters:

FNDCPASS [apps_user]/[apps_password] 0 Y system/[password] SYSTEM \
APPLSYS [new_apps_password]

An example of changing the APPLSYS and APPS passwords to oracle#1 using FNDCPASS:

$UNIX>FNDCPASS APPS/APPS 0 Y system/manager SYSTEM APPLSYS \
oracle#1

▶ *Tip* You must schedule downtime to change the APPS and APPLSYS
passwords for the environment.

Upon completion of changing the APPS and APPLSYS passwords with
the FNDCPASS command, you must run AutoConfig on all nodes in your
environment. This will update the necessary configuration for your
environment to reflect the APPS and APPLSYS password changes. If
AutoConfig is not executed, you will encounter errors with the
application.

▶ *Tip* After changing the APPS password, it is advisable to verify that the
FNDCPASS command has executed properly and that Oracle Applications functions
normally. Review the log file generated by FNDCPASS and, if necessary, correct any
errors. Then, login to the database and application. These steps provide a quick test of
the APPS password change.

Determining Component Versions

Determining versions of the different components is useful for
researching functionality, issues, and certification levels, patching
requirements and providing information to Oracle Support. This section
provides information for obtaining version information for the following
components:

* Identifying Applications file versions

* Identifying Applications component versions

Identifying Applications File Versions

Often you will be required to identify the version of Applications files.
Applications file versions can be obtained with the adident command or
the strings command. This section will outline how to use each of these
commands to obtain Applications version information.

Using adident

The adident command can be used to identify Applications file versions. The syntax for adident is as follows:

adident [pattern] [file1 |, file2, file3, . . .]

In this statement, [pattern] is the identifying pattern that is being searched for in the file, and [file1 |, file2, file3, . . .] is the list of files being reviewed.

Here is an example:

$UNIX>adident Header OA.jsp

```
OA.jsp:
$Header OA.jsp 120.23. 2007/08/16 10:38:06 atgops1 ship $
```

Using the strings Command

The strings command may also be used to retrieve file version information. The syntax for the strings command is as follows:

strings -a [filename] | grep [pattern]

In this statement, [filename] is the name of the file being reviewed, and [pattern] is the pattern being searched for in the file.

Here is an example:

$UNIX>strings -a OA.jsp | grep Header

```
<%! public static final String RCS_ID = "$Header: OA.jsp 120.23. 2007/08/16
10:38:06 atgops1 ship $"; %><jsp:useBean
```

Identifying Applications Component Versions

Oracle has made determining Applications Component versions in Release 12 easier than in previous releases. Many of the technology component versions can be found in *About Page* in the application.

To retrieve information regarding your environment including the OA Framework, Oracle OA Extension, Business Components, UIX, BiBeans Runtime, MDS, XML, AOL/J, Servlet, Java, JDBC Driver and Database simply open an *About Page* screen. To access an *About Page* screen, you must first set the site level profile option FND: Diagnostics to Yes. Once this is set, scroll to the bottom left hand side of any page, including the login page, and click the *About this Page* link. An example of an *About Page* screen is shown in Figure 4-8.

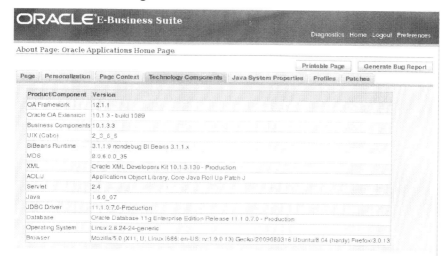

Figure 4-8. *About Page: Used to determine Technology Component Versions*

▶ *Tip*   It is recommended to not set the site level profile FND: Diagnostics to YES in production for long periods of time. Furthermore, FND: Diagnostics should not be set to Yes for extended periods or on a regular basis in development and test instances. For security purposes, the information available from the *About this Page* screen should have limited access.

In addition to the *About Page*, Oracle has provided a Perl script, txkInventory.pl, which can be executed to generate a Technology Stack Inventory report which includes version information. Perl scripts are executed using the ADPERLPRG environment variable. Additional information regarding the txkInventory.pl script can be found in *My Oracle Support Article ID 601736.1*. Additional details regarding the parameters that can be used when executing Perl scripts with ADPERLPRG are described in Table 4-7.

Table 4-7. *Parameters to use when executing Perl scripts with ADPERLPRG*

Parameter	Description
script	Script to be executed. To execute the Technology Stack Inventory report for the application tier, set this parameter to $FND_TOP/patch/115/bin/txkInventory.pl. To execute the report for the database tier, set this parameter to $ORACLE_HOME/appsutil/bin/txkInventory.pl.
txktop	Temporary directory for working files.
contextfile	Name and location of the context file. If not specified, the environment variable $CONTEXT_NAME will be used.
appspass	APPS password.
outfile	Name and location of the output file. The default location is $APPLTMP/TXK.

The following is an example of executing the txkInventory.pl script on the application tier:

```
$UNIX>su – vis
$UNIX>. APPL_TOP/$CONTEXT_NAME.env
$UNIX>$ADPERLPRG $FND_TOP/patch/115/bin/TXKScript.pl \
-script $FND_TOP/patch/115/bin/txkInventory.pl \
-appspass=APPS
```

Oracle HTTP Server Version

The Oracle HTTP Server version may be obtained from any Web Node by executing the httpd -version command. The following is an example of executing this command:

```
$UNIX>cd $IAS_ORACLE_HOME/Apache/Apache/bin/
$UNIX>httpd -version
```

```
Server version: Oracle Application Server-10g/10.1.3.4.0 Oracle-HTTP Server
Server built:  Jul 7 2008 14:58:00
```

Oracle Forms Version

Forms version information may be obtained from the *About* menu of a Forms client session. To obtain the version information from a Forms client session, click on the *Help* → *About* menu. This will display the *About Oracle Applications* dialog box. In the *About* dialog box, scroll to the Forms version information, as displayed in Figure 4-9.

Figure 4-9. *Forms About dialog box showing Forms version information*

Java Class File Versions

Java class file versions may be obtained from the zip files or the class file. To obtain Java class file version information, a combination of UNIX commands is used. The steps to retrieve version information for a Java class from the zip file are as follows:

1. Review the zip file to obtain the full path of the zipped Java class:

    unzip -l [filename].zip | grep [class file]

2. Extract the Java class from the zipped file:

    unzip -j [filename].zip [path/class file]

    where [path/class file] is the path for the class filename retrieved from step 1.

3. Retrieve the header information from the Java class with the strings command:

    strings -a [class file] | grep Header

    where [class file] is the path for the class filename retrieved from step 1.

▶ **Note**   Step 2 in the preceding list extracts the class file to the directory where the unzip command is executed. You should delete the extracted class file once version information has been retrieved in step 3.

For class files that are not contained in zip files, the class file version may be obtained by using the strings command. The following is how to retrieve the version information from a class file:

strings -a [class file] | grep Header

Database Version Query

The version of the database may be obtained simply by reviewing the banner that is displayed when connecting to the instance via SQL*Plus from the database installation $ORACLE_HOME on the database node. Here's an example:

$UNIX>sqlplus

SQL*Plus: Release 11.1.0.7.0 - Production on Sat Jul 10   19:58:41 2010

Copyright (c) 1982, 2008, Oracle Corporation. All rights reserved.

Enter user name: sys as sysdba
Enter password:

Connected to:
Oracle Database 11g Enterprise Edition Release 11.1.0.7 Production
With the Partitioning option OLAP, Data Mining and Real Application Testing options

Additional information regarding the database component installations and versions may be obtained by executing queries against the database. The following examples are the queries to execute to determine database component versions; the results of the queries are displayed in Figures 4-10 and 4-11.

```
SQL>select * from v$version;

BANNER
---------------------------------------------------------------------------
Oracle Database 11g Enterprise Edition Release 11.1.0.7.0 - Production
PL/SQL Release 11.1.0.7.0 - Production
CORE    11.1.0.7.0        Production
TNS for Linux: Version 11.1.0.7.0 - Production
NLSRTL Version 11.1.0.7.0 - Production
```

Figure 4-10. *Results of executing select statement against v$version*

SQL> select comp_name, version, status from dba_registry;

```
COMP_NAME                                                       VERSION         STATUS
---------------------------------------------------------       ------------    ---------
Oracle Application Express                                      3.0.1.00.12     VALID
Oracle Ultra Search                                            11.1.0.7.0      VALID
JServer JAVA Virtual Machine                                   11.1.0.7.0      VALID
Oracle OLAP API                                               11.1.0.7.0      VALID
OLAP Analytic Workspace                                        11.1.0.7.0      VALID
Oracle Real Application Clusters                              11.1.0.7.0      INVALID
Oracle XDK                                                    11.1.0.7.0      VALID
Oracle Database Java Packages                                 11.1.0.7.0      VALID
Oracle Database Packages and Types                           11.1.0.7.0      VALID
Oracle Database Catalog Views                                11.1.0.7.0      VALID
Oracle Multimedia                                             11.1.0.7.0      VALID
Spatial                                                       11.1.0.7.0      VALID
Oracle Text                                                   11.1.0.7.0      VALID
OLAP Catalog                                                  11.1.0.7.0      VALID
Oracle Data Mining                                            11.1.0.7.0      VALID
Oracle XML Database                                           11.1.0.7.0      VALID
Oracle Label Security                                        10.2.0.3.0      OPTION OFF
Oracle Application Server Wireless                            10.1.2.0.2      VALID
Oracle Internet Directory                                    10.1.2.0.2      VALID
Oracle Application Server Certificate Authority              10.1.2.0.2      VALID
Oracle Application Server Integration BAM                    10.1.2.0.2      VALID
Oracle Application Server Integration B2B                    10.1.2.0.2      VALID
Oracle Application Server UDDI Registry                      10.1.2.0.2      VALID
Oracle Business Intelligence Discoverer                      10.1.2.0.2      VALID
Oracle Workflow                                              10.1.2.0.2      VALID
Oracle Application Server Single Sign-On                     10.1.2.0.2      VALID
Oracle Application Server Syndication Services               10.1.2.0.2      VALID
Oracle Application Server Distributed Configuration Management 10.1.2.0.2     VALID
Oracle Application Server Metadata Repository Version-R      10.1.2.0.2      VALID
Oracle Application Server Web Clipping                       10.1.2.0.2      VALID
```

Figure 4-11. *Results of executing select statement against dba_registry*

In addition to the database queries, txkInventory.pl can be executed on the database tier to generate a version information report. The parameters and supporting documentation for this are the same as the application tier script. Please refer to Table 4-6 and *My Oracle Support Article ID 601736.1* for additional details. The following is an example for running the txkInventory.pl script on the database tier:

```
$UNIX>$ADPERLPRG $ORACLE_HOME/appsutil/bin/TXKScript.pl \
-txktop=
-script $ORACLE_HOME/appsutil/bin/txkInventory.pl \
-appspass=APPS
```

UNIX Tips and Commands

There are many UNIX commands that are used frequently in the day-to-day management of the Oracle E-Business Suite. This guide will cover some commonly used UNIX commands and usage tips. This section will cover the following topics:

* Understanding and setting the environment

* Understanding and using X Windows

* Getting UNIX help for commands

* Using common UNIX commands

▶ *Tip*   An Oracle Applications DBA supporting Oracle on a UNIX based system should consider investing in additional reference material specific to UNIX.

Understanding and Setting the Environment

Setting the UNIX environment simply means defining environment variables to specific values that are needed to run Applications and databases. To set the environment in UNIX you can either set variables directly or create and source an environment file. The following is an example of directly setting the ORACLE_HOME environment variable on the database tier:

$UNIX>export ORACLE_HOME=/r12vis/db/tech_st/11.1.0

An environment file may contain a list of environment variables that are set to specific values. Environment files are usually named with an extension of env. The following is an example of the contents of an environment file called custom_VIS_erlinux01.env

```
#####################################################
# File name:      custom_VIS_erlinux01.env
#Description:      This file is an example custom environment file
#####################################################
DB_ADMIN_SCRIPTS_HOME=$ORACLE_HOME/appsutl/scripts/$CONTEXT_NAME
export  DB_ADMIN_SCRIPTS_HOME
DB_LOG_HOME=$ORACLE_HOME/appsutil/log/$CONTEXT_NAME;
export DB_LOG_HOME
#End of File
#####################################################
```

To source an environment file named custom_VIS_erlinux01.env, execute the following:

$UNIX>. custom_VIS_erlinux01.env

After an environment file is sourced, the environment variables can be accessed by the system. For example, you may perform the following to navigate to the DB_ADMIN_SCRIPTS_HOME directory:

$UNIX>cd $DB_ADMIN_SCRIPTS_HOME

▶ *Tip*   All defined environment variables for a session may be reviewed by executing the following: $UNIX>env | sort.

Understanding and Using X Windows

X Windows provides a graphical user interface (GUI) for UNIX systems. X Windows can also be emulated on a Windows PC with X Windows emulation software. An example of X Windows emulation software is Exceed by Hummingbird.

The Oracle Universal Installer and Rapid Install utilities require X Windows. Prior to beginning an install, you must set your DISPLAY environment variable to the machine where the emulator is running. The following is an example of setting the DISPLAY environment variable:

$UNIX>export DISPLAY=erwindows01.erhome.com:0.0

where erwindows01.erhome.com is the name of the workstation where the X Windows session will run.

The Oracle E-Business Suite also uses X Windows for some display items in the application. The DISPLAY variable for the Applications is set in the Applications context file.

Getting Help for UNIX Commands

Prior to discussing additional UNIX commands, this section will offer some guidance for getting help on UNIX commands. The following help options will be covered in this section:

* UNIX man pages

* UNIX command quick help

*   Web searches for UNIX command help

Your system may have the manual (man) pages installed—the man pages tool can provide detailed descriptions of commands. The syntax for the man command is as follows:

man [command]

The following is an example that looks up the man pages for df:

$UNIX>man df

Another option is to use quick help for a command—if the manual pages are not installed in your system, this may be the only available option from the server. It can be accomplished by using the -? parameter with the command. The syntax for this help feature is as follows:

[command] -?

The following is an example of using quick help for the df command:

$UNIX>df -?

Lastly, it is possible to get information about commands by using web search engines. These sites, like Google and Yahoo, may direct you to online versions of manual pages for UNIX commands.

After you develop an understanding for the syntax of a command, you can look for opportunities to use the commands to their fullest potential. One way to accomplish that is to combine the command with other UNIX commands. The pipe character (|) will allow multiple commands to be run together. An example of this is to use the grep command to find information about a specific process ID, such as 2342:

$UNIX>ps -ef | grep 2342

Using Common UNIX Commands

This section will cover common commands used by an Oracle Applications DBA on a UNIX platform. In addition to reviewing the command, commonly used parameter options will also be provided.

Using chown

The UNIX chown command is used to change ownership of a UNIX file. You are required to execute the chown command as the root user or a user with sudo privileges. The basic syntax of this command is as follows:

chown -[R][h] <user>[.group] <directory|filename>

There are many optional parameters that can be used with the chown command. The parameters for chown are described in Table 4-8.

Table 4-8. *Parameters for chown*

Parameter	Description
[R]	Optional parameter used to recursively change ownership for directories and files in directories.
[h]	Optional parameter used to change ownership of a symbolic link, but not the source of the link.
<user>	Mandatory parameter that specifies the new owner of the file.
[group]	Optional parameter that specifies the new group ownership.
<directory|filename>	Mandatory parameter that specifies the name of the directory/ file for which ownership is being changed.

The following is an example of changing ownership of the ORACLE.env file to vis and group ownership to dba:

$UNIX>ls -l ORACLE.env

-rw------- root system ORACLE.env

$UNIX>chown vis.dba ORACLE.env
$UNIX>ls -ltr ORACLE.env

-rw------- oracle dba ORACLE.env

The following is an example of recursively changing ownership of a directory to r12vis and group ownership to dba:

$UNIX>chown -Rh r12vis.dba $INST_TOP/ora/10.1.3

▶ *Tip*   It is recommended that you use the -h parameter with chown so that you do not affect ownership of the source of symbolic links.

Using chmod

The UNIX chmod command is used to change the permissions of a UNIX file. The basic syntax of this command is as follows:

chmod -[R] [u|g|o|a][+|-][r|w|x] <directory|filename>

There are many optional parameters that can be used with the chmod command. The optional parameters for chmod are described in Table 4-9.

Table 4-9. *Parameters for chmod*

Parameter	Description
[R]	Optional parameter used to recursively set permissions for directories and files in directories.
<u|g|o|a>	Mandatory parameter used to specify the setting of the permission for the u (user), the g (group), o (other), or a (all).
<+|->	Mandatory parameter that specifies whether to grant (+) or remove (-) the permission.
<r|w|x>	Mandatory parameter that specifies the permission being set: read (r), write (w), or execute (x).
<directory|filename>	Mandatory parameter that specifies the name of the directory or file for which ownership is being changed.

The following is an example of changing the permissions of the restart_apache.sh file to grant execute permission to the dba group:

$UNIX>ls -l restart_apache.sh

-rwxrw-rw- vis dba restart_apache.sh

$UNIX>chmod g+x restart_apache.sh
$UNIX>ls -ltr restart_apache.sh

-rwxrwxrw- vis dba restart_apache.sh

Additionally, a numeric description can be used to represent the binary value for read, write and execute permissions for a file. This value can be assigned at the owner, group and other levels. The available options are displayed in Table 4-10.

Table 4-10. *Parameters for chmod*

Numerical Value	Binary Value	Permissions
0	000	None
1	001	Execute
2	010	Write
3	011	Write, Execute
4	100	Read
5	101	Read, Execute
6	110	Read, Write
7	111	Read, Write, Execute

An example of changing permissions of the restart_apache.sh file to grant read, write and execute permissions to the owner and group only is as follows:

$UNIX>ls -l restart_apache.sh

-r-xrw-rw- vis dba restart_apache.sh

$UNIX>chmod 770 restart_apache.sh
$UNIX>ls -ltr restart_apache.sh

-rwxrwx--- vis dba restart_apache.sh

▶ *Note*   The other permission setting for files and directories in UNIX is the level of permissions for users other than the owner and the group. For security reasons, it is common to set the permissions for other to 0 in order to prevent access to files by system users who are not members of the appropriate security group.

Using kill

The UNIX kill command may be used to terminate a process on the server. First the process ID must be obtained by using the ps command, and then the kill command can be executed.

The syntax for the kill command is as follows:

kill -9 <process id>

In this command, -9 is an optional parameter used to force kill a process. For additional parameter options that can be used with kill, please refer to your UNIX man pages.

The following is an example of obtaining a process ID and issuing the kill command to terminate the process:

$UNIX>ps -ef | grep xclock | grep r12vis

---

r12vis 10542 6233   0 16:46 pts/1 00:00:00 xclock

$UNIX>kill -9 10542

Using find

The UNIX find command may be used to find files or directories on the server. As with the other UNIX commands that have been presented, there are many options available, but only basic syntax for the command will be given for finding files on the server:

find . name "<filename>" -print

In this command, the period (.) means to search in this directory and all subdirectories; filename is the name of the file or directory that the find command is locating. The asterisk (*) may be used as a wildcard character in the search.

The result of executing the find command is a list of the paths and files that match the criteria. Here is an example:

```
$UNIX>cd  $INST_TOP/ora
$UNIX>find . name "*.env" -print
```

```
./10.1.2/VIS_erlinux01.env
./10.1.2/forms/server/default.env
./10.1.3/forms/server/socket.env
./10.1.3/VIS_erlinux01.env
```

With the find command, it is also possible to locate files based upon size, change date and several other parameters. Familiarize yourself with these options.

Using df

The UNIX df command may be used to obtain filesystem space information. As with other UNIX commands, df has many parameter options, but the use of interest here is the df -m syntax. This will display block information for filesystems. Executing df -m is useful for determining the amount of free space in megabytes and assessing whether additional space is required. The following is an example of using the df command:

```
$UNIX>df –m
```

Using du

The UNIX du command may be used to obtain filesystem space information. This command will return information on space usage by all subdirectories below the location the command was executed from.

Executing a sort command along with the du command is useful for determining which directories are using the most space. This information can help the Oracle Applications DBA resolve issues with space usage. Here is an example:

```
$UNIX>du | sort -n
```

Using tar

Some of the most common uses of the UNIX tar command include archiving directories and files into one single file, extracting files and directories that have been archived with the tar command, and copying directories and files from one location to another. Parameters for the tar command are provided in Table 4-11.

The following tar syntax can be used to compress a directory and its contents:

tar -cvf <tar file name> <directory1 | file1 , directory2 \
| file2 ... directoryn | filen >

The following tar syntax can be used to extract a tar file:

tar -xvf <tar file name>

Table 4-11. *Parameters for the tar Command*

Parameter	Description
<c|x>	Mandatory parameter used to create or extract an archive: c (create), x (extract).
<v>	Optional parameter used to verbosely list the processed files.
<f>	Mandatory parameter used to specify the name of the file or directory to be archived or extracted.
[directory]	Parameter that specifies the name of the directory that is to be archived or extracted.
<tar file name>	Parameter that specifies the file that is being copied or extracted.
[directoryn, filen]	Parameter that specifies the name of the directory that is to be archived.

The following tar syntax can be used to copy a target directory and its contents from one directory to another on the same server:

(cd <source path> ; tar -cf - .) | (cd <target path>; tar -xvf -)

The following example will copy the /vis/oratop/iAS directory to the /newvis/oratop/iAS directory:

$UNIX>(cd /vis/oratop/iAS ; tar -cf - .) | (cd /newvis/oratop/iAS ; tar -xvf -)

Using ping

The ping command will run on UNIX and Windows based machines. The command will connect to another hostname or IP address in order to validate if that address is reachable from your current source.

If you are using a hostname for the target of a ping command and that command fails, then there could be an issue with a DNS entry. You can test this by pinging the IP address instead of the machine name. An example of using ping is as follows:

$UNIX>ping www.oracle.com

```
Pinging a398.g.akamai.net [74.128.20.8] with 32 bytes of data:
Reply from 74.128.20.8: bytes=32 time=7ms TTL=62
Reply from 74.128.20.8: bytes=32 time=18ms TTL=62
Reply from 74.128.20.8: bytes=32 time=7ms TTL=62
Ping statistics for 74.128.20.8:
    Packets: Sent = 3, Received = 3, Lost = 0 (0% loss),
Approximate round trip times in milli-seconds:
    Minimum = 7ms, Maximum = 18ms, Average = 10ms
```

Using uptime

The uptime command will display the length of time since the server was last rebooted. In addition to the time the server has been running, the uptime command will include the average run queues on the system. The load average is listed for the most recent 1, 5, and 15 minutes. These values can give you an indication of the performance of your system; however, to truly gauge system performance you should use other commands such as vmstat or sar as discussed in Chapter 6 of this guide.

Finding and Removing Memory Segments and Semaphores

Shared memory and semaphores being used on a UNIX server can be displayed and removed using the ipcs and ipcrm commands, respectively. These commands are useful when a stopped or killed process does not relinquish a shared memory segment or semaphore. This may become evident if you try to restart a process or try to execute an upgrade or patching step that finds the process is still holding a memory segment or semaphore.

The following is an example of how to use the ipcs command to show all memory segments, message queues, and semaphores:

$UNIX>ipcs -a

```
------ Shared Memory Segments --------
key          shmid   owner  perms bytes     nattch status
0x00000000 6946816 oracle  600    1056768  12     dest
0x00000000 6979585 oracle  600    1056768  12     dest
0x00000000 7012354 vis     600    8589316  10     dest
0x00000000 7045123 oracle  600    1056768  11     dest
0x00000000 7077892 vis     600    1056768  10     dest
0x00000000 7110661 oracle  600    8589316  9      dest


------ Semaphore Arrays --------
key          semid   owner  perms nsems    status
0x00000000 1081344 oracle  600    1
0x00000000 32769   vis     600
------ Message Queues --------
key    msqid  owner  perms  used-bytes  messages
```

To limit the display of the command, you may use it in conjunction with grep to search for a specific process owner, as shown here:

$UNIX>ipcs -a | grep vis

```
0x00000000 7012354  vis  600  8589316  10  dest
0x00000000 7077892  vis  600  1056768  10  dest
0x00000000 32769    vis  600
```

Additional parameters for the ipcs command can be displayed with the following command:

$UNIX>ipcs -help

Once the ipcs command has been executed, the memory segment or semaphore can be removed by issuing the ipcrm command. A memory segment can be removed with the following command:

ipcrm -m

In this command, is the number of the memory segment for the corresponding process displayed in the ipcs command. Here is an example:

$UNIX>ipcrm -m 7012354

A semaphore may be removed with the following command:

ipcrm -s

In this command, is the number of the semaphore for the corresponding the process displayed in the ipcs command.

The following example removes a specific semaphore:

$UNIX>ipcrm -s 32769

Finding and Removing Print Jobs

Applications users may at times accidentally send large print jobs to the printer. When this occurs, the Oracle Applications DBA may be called upon to cancel the print job. This can be achieved by using the lpstat and lprm commands.

To list all of the print jobs for a specific print queue, the following command can be executed:

lpstat –p<print queue>

In this command, <print_queue> is the name of the UNIX print queue where the job to be cancelled has been sent by the user in the application. The following example lists all print jobs for print queue lpl:

$UNIX>lpstat –plp1

```
printer lp1 unknown state. enabled since Dec 06 17:31 2009. available
Printer: lp1@sc 'hp4500' (dest TEXT@hp4500)
Queue: 1 printable job
Server: pid 786 active
Unspooler: pid 788 active
Status: sending data file 'dfA785sc' to TEXT@hp4500 at 17:30:39.443
Rank   Owner/ID      Class Job Files       Size Time
1      oracle@sc+785    A   785 SYSADMIN.10392083   245212 17:30:39
Active connection from  10.0.0.283 lpd Service
```

To remove a job from the print queue, the lprm command can be executed. Parameters for the lprm command are described in Table 4-12. The syntax for the lprm command is as follows:

lprm –P<print queue> <job number>

Table 4-12. *Parameters for the lprm Command*

Parameter	Description
<print_queue>	The name of the UNIX defined print queue. This name will match the definition of the printer in the application.
<job_number>	The number of the print job as displayed by the lpstat command for the submitted job that you wish to cancel.

The following example will remove a specific print job:

$UNIX>lprm -Plp1 785

Removing Database Sessions

At times it is necessary to remove a session from the database. This can be accomplished with the following steps:

1. Obtain the database session ID and serial number, along with the operating system process ID with a SQL statement. This SQL statement will retrieve the sid and pid for a particular condition:

   select sid, serial#, pid from v$session where [condition];

2. Use the sid and serial# to kill the database session:

   alter system kill session '&sid,&serial#';

   In this command, &sid and &serial values are obtained in Step 1.

3. Determine, with the ps command, whether the underlying operating system process has terminated. If the process still exists on the server, terminate it with the kill command. Here is an example:

   ps -ef | grep <process id>
   kill -9 <process id>

   In these commands, the <process id> is the pid that was obtained in Step 1.

User Related UNIX Commands

A list of commonly used user related UNIX commands is provided in Table 4-13. Use your operating system's manual pages for more details about specific features with your system.

Table 4-13. *List of commonly used user related UNIX commands*

Command	Description
finger	Provides descriptions of users connected to the system. This command can be used with a specific user name to get descriptive information about that user.
w	Provides a detailed list of the users connected to the system.
who	Provides similar output to the w command but has less detail.
whoami	Provides the current username for your connection.
who am i	Provides the username for the account used to initially login to the server. If you have used the su command to switch to a different user, this command will return your original username.

Server Related UNIX Commands

A list of commonly used server related UNIX commands is provided in Table 4-14. Use your operating system's manual pages for more details about specific features with your system.

Table 4-14. *List of commonly used server related UNIX commands*

Command	Description
date	This command will provide the current date and time used by the server. This can be used during scripting to perform tasks such as adding timestamps to log files.
hostname	This command will provide the hostname of the server. This can be used during scripting to validate determine the host.
uname	This command used with the -a parameter will output information about the operating system.

Preventative Maintenance

There are many tasks that need to be performed on a regular basis to maintain the overall health of the Oracle E-Business Suite. Many of these tasks should be scheduled with crontab, EM 10*g* Grid Control or a like utility, or as a concurrent request.

The following preventative maintenance topics will be discussed:

*   Gathering statistics
*   Recompiling invalid objects
*   Stopping and restarting the Oracle HTTP Server
*   Perform routine purging

Gathering Statistics

Statistics are gathered so that the cost based optimizer (CBO) can determine the best execution plan for queries that are executed. For Oracle Applications, statistics may be gathered with the fnd_stats package or with a few Oracle standard concurrent requests. Regardless of the method chosen, statistics should be gathered on a regularly scheduled basis. Failure to do so will result in severe performance degradation.

While the frequency with which statistics are gathered is environment specific, it is recommended that you gather stats at least once per week. If an environment experiences frequent data changes throughout the week, this frequency may not be sufficient. Tables with significant changes in data, such as those updated by batch process, may require statistics to be updated on a more frequent basis.

Using fnd_stats

The fnd_stats package is based on the standard Oracle dbms_stats package. It was created to generate statistics for the Oracle E-Business Suite. This package should be executed on the database as the APPS user. Additional details regarding fnd_stats can be found in *My Oracle Support Article ID 368252.1.*

▶ *Caution*   Do not use the standard dbms_stats package to gather statistics for Oracle Applications; only the fnd_stats package should be used.

These are some of the procedures available for gathering statistics with fnd_stats:

* fnd_stats.gather_schema_statistics: Used to gather statistics for schemas

* fnd_stats.gather_table_stats: Used to gather table level statistics

* fnd_stats.gather_column_stats: Used to gather column level statistics

* fnd_stats.gather_index_stats: Used to gather index statistics

The following example will gather statistics for all schemas:

SQL> exec fnd_stats.gather_schema_statistics('ALL')

The following example will gather statistics for all objects in the GL schema:

SQL> exec fnd_stats.gather_schema_statistics('GL')

The following example script can be used to gather statistics:

```
#Script used to generate statistics using fnd_stats
LOGFILE=/tmp/generate_stats_$ORACLE_SID.log
sqlplus -s apps/apps << EOF
 spool $LOGFILE;
 exec fnd_stats.gather_schema_statistics ('ALL)
 spool off;
 exit
EOF
exit 0
```

When running the fnd_stats procedure, it is possible to gather statistics for all or some of the rows in a table. To gather statistics for all rows in a table, the compute option is used with fnd_stats. This is also referred to as *computing statistics*. To analyze a percentage of the rows of the table the estimate option is used with the fnd_stats. This is also referred to as *estimating statistics*.

If the table data is normally distributed, then estimating statistics will provide query optimization. For most objects, either the default of 10 percent, or a value of 30 percent is sufficient for gathering statistics.

When computing or estimating statistics with 50 percent or greater, fnd_stats will analyze all rows of the table. This can be resource intensive for large tables. The following example will execute fnd_stats for the HR schema with the estimate option set to 30 percent:

SQL>exec fnd_stats.gather_schema_statistics('HR',estimate_percent=>30);

Oracle provides a script named coe_stats.sql to assist with automating the gathering of statistics. The latest version of this script, and details regarding it, are provided in *My Oracle Support Article ID 156968.1*. Executing the coe_stats.sql script will generate a report called COE_STATS.TXT and a dynamic script called coe_fix_stats.sql. The COE_STATS.TXT report will list all tables that require statistics to be refreshed. The coe_fix_stats.sql script contains the commands required to generate statistics for the tables listed in the report.

Gathering Statistics with Concurrent Requests

Statistics may also be gathered by scheduling standard Oracle concurrent requests. The following is a list of the concurrent requests available to gather statistics:

* Gather schema statistics: Used to gather statistics for schemas

* Gather table statistics: Used to gather table level statistics

* Gather column statistics: Used to gather column level statistics

* Analyze all index column statistics: Used to gather index statistics

Reviewing Object Level Statistics

To determine when an object was last analyzed, the last_analyzed column of the DBA_TABLES or DBA_INDEXES view may be queried. Here is an example:

SQL> select table_name, last_analyzed from dba_objects
 2 where owner='GL' and table_name='GL_BALANCES';

You may also use the fnd_stats.verify_stats procedure to determine the last analyzed date for an object. Executing fnd_stats.verify_stats will generate a report. The syntax for the fnd_stats.verify_stats procedure is as follows:

fnd_stats.verify_stats ('[schema]', \
'[schema.table_name1, schema.table_name2, . . . , schema.table_namen]')

The following is an example of checking statistics for an object:

```
SQL> exec fnd_stats.verify_stats('GL', 'GL.GL_BALANCES');
```

Recompiling Invalid Objects

Objects in the database will at times become invalid. While most objects will recompile upon access, sometimes dependencies upon other objects hinder this ability. The following script includes a call to a standard Oracle package, utl_recomp.recomp_parallel used for recompiling invalids; it may be scheduled on a regular basis to assist with recompiling invalid objects in your database.

```
#Script used to recompile invalid objects in the database
LOGFILE=/tmp/recompile_parallel_$ORACLE_SID.log
sqlplus -s sys/change_on_install << EOF
  spool $LOGFILE;
  select count(1) from dba_objects where status='INVALID';
  exec utl_recomp.recomp_parallel(8);
  select count(1) from dba_objects where status='INVALID';
  spool off;
  exit
EOF
exit 0
```

The following is an example of executing the recompile_invalids.sh script:

```
$UNIX>sh recompile_invalids.sh
```

The following is an example of scheduling the recompile_invalids.sh script to execute daily—it is scheduled in the instance owner crontab on the database server:

```
# At 06:00 everyday, recompile invalid objects in the database
0 6 * * * /scripts/recompile_invalids.sh 1>/dev/null 2>/dev/null
```

Recompiling invalid objects can also be performed with the adadmin utility. To recompile invalids using adadmin, first select menu option *3 Compile/Reload Applications Database Entities*, then menu option *1 Compile APPS schema*. Recompiling invalids using adadmin is a manual process; however, it allows for a parallel recompile of invalid objects owned by the APPS schema.

Stopping and Restarting the Oracle HTTP Server

With R12, stopping and restarting the Oracle HTTP Server with the adapcctl.sh script does not stop the OC4J container where the JVM is running. The easiest mechanism for stopping all required service components is to utilize OPMN to stop and restart the services. The steps to use OPMN were outlined in the *Application Tier Component Startup and Shutdown Scripts* section in this chapter.

Performing Routine Purging

There are a number of items related to the Oracle Applications that require routine purging. This section covers a range of tasks that should be performed to keep your environment clean and performing well. The following will be covered in this section:

* Purging concurrent requests

* Purging workflow history

* Purging and archiving data

* Rotating or removing log files

* Patching cleanup

* Remove opatch footprint

* Remove pre-upgrade binaries

* Remove $APPLTMP content

Purging Concurrent Requests

When concurrent requests are scheduled, history is kept in tables in the database. Log and output files are also created on the Concurrent Processing Node. Over time, as more and more requests are scheduled and executed, the associated tables and number of log and output files can become quite large. Oracle provides a standard concurrent request, called Purge Concurrent Request and/or Manager Data, or FNDCPPUR, to purge the table history as well as the associated log and output files.

This request should be executed daily. The amount of history maintained will be system dependent. If there are any legislative or legal requirements to maintain the history for longer periods of time, the files can be backed up to tape prior to removal. The job can be scheduled to maintain a specified number of days of history. If this job is not scheduled, performance degradation can be experienced with Concurrent Manager processing.

The first time this job is scheduled, it may be necessary to run several iterations with older history settings in order to prevent errors resulting from excessive undo tablespace usage.

▶ *Tip*   It is recommended that you maintain no more than 30 days of online history for Concurrent Manager processing.

Purging Workflow History

Workflow history is also kept in tables in the database. Based upon the amount of activity in your application, the size of the underlying workflow related tables can increase dramatically. This increase in size will eventually cause performance degradation. Additional details regarding workflow purging can be reviewed in *My Oracle Support Article ID 144806.1*.

Oracle has provided a standard concurrent request called Purge Obsolete Workflow Runtime Data, or FNDWFPR, to purge workflow history. It is recommended that this request be scheduled to execute daily. The job can be scheduled to maintain a specified number of days of history.

Purging and Archiving Data

While it is beyond the scope for this guide to provide details regarding how to purge and archive data contained in the E-Business Suite, it is worth mentioning that a purge and archive strategy should be documented and implemented for your environment. Oracle provides purge routines for many of the primary modules of the application, and these routines may be used to delete data according to the requirements of your organization.

The benefits of controlling data growth include reducing expenses for disk space. More importantly, performance can be vastly improved by reducing the row size of large tables.

Rotating or Removing Log Files

There are many log files associated with the various components of the E-Business Suite. Over time, these log files will grow in size, and this could cause issues with filesystem free space. It is recommended that log files be rotated on a scheduled basis in order to control potential space issues. The following sections provide a script for rotating log files as well as a description of the UNIX provided logrotate utility.

Script for Rotating Log Files

The following sample script will read the contents of a file for a listing of log files and will move each log file listed to $FILENAME.$DATE. The script will also remove any log files named $FILENAME.* that are older than 30 days.

```
#Script used to rotate and remove log files > 30 days old
#Script name is rotate_logs.sh
LOGFILES=$1
NUM_DAYS_RETAIN=30
DATE=`date +%m%d%y`
#read in list of logfiles

awk '{print $0}' $LOGFILES | while read FILENAME
do
  # check that file exists.
  if [ -f $FILENAME ]
  then
    # Make sure the entry does not refer to multiple files
    RESULTS=`ls -l $FILENAME | wc -l`
    if [ $RESULTS -gt 1 ]
    then
      exit 1
    fi
    # backup file and remove old copies
    cp $FILENAME $FILENAME.$DATE
    cp /dev/null $FILENAME
    find . name "$FILENAME.*" -a -mtime +NUM_DAYS_RETAIN -exec rm {} \;
  fi
done
```

An example of the file read by the rotate_logs.sh script is as follows:

```
#########################################
##Example of logfiles.txt, read by rotate_logs.sh
$LOG_HOME/ora/10.1.3/opmn/logs
$LOG_HOME/ora/10.1.3/Apache/logs
$LOG_HOME/ora/10.1.2/forms/logs
#End of file
```

The following is an example of how to execute the script:

```
$UNIX>sh rotate_logs.sh logfiles.txt
```

The rotate_logs.sh script could be scheduled to execute daily in the instance owner crontab as follows:

```
# At 04:00 everyday, rotate logfiles
0 4 * * * /scripts/rotate_logs.sh logfiles.txt >/dev/null 2>/dev/null
```

Using logrotate

There is a UNIX utility called logrotate that can be used to rotate log files on regularly scheduled basis. The utility uses a configuration file to determine what logs should be rotated as well as the directives for rotating each of the logs. The directives are instructions in the configuration file that logrotate uses to determine what to do with each log file. All directives for logrotate can be reviewed by utilizing the man pages on your system.

▶ *Tip*   Read the details of your UNIX systems man pages to determine logrotate options for your environment. You should also work with your UNIX System Administrator regarding installing and scheduling logrotate for your system.

Locations of Log Files

There have been many discussions regarding log files in this guide. For quick reference, the locations and descriptions of log files are provided in Table 4-15. Some of these log files are ideal candidates for rotating and subsequent deletion as discussed in the previous section.

Table 4-15. *Location and description of Oracle Applications log files*

Log File Location	Description
$LOG_HOME/ora/10.1.3/opmn	Log files for OPMN.
$LOG_HOME/ora/10.1.3/Apache	Log files for the Oracle HTTP Server.
$LOG_HOME/ora/10.1.2/forms	Log files for the Forms services.

Table 4-15. *Continued*

Log File Location	Description
$LOG_HOME/appl/admin/log	Log files for the startup and shutdown processes.
$INST_TOP/admin/log/[MMDDH HMI]/adconfig.log	Log files for executions of AutoConfig.

Applications Patching Cleanup

As part of the Applications patching process, a number of items may be purged. Cleanup after patching will also be covered in the *Applications Patching Cleanup* section in Chapter 5 of this guide.

After a patch has been applied, there will be an increase in the used space for the directory where the patch was unzipped. Some of the files here can be cleaned out after the patch has been tested. This will help to control space usage for the filesystem where patches are stored.

The growth is contained in the backup subdirectory of the directory where the patch was unbundled. If you are applying a patch from a common directory to multiple instances, space can be reclaimed in the patch directory by removing files written to the backup subdirectory from previous patch applications. For a large patch that is applied to several instances, this can result in a lot of space.

The patch log directory can also be archived after the patch has been tested. Since these files may be of use as evidence of patch application, you may want to compress the files and move them to another storage system. The patch log files are located in the following directory:

$APPL_TOP/admin/$TWO_TASK/log

Removing opatch Footprint

As part of applying patches with opatch, cleanup can be performed to remove hidden directory information that may have been created as part of the patch application. The hidden directory is called .patch_storage. You may execute the opatch command with the option util cleanup to remove the files in this directory. Executing the opatch cleanup will free up space in the $ORACLE_HOME directory.

Remove Pre-Upgrade Binaries

When upgrades are for components of the Technology Stack, the previous version of the binaries can be removed. After you have successfully upgraded to the new version, you should remove the old version of the software. An example of this is when upgrading from Oracle Database 11gR1 to Oracle11gR2. The Oracle11gR1 binaries may be removed after the upgrade to 11gR2 is successful.

Remove $APPLTMP Content

Temporary files are written to $APPLTMP by various components of the Oracle Applications. You should schedule a job to periodically remove files from this structure to control the content and growth.

Scheduling Scripts

The previous section covered preventative maintenance that should be periodically executed for the overall health of your Oracle Applications environment. This section will cover how you can schedule scripts to perform required maintenance.

Scripts can be scheduled to execute at specific times by using the UNIX crontab, the at command, EM 10g Grid Control, or third-party tools. This section will provide a brief overview of using these utilities to schedule jobs.

Using crontab

UNIX jobs can be scheduled by creating entries in the cron table, or crontab. Entries in crontab are then executed by the cron daemon scheduler. This utility is very useful if a tool like EM 10g is not available for your environment. Through crontab, the Oracle Applications DBA can run custom scripts on a scheduled basis to perform a variety of tasks. Jobs scheduled through crontab will execute on the server as scheduled, unless the server is down.

Each user has its own crontab to schedule jobs. Entries in the crontab have the layout described in Table 4-16.

Table 4-16. *Layout of entries in crontab*

Minute	Hour	Day of Month	Month	Day of Week	Command
[0–59]	[0–23]	[1–31]	[1–12 |Jan–Dec]	[0–6 | Sun– Sat]	[command to execute]

To list the crontab entries for a user, issue the following command:

$UNIX>crontab –l

```
# At 05:00 every Sunday, stop and restart the Apache server
0 5 * * 0 /oracle/admin/scripts/vis/restart_apache.sh 1>/dev/null 2>/dev/null
. . .
. . .
# At 22:30 every night, execute the backup
30 22 * * * /oracle/admin/scripts/vis/backup.sh 1>/dev/null 2>/dev/null
```

Using crontab -e will open the crontab for editing with the standard text editor. After making the appropriate modifications to the file, simply save it as you would a normal text file. The following is an example of the command used to edit crontab:

$UNIX>crontab -e

▶ *Caution*   Only Applications DBAs experienced with UNIX scripting should perform the task of scheduling jobs through crontab. Scripts to be run through crontab should be carefully tested to ensure they perform the desired operations.

Using at

UNIX jobs can also be scheduled by using the at command. This command is more appropriate for running one time jobs. For jobs that need to run on a regular basis, the other utilities described in this section would be more appropriate than the at command.

To use the at command, login to a server as the user you want to execute the command. At a UNIX prompt type the command at followed by a time to execute the command. This will bring up a prompt where you can enter the command you want to run. When you are finished entering the information, press CTRL-D to exit. Consult the manual page for the at command in order to get more details on the formats available for the command execution time. You can schedule jobs to run on specific dates or even a specific number of days from the current time. The following is an example use of the at command which will execute the shell script /home/vis/shell_script.sh at 2:00 PM.

```
$UNIX>at 14:00
at> /home/vis/shell_script.sh
```

Scheduling and Monitoring Tools

There are many database monitoring tools available for managing Oracle database systems. These tools all have similar features for monitoring the database.

One feature of EM 10*g* Grid Control is the ability to schedule jobs to execute in databases or on the servers. Notification can be sent if the job executes successfully or if there is a failure. Jobs can be created and stored in the job library, and they can be copied and easily modified within the browser framework. The job management and scheduling that is offered by EM 10*g* Grid Control is easy to use and manage via a user friendly GUI.

In addition to the basic monitoring and scheduling features, EM 10*g* Grid Control has some advantages over other third-party tools. Oracle provides an Oracle Applications Management Pack for EM 10*g* Grid Control that allow you to manage and monitor other components of the E-Business Suite, including the Oracle HTTP Server and Concurrent Manager. Additional information regarding the Applications Management Pack with EM 10*g* Grid Control is provided in *My Oracle Support Article ID 846628.1*

▶ *Note*   EM Management Packs have additional licensing requirements. Contact your Oracle Sales Representative for additional details regarding licensing fees.

Toolkit Best Practices

A toolkit is a dynamic library that will continue to evolve with an Oracle Applications DBA's environment and as new versions and upgrades are developed by Oracle. It is important to manage and update your toolkit on a regular basis.

Chapter 5

Patching and Upgrading

One of the most important and time consuming aspects of an Oracle Applications DBA's job is to apply patches and perform upgrades to the E-Business Suite Applications and Technology Stack. Patches may be required to resolve problems with the Applications code, to fix production issues, to install new features, or to update components of the Technology Stack. Patching is not a simple one step process, but rather requires careful research in order to determine all of the prerequisite steps, patching steps, and post patching steps required. Upgrades are typically more complicated than patching and will take the code to the next point release. The focus of this chapter will be on Oracle Applications patching, and an overview of Technology Stack components patching and upgrades will also be provided. Oracle E-Business Suite patching and upgrades will be reviewed in the following categories:

* **Oracle Critical Patch Updates (CPUs):** This section will describe security patches that are released by Oracle for the Oracle Applications code as well as the Technology Stack Components.

* **Oracle Applications patching:** This section will describe all patches and upgrades that change the underlying Oracle Applications code.

* **Technology Stack Components patching and upgrades:** This section will describe all patches and upgrades for the Technology Stack components including the Oracle Application Server, Oracle Database Server, JDK and Sun JRE Plug-in.

Oracle Critical Patch Updates (CPUs)

On a quarterly basis, Oracle releases Critical Patch Updates (CPUs). CPUs are released on the Tuesday closest to the 15th of the months of January, April, July and October. Up to date information regarding the CPUs and the schedule can be found on the Oracle Technology Network (OTN). Additional information regarding OTN can be found in Chapter 8 of this guide. CPUs are designed to address security issues with the Applications code and Technology Stack. Code is easily available on the internet that provides detailed information for executing security breaches per the security holes that exist in the Applications or Technology Stack code. It is advisable to download and apply these CPUs on a scheduled basis to protect your environment from the potential security breaches.

▶ *Tip*   Oracle tests the CPUs by applying the CPUs for all components to the environment for the current cycle. You should plan to apply the CPUs to all components of your environment as well to conform to a similar testing model. For example, if the CPU contains patches for your version of the Oracle Database and Oracle E-Business Suite you should apply both patches to the environment at the same time.

For Release 12 of the E-Business Suite, the CPUs are cumulative for the Applications code as well as the Technology Stack components. Since the patches are cumulative, it is sufficient to apply the latest available CPU patches in order to get current. There is still effort required with researching, testing, and scheduling the deployment of the patches given the potential security concerns. At a minimum, a review of the CPUs should occur every quarter when the CPUs are released.

▶ *Tip*   As of the January 2010 CPU, R11i CPUs are also cumulative for the Applications Code.

Oracle Applications Patching

There are a number of important topics related to Oracle Applications patching. In this section we'll discuss the following:

* **Types of Applications patches:** This section provides a description of the various types of Applications patches that are available for Oracle Applications.

* **Preparing to patch:** This section will describe the importance of reviewing the patch README prior to patching.

* **Description of patch drivers:** This section will describe the components of an Applications patch driver.

* **Documenting the patching process:** This section will explain how to document and manage the overall process of applying patches

* **Applying Applications patches:** Applying a patch involves several steps, such as unbundling the patch, enabling Maintenance Mode, applying the patch with adpatch, and implementing manual steps. This section will discuss each of the steps involved.

* **Patching related features in Oracle Applications Manager (OAM):** There are several features available in OAM that assist with managing Applications patches. The OAM functionality that will be reviewed in this section includes patch reporting, patch timing reports, patch wizard, and register flagged files for customized files.

* **Methods for obtaining patch history reports:** In addition to functionality provided in OAM, there are several methods for obtaining patch history reports. This section will discuss using patchsets.sh and querying the database for patch information.

Types of Applications Patches

The concepts of patching in Release 12 are built upon *codelines* and *codelevels*. A codeline is equivalent to a point release of the system. For example, codeline A is Release 12.0 and codeline B is Release 12.1. A codelevel lies on top of a product family in a codeline and is denoted by a number. The first set of fixes for the GL product would be R12.GL.A.1. For additional details regarding codelines and codelevels, please refer to *My Oracle Support Article ID 459156.1.*

There are several different types of Oracle Applications patches. The following are the more common types of patches in order of least complex to more complex:

* **One-off patch:** This is the simplest type of patch. It is created to resolve a specific bug. This is also called an Individual Bug Fix.

* **Product Family Release Update Pack (RUP):** This is a collection of patches on a given codeline for a specific product family. An example of a Product Family Release Update Pack in Release 12.1 is R12.ATG_PF.B.Delta.2.

* **Release Update Pack (RUP):** This is a collection of Product Family RUPs on a given codeline. These RUPs are cumulative. An example of a Release Update Pack in Release 12.1 is 12.1.2.

* **Pre-upgrade patch:** This is a collection of upgrade related, high priority patches for a product family.

* **Consolidated Upgrade Patch:** This is a collection of upgrade related patches for a product family. These patches are used to upgrade an R12 instance from one point release to another.

In addition to the aforementioned common types of patches, the following describes other special types of patches:

* **Documentation patch:** This is a patch that updates online help.

* **Interoperability patch:** This is a patch that is required for Oracle Applications to function with a newer version of a Technology Stack component; for example, you may need to apply an interoperability patch prior to upgrading the database version.

* **NLS patch:** This is a patch that updates language specific information for multi-language installations.

* **Legislative patch:** This is a special patch for HR Payroll customers; it contains legislative data.

As the patch size increases, the complexity of the patch application process also increases. More research is required for Release Update Packs than is required for a one-off patch due to the additional prerequisite and post steps needed.

Preparing to Patch

The first step for applying a patch is to carefully examine the README file provided with the patch. This document will list all steps required by the patch. The patch zip file will typically contain both a README.txt and README.html file.

▶ *Caution*   Before applying a patch, make certain that the README file has been thoroughly reviewed.

The README file will contain prerequisites, installation steps, post installation steps, and other information vital to the successful installation of the patch. The prerequisites may consist of other patches or manual steps. An example of the contents of a README file is shown in Figure 5-1.

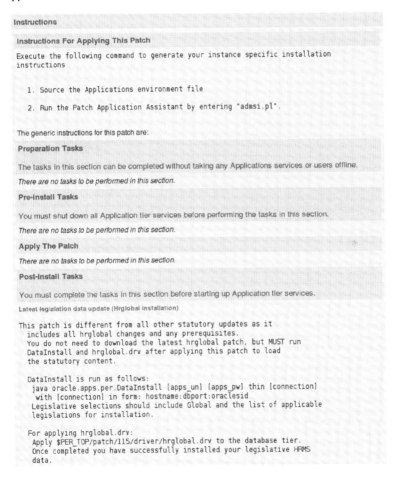

Figure 5-1. *Readme file for patch 9204440*

If prerequisites have not been met, you must add these steps or patches to the overall process of applying the patch. Become familiar with all steps required before attempting to apply the patch.

▶ *Caution*   Removing a patch from Oracle Applications after it has been applied is not usually a feasible option; therefore, a full system backup should be taken before applying patches to an instance.

Description of Patch Drivers

Patches consist of a unified u driver that must be applied to all appropriate nodes using the adpatch utility. The naming convention for patch driver files is u[patch_number].drv.

The unified driver consists of three different phases of patching. – the copy portion, the database portion and the generate portion. The copy portion will copy newer files from the patch directory to appropriate locations, load object modules into the C libraries, apply Java class file changes, and compile new Java Server Pages files. The database portion is used to update database level code and objects. The generate portion is used to generate forms, PL/SQL libraries, reports, menus and other objects.

The adpatch utility allows the Oracle Applications DBA to skip portions of the driver by using a command line switch, such as nocopyportion. Additional details regarding adpatch are provided in the *Using AutoPatch Utility* section in this chapter.

Documenting the Patching Process

Documenting the patching process can be performed manually or by using a utility provided by Oracle. This section describes how you can manually document the patching process as well as how you can use the Patch Application Assistant to document the patching process.

Manually Documenting the Patching Process

It is recommended that you maintain a spreadsheet detailing all prerequisite steps, patching steps and post installation steps required for patch application. By creating such a document, you can eliminate operator error, such as missed steps or steps completed out of order.

The columns in the spreadsheet should be customized to meet your needs. These columns can include information about the node being patched, details about the patch being applied, or the rationale for the patch. At a minimum, it is useful to have columns for patch number, description, and comments, but it is often also useful to include the actual time required to complete each step based upon trial runs in a sandbox instance. Tracking timings allows for an accurate prediction of production maintenance downtime.

An example of a spreadsheet for patches required by Project EOY 2009 Phase 2 that will require 6 hours and 25 minutes to apply is shown in Figure 5-2.

Patches Required for Project EOY 2009 Phase 2				
Patch #	Description	Comment	Time Required (hh:mi)	Task Start Time
	Stop Application processes		0:15	01/12/2010 7:00PM
	Put application in Maintenance mode	use adadmin	0:05	01/12/2010 7:15PM
9204440	US & Canada EOY 2009 Phase 2		2:30	01/12/2010 7:20PM
	Run DataInstaller	post step for patch 9204440	0:15	01/12/2010 9:50PM
	Apply HR Global Driver	post step for patch 9204440	2:00	01/12/2010 10:05PM
	Take application out of Maintenance mode	use adadmin	0:05	01/13/2010 12:05AM
	Recompile Invalid objects	use adadmin	0:30	01/13/2010 12:10AM
	Restart Application processes		0:15	01/13/2010 12:40AM
	Validate Application before contacting testers		0:30	01/13/2010 12:55AM
		Time to complete ->	6:25	01/13/2010 1:25AM

Figure 5-2. *Sample patch documentation spreadsheet*

If timings are included for every step, the Oracle Applications DBA can generate a schedule for applying the patches to production by using time functions in the spreadsheet software. This corresponds to the *Task Start Time* column in Figure 5-2. Identifying shifts is highly recommended for patching efforts that will exceed the duration of a standard shift. Otherwise, a simple summation of the time required for each step should provide an accurate schedule. The times required for applying patches is also tracked by adpatch and can be found in the $APPL_TOP/admin/$TWO_TASK/out/adt*.lst files. Additional details regarding adpatch are provided in the *Using AutoPatch Utility* section in this chapter.

▶ *Tip*   When documenting the patching process for multiple patches, post installation steps such as recompiling invalid objects, regenerating JAR files, and running the AutoConfig utility can be consolidated and executed at the end of the patching process. This helps to streamline the patch process and reduce downtime.

Documenting the Patching Process with the Patch Application Assistant

Oracle has created the *Patch Application Assistant* (PAA) to assist with the tedious and mistake prone task of tracking manual steps required with some patches. The patch's README file will have instructions to run the PAA if needed.

The PAA is executed with the Perl script admsi.pl. Prior to executing the Perl script, first set the DISPLAY variable so that the screen will be displayed on your desktop. An example of the initial screen for PAA is shown in Figure 5-3.

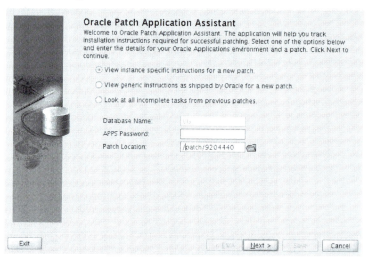

Figure 5-3. *The Oracle Patch Application Assistant (PAA) Main Menu*

The PAA will use information from the patch directory to create the list of steps to be executed with the patch specified in the patch location field. As the steps are finished, they can be marked as *Completed* in the PAA interface.

Applying Applications Patches

After the README file has been reviewed and all of the required patching steps have been documented, you can begin the process of applying the patch. Be sure to run steps as the owner of the Applications software with the appropriate environment settings in place. The patching process generally involves the following logical steps:

1. Download and unbundle the patch.

2. Run the Oracle Patch Application Assistant, if needed.

3. Shut down the Applications services.

4. Place the instance in Maintenance Mode or apply as a hotpatch.

5. Use the AutoPatch utility to apply patch driver file.

6. Review log files to ensure patch completed successfully.

7. Perform any manual steps that may be required.

8. Perform post patching steps.

9. Restart the Applications services.

A sandbox instance is a must for applying patches. This instance gives the Oracle Applications DBA a place to apply patches and resolve issues with the patching process without impacting production or test instances. Ensure that the sandbox instance is a recent clone of production, so that this environment matches the production environment. All steps should be practiced multiple times and be thoroughly tested before applying the patch in production. The patch documentation spreadsheet should be updated as needed based upon the application of the patch.

Downloading and Unbundling the Patch

The first step for applying a patch is to download and unbundle it using an unzip utility. If errors are encountered while unzipping large zip files, you may require an updated version of the unzip program. Review operating system specifics and release notes regarding the unzip utility.

It is advisable to have a separate filesystem for storing and unbundling patches. When a large patch, such as a Consolidated Upgrade Patch, is released, a temporary filesystem may need to be created to store the unbundled patch. When sizing the filesystem, be sure to include an extra 20 percent for backup information that is written to the patch directory.

Once the patch has been downloaded and unbundled, you should change to the directory where the patch driver is located. If the same patch is to be applied to multiple instances, there is no need to unbundle the patch more than once. The initial unbundling of the patch can be used for multiple applications. You may need to change permissions on the directory so that the instance owner has the ability to read and write to the unbundled area. This prepares you for the next step of using the adpatch utility to apply the patch. Before applying the patch, the instance should be placed in Maintenance Mode. Additional details regarding Maintenance Mode are covered in the next section.

▶ *Tip*   Before applying a patch, confirm that there is enough space allocated to the instance filesystem, as well as to the filesystem where the patch has been unbundled. Exhausting filesystem space is a common error that occurs while applying patches.

Shutting Down the Applications and Enabling Maintenance Mode

Most patches require the Applications processes be shut down prior to applying the patch. Additional details regarding stopping and starting Applications processes are provided in Chapter 4 of this guide. The system is also required to be in *Maintenance Mode* prior to applying patches. Maintenance Mode places the system in a state that allows for administrative tasks to occur while restricting user access to the system.

The instance can be placed in Maintenance Mode by running adadmin and selecting the appropriate menu options. Alternatively, executing the SQL script $AD_TOP/patch/115/sql/adsetmmd.sql with the ENABLE parameter will also place the instance in Maintenance Mode without using adadmin. When the patching has been completed, be sure to take the instance out of Maintenance Mode by using the adadmin utility or by executing $AD_TOP/patch/115/sql/adsetmmd.sql with the DISABLE parameter. If the instance is in Maintenance Mode, users are redirected to a system downtime URL upon logging into the system.

A patch can also be applied using the hotpatch parameter with adpatch. This option does not require the instance to be in Maintenance Mode; however, Oracle recommends using Maintenance Mode to improve patching performance.

Using AutoPatch Utility

The administrative tool used to apply Applications patches is AutoPatch, also referred to by its command line executable, adpatch. Basic information about the AutoPatch utility can be found in *My Oracle*

Support Article ID 459156.1. The AutoPatch utility will spawn off a user determined number of patch worker processes to update Applications code by copying later versions of programs to the application tier, updating database objects, regenerating Applications forms and reports, and performing some post patching steps. The code changes are determined by the patch's driver file.

▶ *Tip*   Prior to executing adpatch, disable any password constraints defined within the Applications or database. These constraints could cause errors if the patch creates a new user account. Some patches use default database passwords when make updates; therefore, you may also need to reset some standard Oracle passwords for accounts such as CTXSYS.

An Oracle Applications DBA needs to be familiar with the options available for the AutoPatch utility. The parameters supported by the adpatch command differ depending upon the codelevel of the AD product. When upgrading the AD product group, be sure to identify and understand any new features of the AutoPatch utility. Review the adpatch command parameters for benefits. Use the command adpatch help=y to see the available options. Commonly used adpatch options shown in Table 5-1.

Table 5-1. *Commonly Used adpatch Options*

Option	Purpose
novalidate	Prevents adpatch from validating all schema connections. This is a default setting.
noprereq	Prevents adpatch from checking the existence of prerequisite patches. This is a default setting.
nocompiledb	Prevents adpatch from compiling database objects.
nocompilejsp	Prevents adpatch from compiling JSP objects.
noautoconfig	Prevents adpatch from running AutoConfig after patching.
nogenerateportion	Prevents adpatch from regenerating objects after patching.
parallel	Allows adpatch to perform certain steps in parallel. This is a default setting.
hotpatch	Allows adpatch to be run when not in Maintenance Mode.

▶ *Tip*   If you are applying a large number of patches, use the options nocompilejsp, nocompiledb and noautoconfig to speed up the application of the patches. Recompiling Java Server Pages (JSPs) and database objects and running AutoConfig can also be performed at the end of the patching process. Placing the database in noarchivelog mode may also improve patching performance. In addition to noarchivelog mode, you may also want to adjust database initialization parameters that control database memory settings to improve patch application performance.

Having changed directories to the location where the patch driver(s) is located, you can then start the patching session as the instance owner by executing adpatch with the desired options: The following is the syntax for using options with adpatch:

adpatch options=[option1, option2..]

The following is an example of executing adpatch with the nocompiledb and noautoconfig options:

$UNIX>adpatch options=nocompiledb,noautoconfig

▶ *Note*   The adpatch utility must be executed as the owner of the Applications software after appropriately setting the environment.

By default adpatch is started in interactive mode and the user must respond to several questions. These questions serve to verify Applications file settings, database connectivity, and patch driver options. For example, the user may set adpatch to send an email upon failure. The following questions from adpatch require additional explanation:

Question: Filename for AutoPatch Log

Recommended response: Rather than use the default name of adpatch.log, use a more descriptive name, such as u[patch#].log. For multi-node or multi-language patching, you should consider including the server name and language in the filename. Additional descriptions may also be added depending on your environment.

Question: The default directory is [current working directory]

Recommended response: It is advised that for one-off patches you run the adpatch utility from the directory where the patch has been unbundled. By doing this, the default value for this question can be chosen. Otherwise, enter the directory where the patch was unbundled.

Question: Please enter the name of your AutoPatch driver file

Recommended response: This depends upon the patch being applied. Most patches from Oracle now contain a single u driver. A case where this would change is the hrglobal driver or hrglobal.drv file for legislative patches.

Question: Number of parallel workers

Recommended response: This value is environment specific and should be adjusted accordingly.

Using a defaultsfile will allow for non-interactive patching by providing responses to the adpatch questions. Non-interactive patching will allow you to apply a patch without having to manually respond to prompts. This mode is beneficial if the patch is being applied by a script. The defaultsfile option of adpatch must point to a file in the $APPL_TOP/admin/$CONTEXT_NAME directory. When the utility is run in this mode, the Oracle Applications DBA responds to the prompts with common answers until the directory location of the patch is requested. Enter abort at this prompt to create and save the defaultsfile. This option is typically used with the mode interactive=no.

▶ *Tip*   Uploading patch information to the database can be done after the system is out of Maintenance Mode. For large patches this can help to reduce downtime to the application. Review the Oracle Applications Patching Procedures document, available on My Oracle Support, for details on these steps.

Additionally the AutoPatch utility can run in two different modes. The preinstall mode is used during the upgrade process to update AD utilities as well as for other special circumstances. For those special cases the README file will have instructions to apply with this mode. The preinstall mode is run by using the command adpatch preinstall=y.

The other mode for AutoPatch is test mode. When run in this mode, AutoPatch will not apply the patch. Running it in test mode is used to determine patch application file changes. The driver file is read and a list of files that would be impacted by the patch is produced in the patch log file. The test mode is run by using the command adpatch apply=no.

Performing Environment Specific Manual Steps

In addition to manual steps required by the patch, there may be additional steps required by the organization. For example, it may be necessary to track new users or new objects due to audit requirements. In those situations it is useful to create scripts to automate the manual commands. This can not only help reduce the chances of human error during the patching process, but scripting can also speed up the process.

For ease of management, you should create a special directory to be the home directory for such scripts. During the creation of the scripts, be sure to include logging commands as well as parameters for values such as instance name. When you parameterize such values, the scripts can be executed with each patching effort without requiring modifications.

For example, you may build a script of manual steps that looks similar to the following template:

```
SCRIPT_TOP=/patch/scripts/project_a
INSTANCE_NAME=$1
LOG_TOP=$SCRIPT_TOP/logs
script_1.sh > $LOG_TOP/post_steps.log
command_1 >>$LOG_TOP/post_steps.log
script_2.sh $INSTANCE_NAME >> $LOG_TOP/post_steps.log
exit
```

In the preceding example, script_1.sh may be a script that collects filesystem space usage changes, and script_2.sh could be a script that collects information about new users created by the patch.

When the script has executed, thoroughly review the log files generated by the script. New failures may be encountered on some instances that had not occurred during past patch applications. Resolve any errors before proceeding to the next steps. These log files should be saved as part of the patching results in case they need to be reviewed at a later time.

Scripts created for such steps should contain error handling, such as checking the number and types of parameters. Custom scripts should also contain documentation to describe the purpose of the script.

The scripts you create should be included in the spreadsheet as part of the process for applying the patch. Part of the documentation process for the patching effort involves using descriptive script and variable names.

▶ *Tip*   Writing scripts is a useful skill set for Oracle Applications DBAs. We recommend you practice coding scripts on test severs while connected as a user with a low level of permissions until you become more comfortable with scripting. Always test your scripts thoroughly before running them on production systems.

Post Patching Steps

Many patches require post patching steps to be executed to complete the patching process. In addition to this, if the patch was applied using options such as nocompiledb, noautoconfig, nogenerateportion or others, those steps need to be performed as part of the post patching steps. Typical post patching steps include generating message files, regenerating JAR files, regenerating menu options, relinking executables, recompiling invalids, and recompiling flex fields. Most of the post patching requirements can be performed with the AD Administration utility, adadmin. As an Oracle Applications DBA, you should be familiar with the menu options available in the adadmin utility. Details regarding the adadmin utility are available in the Chapter 4 of this guide.

Resolving Patching Problems

Patching problems manifest themselves in many different ways. Typically, the adpatch session will display an error or will appear to be hung on one task for a long period of time. The first step in resolving the issue is to review the adpatch log file and associated worker log file. Next, the reason the worker failed must be determined and resolved. After resolution has been obtained, adctrl can be used to continue the patching process.

Reviewing Patch Log Files

During and after the application of patches, it is helpful to review log files of the adpatch session and its workers. These files are found in the $APPL_TOP/admin/$TWO_TASK/log directory. The adpatch log filename is specified during the patch process. See the *Using AutoPatch* section earlier in the chapter for more details.

In order to monitor the patch from a telnet session other than the one where the patch was started, a simple UNIX command such as tail -f u[patch#].log can be used to display information as it is written to the log file. This is a useful means for monitoring the progress of a patch that is being applied.

The log files for the workers will be named adwork[xxx].log, where [xxx] is the number of the patch worker process. If a particular worker has failed, examine the related log file for detailed information. This information can be researched on My Oracle Support or used to open an SR with Oracle Support.

▶ *Tip*   Patching log files may contain sensitive data such as passwords. For security purposes, keep these log files in a directory that is not viewable by all users.

An example of the log file listing for the u driver of patch 9204440, applied through adpatch using 5 workers, may look like this:

$UNIX>ls

```
adwork001.log
adwork002.log
adwork003.log
adwork004.log
adwork005.log
u9204440.log
```

Using AD Control

The administrative tool used to manage patch workers is AD Control, or adctrl. Occasionally workers will fail or hang, which will require the Oracle Applications DBA to interface with adctrl. Common patching errors will be covered later in this chapter.

AD Control menu options will vary depending upon the AutoPatch version applied to the instance. When logged in as the Applications owner on any of the Applications nodes in your environment, execute adctrl to display the AD Control menu options. An example of the menu options are shown in Figure 5-4.

```
                    AD Controller Menu
- - - - - - - - - - - - - - - - - - - - - - - - - - - - - - - - - - - - - - - -

1.    Show worker status

2.    Tell worker to restart a failed job

3.    Tell worker to quit

4.    Tell manager that a worker failed its job

5.    Tell manager that a worker acknowledges quit

6.    Restart a worker on the current machine

7.    Exit




Enter your choice [1] :
```

Figure 5-4. *AD Controller Main Menu*

To execute an adctrl menu option, simply type the menu option and press *Enter*. If options 2–6 are chosen, either specify the number of the worker that requires action, or enter "all" for the action to be executed for all workers.

The *Skip Worker* menu option is a hidden adctrl menu option. If a worker needs to be skipped, start adctrl, enter 8, and then enter the worker number. Only use this option if advised by Oracle Support.

Resolving AutoPatch Worker Failure

If a worker has failed, the adpatch session will normally display a failed worker message. The status of the worker may also be determined using adctrl. If a worker has failed, the worker error can be obtained by viewing the worker log file. Once the worker issue has been resolved, use adctrl to restart the worker.

If a worker has failed, and it is determined that the step the worker was trying to execute may be skipped, the hidden option 8 of the adctrl menu, *Skip Worker*, may be used to skip the worker. It is only advisable to skip a worker if the step is not critical to the environment being patched and is recommended under the direction of Oracle Support.

▶ *Tip*   It may be necessary to research My Oracle Support or open a Service Request (SR) to resolve issues with failed workers. For additional information on My Oracle Support and the SR process, see Chapter 8 of this guide.

The following are common worker failures that may be seen by the Oracle Applications DBA during patching. The error messages will be displayed by the adpatch session or in the worker log file:

Error message: ORA-01013: user requested cancel of current operation

Resolution to error: If this error occurs, simply use adctrl to restart the worker on the current machine.

Error message: Patch not applied successfully, **adpatch** did not cleanup its restart files (*rf9).

Resolution to error: If this error occurs, execute the following commands as the instance owner to archive restart files then restart the adpatch session:

```
$UNIX>cd $APPL_TOP/admin/$TWO_TASK
$UNIX>mv restart restart_old
$UNIX>mkdir restart
Restart the adpatch session
```

▶ *Tip*   A command line option of abandon=yes can be used to begin a new patching session if adpatch failed. Running the utility with this option will allow it to remove the restart files automatically.

Error message: No error message is displayed; rather, the worker log file states that the worker is complete, yet adctrl indicates that the worker is still running.

Resolution to error: This patching problem occurs when the worker is complete, but did not update patching tables correctly to notify the adpatch session that it has finished. In this scenario, the adpatch session is still waiting for the finish return code from the worker. When this occurs, use adctrl to fail the worker, and then restart the worker.

▶ *Tip*   Any form, library, or report that fails to generate during the patch process can be regenerated manually after all patching and post patching steps have completed. If the object still fails to compile, open an SR.

Additional Tips for Resolving Patching Issues

If a patch has hung or workers have failed, and the reason for this failure cannot be determined, it is advisable to check the number of invalid objects in the database. If the number of invalid objects is high, recompile the invalid objects in parallel and restart the patching session.

If the adpatch session is hung, and all other methods for resolution have been executed, it may be necessary to bounce the database and restart the patch session. This method for resolving patching issues is sometimes necessary, especially when applying large patches, such as Consolidated Upgrade Patches.

If a failure occurs during the application of a patch, it may be necessary to apply another patch to resolve the issue. If this type of issue occurs during the application of a large patch, you may want to be able to restart the original patch from the point of failure. The *Oracle Applications Patching Procedures* document provides details for applying a patch with adpatch already running.

Using AD Merge Patch

When applying a large group of patches, some performance benefits can be incurred by using the AD Merge Patch utility to combine the patches into one patch. Merging the patches eliminates the need to run AutoPatch and respond to its prompts for every patch.

▶ *Tip*   Some patches are not able to be merged using AD Merge. The patch README will contain information if the patch cannot be merged with AD Merge..

The set of patches to be merged should be copied to a common directory. After the patches are unbundled in this source directory, the AD Merge Patch utility can be run against the patches to output a merged patch into a destination directory. The source and destination directories must exist under the same base directory. The following is an example of the syntax for using Ad Merge Patch by running admrgpch:

$UNIX>admrgpch /source_dir /destination_dir

The completed merged driver files found in the destination directory can be applied the same way an unmerged patch is applied. The merged driver files will have a name like u_merged.drv unless the merge_name option is specified. A log file, admrgpch.log, will be created in the directory where the utility was run.

▶ **Note**   When using Ad Merge, be sure to thoroughly test the patching effort.

For more information, see the *Oracle Applications Patching Procedures* document. Note that these commands can also be run through the Oracle Applications Manager (OAM) user interface. The admrgpch utility can be run with several parameters, shown in Table 5-2.

Table 5-2. *admrgpch Options*

Option	Purpose
s	Specifies the source directory containing compressed patch files.
d	Specifies the destination directory for merged patch files.
verbose	Controls the level of detail included in admrgpch output.
preinstall	Specifies the utility run in preinstall mode where it will only merge driver files in the preinstall directory. With this mode AutoPatch must be run in preinstall mode.
admode	Specifies only AD patches will be merged. Default value is non-ad mode.
driveronly	Specifies that only driver files are merged. The files will not be copied to the destination directory
master	Specifies the master upgrade driver to be merged with preinstall upgrade drivers. This option is used with preinstall or driveronly options.

Table 5-2. *Continued*

Option	Purpose
manifest	Specifies a text file containing the list of patch files to be merged. This is useful if the source directory includes a large number of patch files.
logfile	Specifies the log file to contain the output from admrgpch utility.
merge_name	Specifies the name of the merged file. This defaults to "merged", and it should be changed to be more descriptive.

▶ *Tip R12 Concepts*   AD Merge Patch has several new parameters with R12. Review the documentation to ensure you fully understand the new functionality before using the utility.

Special Patching Considerations

There are some additional items that you may need to consider as part of the patching process for your environment. A class of patches that contain legislative data has an additional driver called hrglobal which may need to be applied. For some groups of patches, it may be beneficial to merge the patches into one set of driver files. Depending upon the implementation, there may be a need to deploy multi-language patches. In addition to this, a multi-node environment requires special patching considerations. These topics are discussed in the following sections.

Applying Legislative Patches

For Oracle Payroll, HR and Oracle Time and Labor (OTL) customers, there is another category of patch required by the system. The hrglobal patch supports the legislative requirements of multiple countries. Given the nature of this patch, it is updated frequently by Oracle. It is often a post patch requirement for the mandatory patches released for Oracle Payroll.

Oracle includes the hrglobal patch with the legislative patches. However, if it is ever required to obtain the patch outside of the legislative patches, consult *My Oracle Support Article ID 145837.1*. This note will contain useful information for the hrglobal patch, along with a link to the patch installation instructions and a change history for the patch.

▶ *Tip*   Oracle provides a mailing list that will notify North American HR Payroll customers when key mandatory patches are released. To sign up for this service, send an email to cshrdev_uk@oracle.com with the subject "Oracle North American Payroll World Contact Update" and put your contact name, Customer Support Identifier (CSI) number and company name in the body. For other locations, use the appropriate Legislative Code in the subject line. See *My Oracle Support Article ID 856035.1* for more details.

After unpacking a legislative patch containing a hrglobal driver, the adpatch utility can be run to install the patch's u driver. In addition to the standard u driver, these patches contain a special driver called hrglobal.drv.

The hrglobal.drv has additional requirements for application. Once the u driver has been applied, the DataInstall Java utility needs to be run in order to select the required legislative updates for the install. Details on these steps can be found in *My Oracle Support Article ID 140511.1*. The syntax for this command is as follows:

```
java oracle.apps.per.DataInstall apps apps_password thin --
[hostname]:[dbport]:[oracle_sid]
```

The main menu for the DataInstall utility is shown in Figure 5-5.

```
+----------------------------------------------------+
|               DataInstall Main Menu                |
+----------------------------------------------------+

1.    Select legislative data to install/upgrade

2.    Select college data to install/upgrade

3.    Select JIT or OTL to install/upgrade

4.    Exit to confirmation menu

Enter your choice : █
```

Figure 5-5. *The DataInstall Main Menu*

Using the DataInstall utility, the Oracle Applications DBA will need to select all relevant legislations to be applied. Select option *1.* to choose which legislative data to install or upgrade. From resulting menu, you should choose to install any legislative data marked as *Installed.* These options are shown in Figure 5-6.

```
# Localisation        Product(s)                   Leg. Data? Action
-- -----------------  -------------------------    ---------- -------------
1  Global             Human Resources              Installed
2  Australia          Human Resources
3  Australia          Payroll
...
55 United States      Human Resources              Installed
56 United States      Payroll                      Installed

<Product #><Action>  Change Action
 where <Action> is [I : Install, C : Clear]
```

Figure 5-6. *The DataInstall legislative data submenu*

▶ *Tip*   The selection numbers for the installed legislative choices in Figure 5-6 may differ depending upon your version of the hrglobal patch and your environment. Carefully review the selections and make appropriate choices for your installation.

Select the legislative data to be installed by entering the localization number and I. If an incorrect number is selected, you can correct the mistake by entering that number with a C to clear the action.

After all legislative data is marked for install, return to the main menu to select any required college data. When all college data is selected, return to the main menu and select 4 to exit the utility. Upon exiting, an Actions Summary will be displayed. Review that summary to ensure that all required actions have been selected.

The final stage of the legislative patch is to run the adpatch utility to apply the hrglobal driver. This driver is copied to the $PER_TOP/patch/115/driver directory by the patch's u driver. The same adpatch options for applying other drivers should be used for the hrglobal driver.

NLS Patching

For E-Business Suite installations with multiple language enabled, there are patches available for each additional language. Each required NLS patch needs to be applied to Oracle Applications. Oracle provides some recommendations for dealing with NLS patches and Globalization issues; these are outlined in *My Oracle Support Article ID 393861.1*.

The U.S. version of the patch should be applied before any of the translation patches. The translation patches may be applied without downtime to the entire system if users of the affected language are not active.

Using admrgpch, it is possible to merge all U.S. patches into one patch, and then merge all non-U.S. patches into a separate patch. Depending upon the Applications configuration, some variation of this approach may be necessary. It is also possible to create a single, merged patch for all languages required. AD Merge was discussed previously in the *Using AD Merge Patch* section in this chapter.

Translation Synchronization patches allow you to synchronize your existing translations with the American English file versions of the instance. This feature will bring the translations up to date by applying just one patch for each language. The steps to request and apply this patch are described in *My Oracle Support Article ID 252422.1*.

Multi-Node Patching

There are a couple of options available in order to optimize patching for multi-node environments. The system can be designed with a Shared Application Tier Filesystem. The Shared Application Tier Filesystem contains the application's APPL_TOP, COMMON_TOP, and ORACLE_HOMEs for the Java and Tools Tech Stacks. When using a Shared Application Tier Filesystem, APPL_TOP, COMMON_TOP, and ORACLE_HOMEs are installed on a shared disk which is mounted on all of the Applications nodes. *My Oracle Support Article ID 384248.1* describes how to implement a Shared Application Tier Filesystem. As a result of this configuration, patching the shared filesystem applies the patch to shared disk, making the updates available to all nodes at once.

In order to increase the performance of the patching process, Distributed AD will execute workers on remote nodes in a multi-node implementation. Distributed AD improves scalability and resource utilization. More information on this feature can be found in the *Oracle Applications Patching Procedures* document.

If a Shared Application Tier Filesystem is not in use, then a unified APPL_TOP is in place. In this environment each node has its own copies of the filesystems. With a unified APPL_TOP each node must be patched separately. A patched filesystem can be cloned to another node if the downtime required to patch the node exceeds the time required to clone the filesystem.

Applications Patching Cleanup

Patching cleanup was previously covered under the *Applications Patching Cleanup* section in the Chapter 4 of this guide. It is worth reviewing the patching cleanup recommendations in this section.

After a patch has been applied, there will be an increase in the used space for the directory where the patch was unzipped. Some of the files here can be cleaned out after the patch has been tested. This will help to control space usage for the filesystem where patches are stored.

Cleanup can occur by removing the contents of the backup subdirectory of the directory where the patch was unbundled. If you are applying a patch from a common directory to multiple instances, space can be reclaimed in the patch directory by removing files written to the backup subdirectory from previous patch applications.

The patch log directory can also be archived after the patch has been tested. Since these files may be of use as evidence of patch application, you may want to compress the files and move them to another storage system. Patch log files are located in the directory:

$APPL_TOP/admin/$TWO_TASK/log

Patching Related Features in Oracle Applications Manager (OAM)

OAM provides a wide variety of functionality related to Applications patching. The following sections will provide an overview of the following OAM patching features:

* Patch Reporting
* Patch Timing Report
* Patch Wizard
* Register Flagged Files
* File History

Patch Reporting

In OAM, the Applied Patches functionality will allow searches by Patch ID, Applied Within Last *x* Days, Applied From Date, and Applied to

Date. Once a search result is returned, additional details regarding the patch can be displayed. The Simple Search screen for patches in OAM is shown in Figure 5-7.

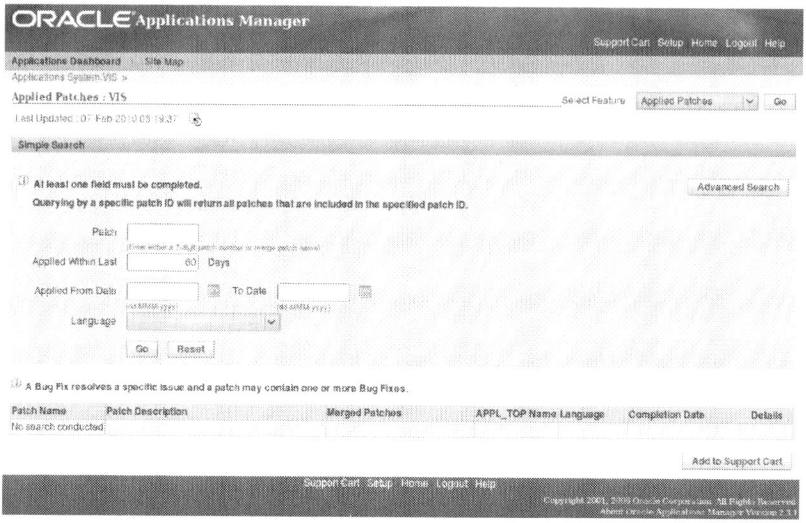

Figure 5-7. *OAM Simple Search screen for patches*

The Advanced Search screen offers additional search criteria. Use this screen if you need to search for certain product families, patches applied only to certain nodes, or patches for different APPL_TOPs. This screen also has the option to search for language specific patches. This feature is useful for multi-language installations. The Advanced Search screen is shown in Figure 5-8.

When a patch is returned to the result screen, you can select the Details cell to see a patch impact analysis screen. This information can be useful to testers for determining functionality that was altered by the patch. For large patches, the patch impact analysis may be too lengthy to be of much value. Some of the information included with the Details screen is a breakout of the timings for each step of the patch, as well as a list of bug fixes and files copied by the patch

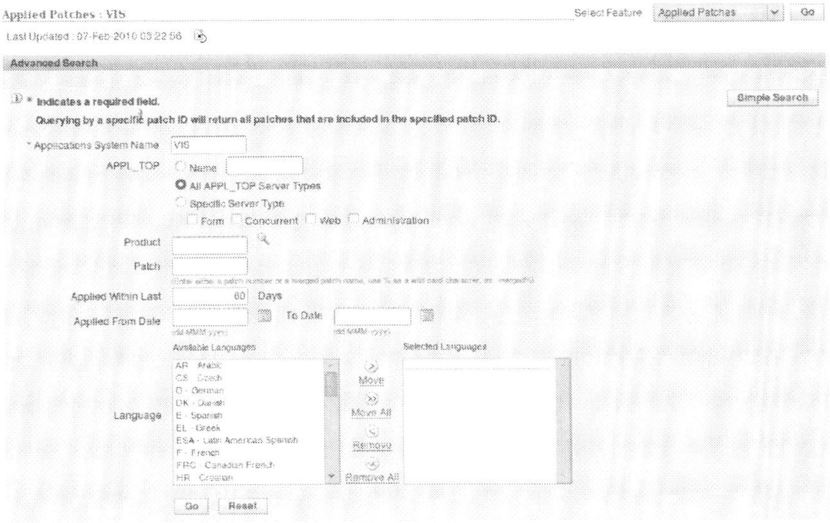

Figure 5-8. *OAM Advanced Search screen for patches*

Patch Timing Report

In OAM, the Timing Reports functionality will display job timing information for both AutoPatch and AD Administration sessions. This information can be useful when reviewing maintenance that had a longer than expected runtime. The Timing Reports can identify which jobs had the longest run times.

The Timing Reports listing also contains a link to the log files generated by each maintenance session. Additional information about the Timing Reports is available with the OAM help screen.

The main listing in Timing Reports will also include sessions that failed. The listing can include active sessions if there is anything running. The list can be filtered based upon the status desired. Sample output from the Timing Report is shown in Figure 5-9.

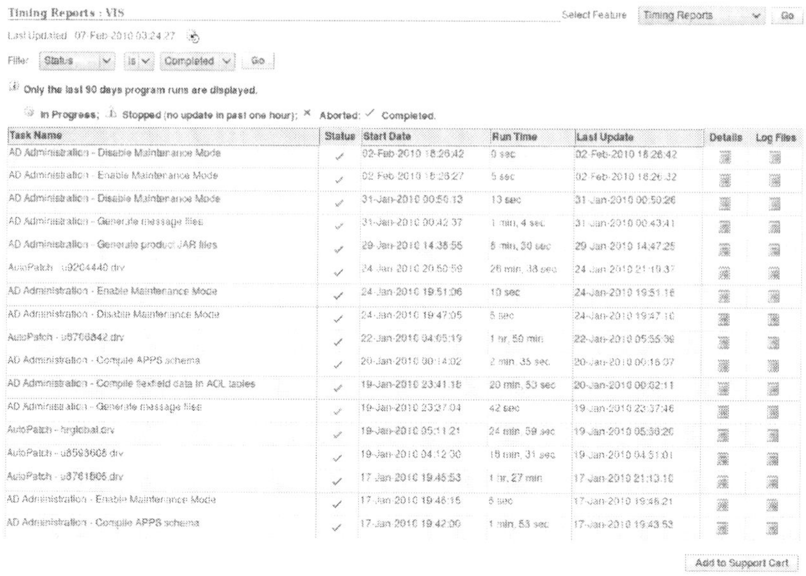

Figure 5-9. *Results from the Timing Reports*

Additionally, job timing information about active sessions can be obtained from running the SQL script $AD_TOP/sql/adtimrpt.sql. The session id is a required parameter for the script. This script will output a file, adt<session_id>.lst, with the timing data.

Patch Wizard

One of the most feature rich sections of OAM is the *Patch Wizard*. The *Patch Wizard* can determine if there are Oracle recommended Applications patches that need to be applied to an instance. These recommended patches can range from high priority one-off patches to product family RUPs. Select the Patch Wizard Tasks menu in OAM to see the options shown in Figure 5-10.

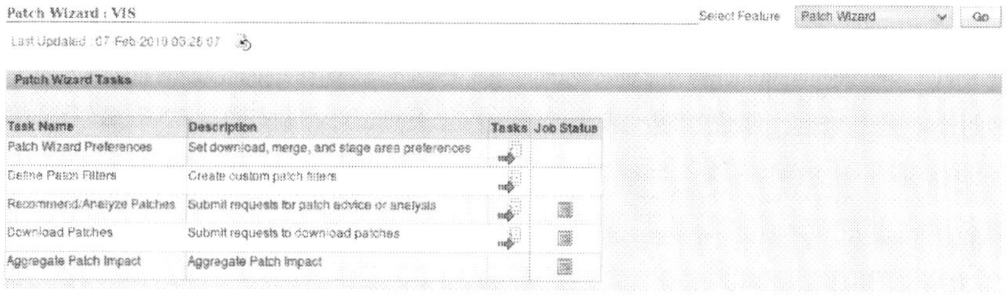

Figure 5-10. *Patch Wizard Tasks menu*

Select *Patch Wizard Preferences* to define your work environment. These options include the staging directory for patches, as well as language and platform defaults. The *Patch Wizard* will use these details to download information from My Oracle Support in order to create recommendations or patch analysis.

In order for *Download Patches* to function, the My Oracle Support Account information must be populated in the *OAM Update Metalink Credentials* page in the *Setup* page of the *Patch Wizard*. The *Recommend/Analyze Patches* utility can still work without a My Oracle Support account specified in the Applications by transferring the *Patch Information Bundle* from another machine where the file was downloaded. The Patch Information Bundle is a daily updated file from Oracle that contains information on the latest recommended patches, codelevel patches and product family patches.

The *Patch Wizard* schedules a set of concurrent programs to accomplish its tasks. In addition to analyzing and downloading patches, the *Patch Wizard* can also merge the downloaded patches into a single patch. The option to merge patches can be performed on the *Patch Wizard Preferences* screen.

Another important function of the *Patch Wizard* is the *Patch Impact Analysis*. The analysis will include a list of new files introduced by the patch as well as existing files that were changed by the patch. This is very useful information to have when preparing to install a patch. This type of information can be shared with functional users to assist them with developing their test plans. It can also be shared with developers to determine impacts to customizations that have been deployed. A scheduled job can be created to perform these tasks on a regular basis, as shown in Figure 5-11.

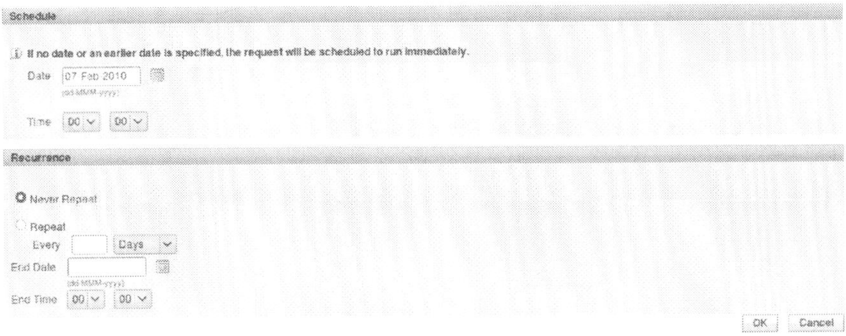

Figure 5-11. *Scheduling options for patch analysis*

Register Flagged Files

In previous versions of Oracle Applications tracking customized files was an error prone process. If the applcust.txt file was not kept up to date, then customizations could be lost. Oracle has improved the process of tracking these files with the OAM *Register Flagged Files* feature.

With *Register Flagged Files*, the customized files can be imported, exported, added, deleted and viewed. The information included lists not only the name and location of the customized file but also the product abbreviation and a comments section. Figure 5-12 shows the main menu for *Register Flagged Files*.

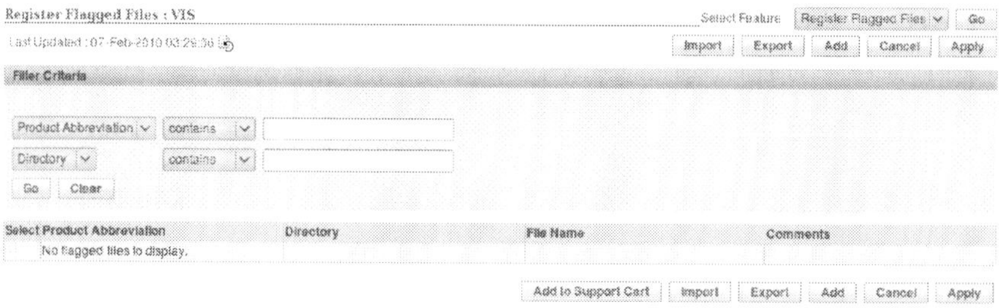

Figure 5-12. *Register Flagged Files menu*

The list of customized files is written to the applcust.txt file by OAM. *Register Flagged Files* is an OAM utility for maintaining the list of customized files. Customized files can be added through the utility which is useful for one-off files. A larger list of files can be imported from one or more files in csv format.

File History

When troubleshooting issues, it is sometimes useful to have detailed knowledge of what changes have occurred to a file and when those changes occurred. The OAM feature *File History* makes this task very easy.

In *File History* a lot of information can be obtained about a file. From this interface, the name, location, and product owner can be seen as well as the file version, date the file was changed, and a details report on what has changed.

The *File History* feature has a *Simple Search* screen and an *Advanced Search* screen. The *Simple Search* screen is shown in Figure 5-13. The *Advanced Search* screen has additional options such as the ability to select multiple languages and return only the latest version of the file or all versions.

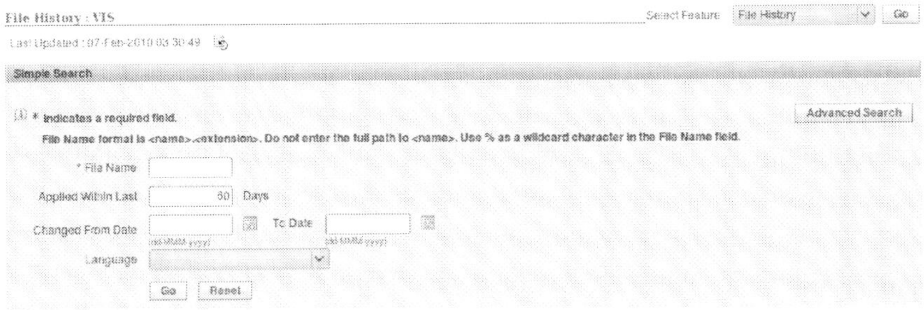

Figure 5-13. *File History menu*

From the results list of the *File History* search an action link is available to drill down into more details about the file history. The results list will include the *Version* and *Changed Date* of the file as well as the *Patch Number* that changed the file.

Methods for Obtaining Patch Reporting

Patch reporting is used to determine whether or not a specific patch has already been applied to the instance or what version of a product is currently installed. OAM features for patch reporting have already been discussed. The following sections will discuss additional methods for determining patching levels:

* Using the patchsets.sh utility
* Querying the database

Using patchsets.sh

The Oracle provided patch comparison utility, patchsets.sh, is a useful tool for reviewing patchset levels. Family Pack versions, fully installed products, and shared installed products, along with the latest version available, are displayed in the output. Information about the latest version of this utility can be reviewed in *My Oracle Support Article ID 139684.1.*

This utility is updated frequently by Oracle. Before running the script, download the current version from the following FTP site:

ftp://ftp.oracle.com/support/outgoing/PATCHSET_COMPARE_TOOL/patchsets.sh

The syntax for executing patchsets.sh as the instance owner is as follows:

patchsets.sh connect=[userid]/[password]

The following is an example of executing patchsets.sh:

$UNIX>patchsets.sh connect=apps/apps

More details about the parameters available for this script can be found by using the -h parameter for online help. The output file created is named Report_R12.txt. The output for the file will contain the following columns for each product group:

* **Baseline Version:** Displays the version provided with the release.

* **Running Version:** Displays the current version installed for each product.

* **Latest Available:** Displays the current version available for the product. The Status portion of the column consists of two parts: the patchset status (Rel is short for released, Sup for superseded, and Obs for obsoleted) and the distribution status (By_Metal indicates it is on My Oracle Support, Not_Dist means it is not available, and By_Dev means it is available from development only).

* **Status:** Displays the current version available for the product. The Status portion of the column consists of two parts: as described by the Status portion in above Latest Available status portion.

The output of the report can be reviewed to find products that have available updates. An example of the output of patchsets.sh from as described in *My Oracle Support Article ID 139684.1* is shown in Figure 5-14.

```
FAMILY PACK PATCHES
Product Baseline               Running Version          Latest Available         Status
atg_pf  R12.ATG_PF.B.1(7307198) R12.ATG_PF.B.1(7307198) R12.ATG_PF.B.2(7651091) Rel-By_Metal
bis_pf  R12.BIS_PF.B.1(7458599) R12.BIS_PF.B.1(7458599) R12.BIS_PF.B.2(8525503) Rel-Not_Dist
cc_pf   R12.CC_PF.B.1(7389432)  R12.CC_PF.B.1(7389432)  R12.CC_PF.B.2(8522000)  Rel-By_Metal
....


FULLY INSTALLED PRODUCTS
Product Baseline               Running Version          Latest Available         Status
fnd     R12.FND.B.1(7307224)    R12.FND.B.1(7307224)    R12.FND.B.2(7651104)    Rel-Not_Dist
hz      R12.HZ.B.1(7389406)     R12.HZ.B.1(7389406)     R12.HZ.B.2(8521996)     Rel-Not_Dist

SHARED INSTALL PRODUCTS
Product Baseline               Running Version          Latest Available         Status
ad      R12.AD.B.1(7461070)     R12.AD.B.1(7461070)     R12.AD.B.2(8502056)     Rel-By_Metal
ak      R12.AK.B.1(7307331)     R12.AK.B.1(7307331)     R12.AK.B.2(7651136)     Rel-Not_Dist
```

Figure 5-14. *Output from the patchsets.sh script*

For R12, the execution of patchsets.sh will also create a file called Applied_Patches_R12.txt. This file includes a list of current Maintenance Packs, Product Family Code Levels and specific bug fixes applied.

Querying the Database for Patches

In order to determine whether a specific patch has been applied, a query can be executed against the ad_bugs table. The following SQL will return results if the patches included in the IN clause have been applied to the instance:

```
SELECT bug_number
FROM ad_bugs
WHERE bug_number IN ('patch_number', 'patch_number', . . .)
ORDER BY bug_number DESC;
```

Technology Stack Components Patching and Upgrades

In addition to Applications Patching, the Technology Stack components of Oracle Applications also require patching and upgrades. This section will review patching and upgrade requirements for the following components:

* **Oracle Application Server patching and upgrades:** This section provides details for patching and upgrading the Oracle Application Server installations in the Technology Stack.

* **Database patching and upgrades:** This section provides details for patching and upgrading the database component of the Technology Stack.

* **Additional components to upgrade:** This section provides details for upgrading JDK and the Sun JRE Plug-in.

▶ *Tip*   Upgrades to the Oracle Applications Technology Stack typically require an interoperability patch to be applied to the application tier. Information regarding interoperability requirements is denoted in the upgrade documentation on My Oracle Support for the upgrade that is under consideration.

Oracle Application Server Patching and Upgrades

For every Oracle R12 installation there are two installations of the Oracle Application Server. One installation is for the Java Tech Stack; the other is for the Tools Tech Stack. Each installation requires patching and upgrades to occur independently. A patch for the Oracle AS is a fix for the existing version that is installed. An upgrade will increase the point level release or patchset to a higher level. It is important to stay current with certified releases of the Oracle Application Server.

Patching the Oracle 10gAS

As previously stated, there are two Oracle Application Servers with the R12 Technology Stack. The Java Tech Stack is version 10.1.3 and the Tools Tech Stack is version 10.1.2. Both of these installations may need to be patched with any critical updates from Oracle.

One-off patch fixes for the OracleAS are applied using the opatch utility. This is true for both of the OracleAS homes. The larger patchsets described in the next session are applied using the Oracle Universal Installer.

Upgrading the Oracle 10gAS

Upgrades for the Oracle 10gAS are deployed as patchsets. Patchsets will increase the point release of the Oracle 10gAS. Patchsets will include a variety of bug fixes and other improvements to the software. These efforts will need to be coordinated to ensure that proper testing occurs.

My Oracle Support Article ID 454811.1 outlines the steps to upgrade to the latest OracleAS 10.1.3.x Patch Set with Oracle E-Business Suite. This document contains the steps to perform the upgrade along with a list of post installation tasks and known issues. Reviewing Applications specific documentation like this is critical to being successful with Technology Stack upgrades. The 10.1.2.x version of the OracleAS provides the Forms services. *My Oracle Support Article ID 437878.1* outlines the steps required to upgrade this version of the Oracle 10gAS. Review these notes along with the appropriate README file.

Oracle Database Patching and Upgrades

Database patching consists of either interim fixes, also known as one-off patches, patchset updates (PSUs) or Critical Patch Updates (CPUs) and upgrades. The following sections describe interim fixes, patchset updates, and database upgrades.

Interim Fixes

Interim fixes are patches that are applied to the current version of the database. Upgrades increase the point release level of the database, for example from 11.1.0.6.0 to 11.1.0.7.0, or are a major point release, for example 11gR1 to 11gR2. Database upgrades can also upgrade from one version to the next major version of the database, for example from 10.2.0.1 to 11.1.0.6.

Interim patch fixes for the database are applied as the owner of the database install with the opatch utility or by running an operating system script. Details on how to apply database patches are outlined in the patch's README. Additional details regarding opatch are provided in *My Oracle Support Article ID 242993.1*.

The opatch utility is included in the standard install of the database software. However, it can also be downloaded from My Oracle Support as patch number 6880880. The opatch utility requires Perl and JDK to function, and they must be installed and specified in the path and library environment variables. Once the opatch utility has been downloaded and unbundled, the OPatch directory of the opatch unbundled patch should be added to the PATH, as in the following example:

export PATH=$PATH:/[path_of_6880880]/OPatch

The library path of Perl must also be specified with the following PERL5LIB environment variable, as in the following example:

export PERL5LIB=[path_of_PERL]/lib

To validate that opatch is functioning properly; execute the following command with the lsinventory option:

$UNIX>opatch lsinventory

Once opatch has been successfully set up, the database interim patch fix may be applied. To prepare for patching, perform the following preliminary tasks:

1. First review the README file for the patch.

2. Make certain that all prerequisites have been met.

3. Document any pre and post patching steps that are required.

4. Download the patch and unbundle it.

5. Change to the directory where the patch has been unbundled.

6. Verify that the database has been shut down.

7. Verify that the /etc/oraInst.loc file has the correct inventory listed.

8. Verify that the inventory directories are writeable by the database owner.

After the required preparation has been completed you are ready to begin applying the patch. Apply the patch by executing opatch as the database owner with the apply parameter, as in the following example:

$UNIX>opatch apply

To verify that a patch has successfully been applied, the lsinventory option can again be executed. This will display all patches that have been applied to the database. The recently applied patch should now be included in the output.

▶ **Note**   If opatch fails, there may be a patch_locked file located under the hidden directory $ORACLE_HOME/.patch_storage. The opatch utility may not be executed until the patch_locked file is removed.

After a database patch has been applied, backup files may be created in the hidden directory called .patch_storage. The opatch command can be run again with the option util cleanup to remove these files. This should be done to free up space in your ORACLE_HOME on the database node.

Oracle Patch Set Updates

Oracle releases *Patch Set Updates* (PSUs) for the database software and EM Grid Control. This section will describe PSUs for the database. PSUs for EM Grid Control are out of scope for this guide. As with the CPUs, the PSUs are released on the same quarterly basis. PSUs contain all of the security fixes in that quarter's CPU. PSUs also include other interim fixes for critical issues which are likely to be encountered by multiple customers. The one-off patches included in the PSU should not require recertification or any configuration changes The PSUs are tested by

Oracle prior to release. The PSU will be installable to RAC instances as rolling install.

▶ *Note* Oracle does support but does not test PSUs for the Oracle EBS database. Please be aware of this as you consider applying PSUs to your Oracle EBS database.

You should choose a patching strategy for the database where you apply either CPUs or PSUs. Once a PSU is installed, it is not easy to revert back to CPUs as your patching strategy. If a PSU is installed, this should become your direction for installing the quarterly security fixes. Additional details about Patch Set Updates can be found in *My Oracle Support Article ID 854428.1*. This article contains numerous sections devoted to different aspects of the PSU.

Database Upgrades

Database upgrades are typically complex in nature and require installation of new software when upgrading from one point release to another. Obsolete and new initialization parameters must be reviewed when upgrading to a new release of the database. For additional details regarding database initialization parameters, review *My Oracle Support Article ID 396009.1*.

Database upgrades can be accomplished manually or by using dbua, the database upgrade assistant. Since the method for upgrading the database is version and platform dependent, the associated README file for the upgrade must be reviewed, and the steps required to perform the upgrade should be documented. Before upgrading or applying a patch to the database, the oraInst.loc file must point to the correct Oracle inventory location for the database ORACLE_HOME. It is also important to cleanly shut down the database before proceeding, and to perform a cold database backup.

Additional Components to Upgrade

Two additional components that require upgrading are the Java Development Toolkit (JDK) and the Sun JRE Plug-in. Additional details regarding how to perform these upgrades are provided in this section.

Upgrading JDK

On the application tier of the E-Business suite there is an installation of the Java Standard Edition Development Kit. It is recommended to keep this software updated for performance and security reasons.

For information about upgrading the version of JDK used by the Applications review *My Oracle Support Article ID 418664.1*. This document contains links to specific documents containing instructions for upgrading to different releases of JDK.

Upgrading the Sun JRE Plug-in

For the client tier to access forms in E-Business Suite installations, it needs to have the Sun Java2 Standard Edition Java Runtime Engine, also referred to as the Sun JRE Plug-in, installed. Oracle certifies EBS with minimum Sun JRE Plug-in releases. Users can run higher releases of the JRE stream. For example, if JRE 1.6.0_03 is certified then the clients can run JRE 1.6.0_17.

Before upgrading, be sure to review *My Oracle Support Article ID 393931.1*. This document contains certification information along with instructions for configuring the Sun JRE Plug-in. Another useful part of the document is the Known Issues section. This section can assist with troubleshooting problems with the Sun JRE Plug-in.

Patching and Upgrading Best Practices

A proactive approach to patching is highly recommended. The Server Technologies Division of Oracle has a policy of creating bug fixes for only the two most current versions of software releases. Please refer to *My Oracle Support Article ID 209768.1* for additional details regarding Oracle's error correction support policies. Patch fixes and upgrades will not only provide new functionality, but will also fix bugs for issues that may only come to light at the least opportune time. It is advisable to apply Consolidated Upgrade Patches routinely and to not fall more than two point releases behind the most current release available. An automated approach to testing will facilitate patching efforts. When performing large patching efforts, it is recommended that you download and apply the latest Release Update Packs available for your environment

Technology Stack components and product groups such as ATG are often prerequisites for future patches, such as Consolidated Upgrade Patches and mandatory Release Update Packs. Therefore, it is important to stay current on these items. By applying such upgrades on a proactive basis, the time requirements for later patch sets may be greatly reduced. In order to minimize testing, Technology Stack updates such as a JDK upgrade and Application Server patches can be applied at the same time. With changes to the Technology Stack components, it is not possible to narrow the testing focus to specific items as those elements have a broad impact to the system.

Applying patches often creates a need for changes in configuration and/or process. After applying patching to your patching your environment, it is important to document these required changes. Where possible use the tools available from Oracle, such as the OAM patch reports, to simplify your steps. If needed, prepare custom scripts and documentation procedures to assist with maintenance.

Run through maintenance efforts several times in recent clones of your production instance. This will help to reduce the possibility of unexpected errors in the application of patches to production. Explore options available to reduce system downtime with maintenance and include those steps in your application of patches to a test instance.

Chapter 6

Monitoring and Troubleshooting

The Oracle E-Business Suite is a large and complex environment. The typical Oracle Applications DBA spends a considerable amount of time monitoring and troubleshooting the multiple components of the applications. Through proactive monitoring, many troubleshooting requirements and performance issues can be identified or eliminated. Due to the overwhelming benefit of such monitoring, the Oracle Applications DBA should invest time in developing an extensive proactive monitoring process. This chapter focuses on the following monitoring and troubleshooting processes for different components of the system:

* **Server**: The Oracle Applications DBA must be familiar with UNIX commands that can be used to monitor and troubleshoot issues on the physical servers. This section will review the key things to monitor along with the most commonly used basic commands.

* **Application tier**: There are many processes running on the application tier of the E-Business Suite. This section will review monitoring and troubleshooting steps for Web and Concurrent Manager processes. Some tools that can be used by the Oracle Applications DBA such as Oracle Applications Manager (OAM) and the Oracle Enterprise Grid Control Applications Management Pack will be covered.

* **Database tier**: This section will focus on monitoring and troubleshooting options available for the database tier. Standard options will be reviewed along with some Oracle Enterprise Grid Control features.

* **Additional items**: Monitoring and troubleshooting steps for the client tier and the Oracle Applications will be covered in this section. Some commands for network issues will also be included in this section.

Server Monitoring and Troubleshooting

Depending on the size of your organization there may be other groups responsible for monitoring different components of the Oracle Applications environment. For example, server system administrators in your organization may have responsibility for monitoring the physical servers. Even with this added support, the Oracle Applications DBA should be familiar with steps to monitor and troubleshoot issues on the servers. This can assist with resolving issues quickly. With multi-node configurations, there may be a large number of physical servers deployed to support the application.

This section will cover the key aspects to monitor and troubleshoot server issues. Some basic commands for the servers will be covered with respect to the functionality of the commands. Additional details on these commands can be found in the server specific documentation provided by your vendor.

The server system administrators may perform some of the system monitoring, but the Oracle Applications DBA needs to be aware of any issues occurring on the system as this can impact the health of the Oracle Application. Monitoring and troubleshooting the server should be coordinated with the system administrators as needed or required by your organization.

Monitoring Availability

A key starting point for monitoring servers is to validate that the server is available. This can be accomplished through establishing connections from another server or pinging the target server from another system. A server cannot be relied upon to monitor itself for availability. If another system is used to monitor availability of servers, then that monitoring system should also have monitoring defined on it.

When connecting to a server, the uptime command will return the amount of time the server has been running. If a server was unavailable for a period of time, this command will help to identify if the server had been rebooted. If the uptime indicates the system has been running for a while, then being unable to access a server may be contributed to a network issue. Keep in mind that a server that has no available CPU may not allow connections and therefore appear to be down. Additional details regarding the ping command and uptime commands can be found in Chapter 4 of this guide.

Monitoring Resource Consumption

There are several areas of resource consumption that need to be monitored at the server level. The key areas are CPU usage, memory usage and storage availability. Examples of each of these will be provided in this section.

The server should be monitored for CPU resource usage. Typically a server should not be more than 80% busy on a consistent basis. Some environments will run at high levels of CPU consumption; however, that does not leave much buffer for peak activity or for growth of the environment. The run queue length can also be monitored to determine if the server is too busy. This is the case when the run queue exceeds the number of CPUs on the server. UNIX commands such as vmstat and top can be used to monitor the size of the run queue.

Memory usage should also be monitored for every server. If the physical memory is consumed then the server may begin swapping memory with the swap space on disk. Several UNIX commands such as sar or vmstat will display usage of swap space. As the amount of paging increases, performance impacts can occur on the system. This can result in very high CPU consumption. Adding more CPU to this situation will not really resolve the problem as it is more of a memory issue.

The amount of available disk space should be also be monitored. Identify and track disk space requirements for all key filesystems on the server. Failure to do so could lead to unplanned outages. For example, if the archive destination becomes full for a database running in archivelog mode, then the database will hang until space is made available in this filesystem. Failures to obtain disk space for datafiles can result in errors in the database. With the Concurrent Manager, a lack of free space can cause log and output files to not be created. It may also be beneficial to monitor for rapidly growing filesystems or for large objects being created on disk. UNIX commands such as du and df can provide details on disk usage.

Monitoring Setup

The UNIX system has several setup items that you should consider monitoring. This section is not intended to be a complete inventory of items to monitor on the server, but provides direction on some important items. Some of the details here may depend upon your business requirements. A few common items will be provided as examples. The items to be under consideration are file permissions, group and user definitions, and printer definitions.

File permissions may need to be adjusted for certain directories or files. For example the directory, defined as the ORACLE_HOME for the database tier may be set to only be readable, writeable and executable at the owner level. Setting the aforementioned privileges would result in the directory permissions of rwx------. If the directory was changed to be accessible by the world, then the Oracle Applications DBA should be notified of the change as this could create a security risk. You should identify and document all files and filesystems that require specific permissions and monitor these settings on a regular basis.

Group and user definitions are another item that should be considered for monitoring. There are several issues here that could be of concern. For example, the Oracle Applications DBA may wish to be notified if a user is added to the dba group on the server. This can be accomplished by monitoring the /etc/groups file on the server for changes to the dba entry. Other items which should be monitored include the creation of new user accounts and the time period between password changes for certain accounts, such as the instance owner.

► *Tip*   If users on the UNIX system are managed on an LDAP server, then to print out group information you can use the following command: $UNIX>getent group.

The status of a printer can also be monitored at the server level. If a printer is no longer active, then that could cause issues with printing reports from concurrent requests. The UNIX command lpstat -p can be run to get more information about the printers defined on your server. Additional details regarding lpstat may be found in Chapter 4 of this guide.

Application Tier Monitoring and Troubleshooting

Monitoring and troubleshooting on the application tier will cover several different items related to the processes and services running on this tier. The application tier runs web and forms processes along with Concurrent Manager processes. Steps for monitoring and troubleshooting these processes will be provided.

Web and Forms Services

This section will cover topics such as monitoring the status of the web and forms services, determining the location of log files, debugging and diagnostic steps for these processes and enabling tracing for these processes.

Process Status

Monitoring the process status for web and forms processes will not only determine if the processes are running, but will also return how long the processes have been running and if the processes are in a bad state. This is often a starting point with troubleshooting any related issues.

Running the $ADMIN_SCRIPTS_HOME/adapcctl.sh script with status as a parameter will return information about the Oracle HTTP Server components. An example of executing adapcctl.sh with the status parameter is shown in Figure 6-1.

```
Processes in Instance: VIS_erlinux01.erlinux01.erhome.com
------------------------------------+---------------------+---------+---------
ias-component                       | process-type        |     pid | status
------------------------------------+---------------------+---------+---------
OC4JGroup:default_group             | OC4J:oafm           |    6628 | Alive
OC4JGroup:default_group             | OC4J:forms          |    6559 | Alive
OC4JGroup:default_group             | OC4J:oacore         |    6480 | Alive
HTTP_Server                         | HTTP_Server         |    6428 | Alive
```

Figure 6-1. *Using adapcctl.sh to display the HTTP Server status*

You can use the ps command on one of the pids listed in the output to get information on how long the process has been running. From the previous example, the HTTP Server process has a process id of 2003. The following is an example of using the ps command to show information regarding this process:

$UNIX>ps –p 6628 –f

UID   PID PPID C STIME TTY   TIME CMD
vis   6628 16839 0 May31 ?   00:00:05
/r12vis/apps/tech_st/10.1.3/Apache/Apache/bin/httpd -d
/r12vis/apps/tech_st/10.1.3/Apache/Apache -DSSL -f
/r12vis/inst/apps/VIS_erlinux01/ora/10.1.3/Apache/Apache/conf/httpd.conf

Location of Log Files

A necessary aspect of monitoring and troubleshooting processes is to
identify the location of the log files created by the processes. Log files
may contain critical information for resolving an active issue.

As mentioned in Chapter 2 of this guide, many of the log files for the
application tier are stored in a centralized location. The directory
$LOG_HOME is the base location for these files. The environment variable
$LOG_HOME is based upon the value of the context variable s_logs_dir.
The key log file directories for Oracle HTML and Forms processes are:

$LOG_HOME/10.1.3/opmn
$LOG_HOME/10.1.3/Apache
$LOG_HOME/10.1.2/forms

Tracing Sessions

Generating trace files is a method to capture additional information for
the various components of the environment. Depending upon which
component you need to trace, there are different steps necessary to
generate the trace files. This section provides instructions for tracing
Oracle HTML Applications and Forms sessions.

Oracle HTML Applications Tracing

To enable Oracle HTML Applications tracing, a series of steps must be
executed. Additional information regarding these steps may be found in
My Oracle Support Article ID 438652.1. The steps are as follows:

1. Log into the application.

2. Navigate to *Profile* → *System.*

3. Select the *User* checkbox and enter the user name.

4. Query the profile FND: Diagnostics.

5. Set FND: Diagnostics to Yes at the user level.

6. Login to the Applications as the user for which the diagnostics profile was set.

7. Click the *Diagnostics* icon, select *Set Trace Level*, and click *Go*.

8. On the next page, select *Trace with Binds and Waits*, and click *Save*.

Perform the steps required to duplicate the problem. When this has been completed, there will be a trace file generated. The resulting trace file will be written to the trace directory located in the diagnostic destination on the Database Node. An example of the screen to generate the trace file is displayed in Figure 6-2.

Figure 6-2. *Generating trace files for OA HTML Applications*

Forms Tracing

To generate a trace file for a Form, be sure to have the profile options Utilities: Diagnostics set to Yes and Hide Diagnostics Menu Entry set to No. The steps to start tracing are as follows:

1. Login to the application.

2. Select the *Help* → *Diagnostic* → *Trace* → *Trace with Binds and Waits* menu option.

An example of the steps necessary to enable forms tracing is provided in Figure 6-3.

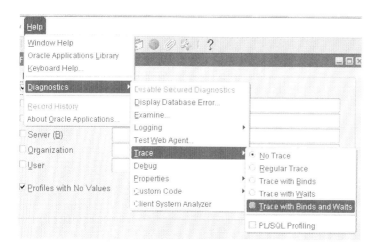

Figure 6-3. *Generating trace files for Forms*

Once forms tracing is enabled per the previously outlined steps, you should set the trace size to unlimited by selecting the following menu options: *Help → Diagnostics → Trace → Unlimited Trace File Size*. The forms trace will be written to the trace directory located in the diagnostics destination on the Database Node.

Analyzing Trace Files

Once the raw trace file has been generated, execute the tkprof or trcanlzr utilities to translate it into a readable format. Descriptions for using these utilities are provided in the following sections.

Using tkprof

In order to run tkprof on the raw trace file, obtain the name of the generated trace file. Note that tkprof may only be executed in the database from which the trace file was originally generated. Execute tkprof as the instance owner in a directory with write permissions as follows:

tkprof <raw trace file name> <output filename> explain=apps/<apps password>

The trace file generated by tkprof will contain important information regarding the SQL statement. Included in the trace file is diagnostics information such as CPU and elapsed time, disk and logical reads and the number of rows returned in the query. The trace file also includes the SQL execution plan. Most likely, this file will need to be uploaded to

Oracle Support for assistance in resolving the underlying performance issue.

Using trcanlzr

The Trace Analyzer utility, also know as trcanlzr, reads a raw trace and generates an HTML report that includes tkprof analysis data as well as other statistics. The HTML file that is generated can be used by Oracle Support to assist in resolving performance issues.

To generate the HTML file, the trcanlzr utility must be downloaded from Oracle Support. It is available by referencing *My Oracle Support Article ID 224270.1*. Once the utility has been downloaded, you will need to install it by following the instructions in the download.

Concurrent Manager

A large number of critical processes are run by the Concurrent Manager. Monitoring and troubleshooting this component of the Applications is an important skill set for an Oracle Applications DBA. In large deployments, the Concurrent Manager can run tens of thousands of requests on a daily basis.

Process Status

The Internal Concurrent Manager can be checked by running the script $ADMIN_SCRIPTS_HOME/adcmctl.sh with the status parameter. This script will return information about the processes. The script will require the apps username and password to run. The following is an example of executing adcmctl.sh with the status parameter:

$UNIX>adcmctl.sh status

```
You are running adcmctl.sh version 120.17.12010000.3

Enter the APPS username : apps

Enter the APPS password :
Internal Concurrent Manager is Active.

adcmctl.sh: exiting with status 0
```

adcmctl.sh: check the logfile
/oraprod/oracle/VIS/inst/apps/VIS_hostname/logs/appl/admin/log/adcmctl.txt for
more information

The status of all Concurrent Manager processes can also be viewed
from within the application. From the main menu select *Concurrent
Manager* →*Administer*. This screen will show *Actual* and *Target* values
which will show if the manager is running. If the manager is not running
then the Actual column will be 0. An example of the *Administer
Concurrent Managers* screen is shown in Figure 6-4.

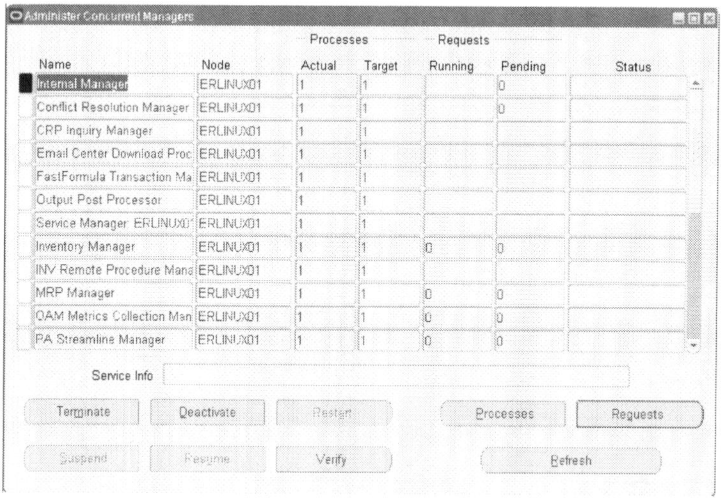

Figure 6-4. *The Administer Concurrent Managers screen*

There are several scripts in the directory $FND_TOP/sql. These scripts
provide important information on the Concurrent Manager, workflow and
other parts of the application. The script afcmstat.sql will return status
information of all of the managers. Another useful script is afcmrrq.sql
which returns the requests that are running at the time the query is
executed.

Location of Log Files

The log files for the Concurrent Manager can be found in the directory
$APPLCSF/$APPLLOG. There may be a large number of files in this
directory. The manager files to review will be named with the extension
of mgr. Other files located in that directory are created by individual

requests. These will have the extension of req. Additional log files are present with the extension of txt.

Tracing Concurrent Requests

As with other Oracle Applications processes, the Oracle Applications DBA may need to generate tracing information in order to diagnose or troubleshoot issues with the Concurrent Managers. Oracle Support may request tracing information when opening a Service Request for issues with a particular request. *My Oracle Support Article ID 453527.1* provides details on how to generate a trace file for concurrent requests. The following is an overview of the required steps:

1. Login to the Applications with S*ystem Administrator* responsibility.

2. Navigate to the *Concurrent Program Definition* for the program you want to trace.

3. Select *Enable Trace* in the definition screen and save your change.

4. Select *Profiles* → *System.*

5. Choose the profile option *Concurrent: Allow Debugging.*

6. Set that profile to *Yes.*

7. Switch to the responsibility that executes the concurrent request.

8. In the *Submit Request* Screen select *Debug Options.*

9. Select the checkbox for *SQL Trace.*

▶ *Tip*   Concurrent request trace files are located in the trace directory of the diagnostic destination. Some Oracle articles may still refer to the user dump location which predates version 11g of the database.

Additional Monitoring

The Concurrent Manager processes can be monitored for common issues. These can be monitored through custom scripts. Some of the items can also be monitored using OAM or Applications Management Pack in Enterprise Manager.

Additional items to monitor for Concurrent Managers include the number of pending requests as well as the length of time pending requests wait. Issues like this can indicate that additional managers need to be created, or there could be issues with the time periods requests are scheduled.

Monitoring concurrent request run times can identify potential issues with performance of an individual request. It is important for the Oracle Applications DBA to have an understanding of the long running requests on the system. If a request takes much longer to run than expected, then the DBA may need to be notified.

Using Oracle Applications Manager (OAM) Features

Included with the Oracle E-Business Suite installation is the Oracle Applications Manager (OAM). OAM is a web based tool that provides a great deal of functionality to the Oracle Applications DBA.

Using OAM, you can perform several tasks including monitoring OA HTML Applications and Forms sessions as well as concurrent requests. All of this can all be performed using the OAM graphical interface. Database sessions can also be monitored with OAM.

Useful information about the Applications configuration can also be monitored with OAM. For example, from the *Dashboard* screen you can view if any profile option values have changed in the past 24 hours.

Using Oracle Applications Diagnostics Tool

The *Oracle Applications Diagnostics Tool*, provided by Oracle as part of the E-Business Suite, allows for the collection and analysis of system information. The *Diagnostics* tool will collect setup information as well as run tests against specific functionality in the system.

Users who need to run this tool are required to have the *Applications Diagnostics* responsibility. As there may be overhead to executing the diagnostic processes, the responsibility should be granted to a limited number of users.

The output generated by this tool can be easily reviewed with a web browser. If a Service Request has been opened with Oracle, the output can be uploaded to the SR. The output generated can be reviewed by the user who generated the output or by a system administrator. Additional details regarding the Oracle Applications Diagnostics Tool can be found in *My Oracle Support Article ID 235307.1*. An example of the *Diagnostics* screen is displayed in Figure 6-5.

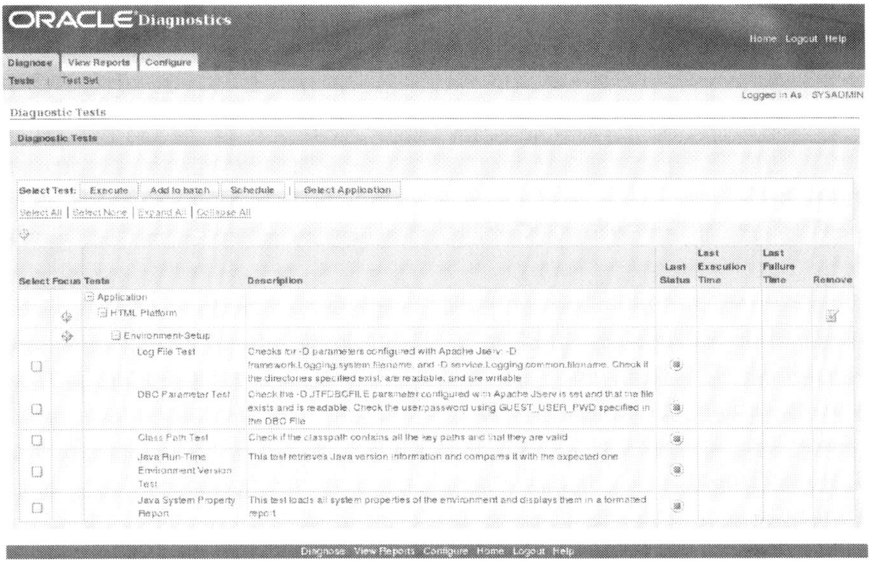

Figure 6-5. *Oracle Diagnostic Tests screen*

The Oracle Applications DBA should be aware of the features available with this tool. Using this tool can provide a faster resolution to common issues with the application.

Using EM Grid Control's Applications Management Pack

Oracle has developed a GUI tool for monitoring and troubleshooting application tier components with the *Applications Management Pack* for Oracle E-Business Suite. The Applications Management pack deploys as a on top of an existing EM Grid Control deployment. Additional details regarding the Applications Management Pack for Oracle E-Business Suite can be found in *My Oracle Support Article ID 846628.1.*

The Applications Management pack has several tools that will assist the Oracle Applications DBA with managing the complex E-Business Suite environment. Two of these tools are *Configuration Management* and *Service Level Management.*

The Configuration Management tool will allow you to search for details on the Oracle Applications Configuration. Some examples of this include Concurrent Manager and workflow configuration, patch levels, context files, and Technology Stack inventory. Using this feature you can also compare the configuration details between instances.

The Service Level Management tool includes metrics that will monitor both availability and performance of many Applications components. This allows for the Oracle Applications DBA to quickly enable automated monitoring for the application. When issues are discovered, the Oracle Applications DBA can start performing root cause analysis with this tool.

▶ **Note**   Contact your Oracle Sales Representative regarding licensing requirements for the Applications Management Pack.

Database Tier

An Oracle Applications DBA needs to be aware of the database activity in the system – over time, trends will develop in the database that enable the DBA to proactively monitor the database. This section will assist you in identifying and monitoring common database trends and events.

Database Log Files

When monitoring the database, it is important to review the associated database log files, particularly the database alert log file and the database listener log file. These files should be monitored for error messages. This section will describe the key files to review.

Database Alert Log and Trace Files

One of the most important tasks for a database administrator is monitoring the database alert log and trace files. The location of the alert log and trace files is specified by the diagnostics_dest parameter.

Errors or important informational messages are written to the database alert log. The alert log should be monitored for any ORA-messages that are added to the log. These errors can indicate a problem with the system that needs to be addressed as soon as possible.

In addition to monitoring the alert log, the trace directory should be monitored for the creation of trace files. The trace files provide additional information useful for troubleshooting issues. New trace files should be reviewed as they are created. Bugs in the database may cause an abnormal number of trace files to be created. Some trace files can be ignored. For monitoring purposes, a white list can be created to screen out trace files that do not contain useful information.

Database Listener Log

The database listener will also store information in a log file. The location of the log file can be controlled by the log_directory variable defined in the $TNS_ADMIN/listener.log file.

The listener logging level can also be controlled in the listener.log file. Listener logging can assist when troubleshooting database connection issues.

Database Availability

Basic availability applies to both the database and the database listener. The up/down status of the database and database listener should be monitored so that you are the first person aware of any outages. If the listener is down then external users will not be able to access the database which will make the system unavailable.

Database Session Monitoring

Another key aspect of database monitoring is to monitor session behavior. Issues here can have a negative impact on the system. Identifying and troubleshooting any problems with sessions can prevent more serious problems from occurring.

The overall system performance should be monitored for any changes. There are several metrics that can comprise this item. Some key metrics are the number of active sessions, total number of sessions, SQL response time, and wait times.

Additional metrics can be monitored to prevent problems from occurring in the system. Long running sessions can be monitored, as that may indicate an issue with a query or process. The definition of a long running session will vary from system to system. Some batch jobs running as concurrent requests will account for the longest running sessions. The majority of the transactional sessions should complete within seconds or minutes.

Blocking sessions can cause issues in the database. If a Forms session or a concurrent request is being blocked, then the Oracle Applications DBA will get a call from users complaining about response time. To avoid this call, you should proactively monitor for database blocking sessions.

High resource consuming sessions should be monitored. You should be familiar with the resource consumption that occurs in the system. Based upon your baselines, you can define metrics for sessions that consume a high amount of memory or CPU time. These sessions may indicate a problem in the system. If the sessions are expected then the metrics can be adjusted appropriately.

▶ *Tip*   Thresholds should be periodically evaluated to determine whether they are still relevant to your system.

Additional Database Monitoring

If archiving is enabled, then it is important to monitor the archiving process. If the archive destination has no available space or the permissions on the directory are changed so that the database owner cannot write to the destination, then the database will hang. If a standby database is in place, then the Oracle Data Guard processes should also be monitored.

The system backups should be monitored for successful completion. If you perform frequent clones then you are testing the validity of your backups. If you do not perform clones often, then you should perform a regular test of your backup to make sure it is recoverable.

Monitoring object growth is also important. This includes several aspects of object growth. Creation of new objects should be monitored so they can be tied back to specific activities in the database. The space consumption of objects should also be monitored. If an object starts growing at an abnormal pace, then the system should be investigated for the cause of the object growth. The extents of an object should be monitored for both objects that are near their maximum number of extents as well as objects that do not have room for their next extent. If you have multiple copies of the database for development, test, and QA, then the space growth of the production system should be multiplied by all of the copies used to determine disk requirements.

Using Oracle11g Diagnostic Features

Additional diagnostic features are available with Oracle11g. One of the key changes is the addition of the Automatic Diagnostic Repository (ADR). This feature is more than just a relocation of the alert log and trace files to the diagnostic_dest directory. ADR is a comprehensive set of tools to assist with database diagnostics.

The ADRCI command line interface will allow the Oracle Applications DBA to easily interact with the ADR. The interface for ADRCI is text based. The SHOW ALERT command can be executed to view alert log entries. The HELP command will display commands available in ADRCI.

Oracle11g includes the concept of an *incident*. An incident can be the occurrence of an error which is logged in the alert log. When this happens, an incident is created which can be packaged and sent to Oracle Support. The process for creating an incident package is listed below.

Oracle provides an *Incident Packaging Service (IPS)* with ADRCI. The IPS can be used to create a package to be uploaded to Oracle Support. The software will bundle the required information for a problem or an incident. Then IPS can be used to generate the package to be sent to Oracle Support.

To start the ADRCI command line interface enter adrci at a UNIX command prompt. At the adrci> prompt, you can enter ADRCI commands. The following will display all commands available for ADCRI:

adrci> help

The following will display the content of the database alert log:

adrci> show alert

The following command will display any registered incidents:

adrci> show incident

Using EM Grid Control's Database Diagnostic Pack

Users of EM Grid Control can make use of the add-on tool Diagnostics Pack to assist with monitoring and troubleshooting database issues. The tools available with this pack include *Automatic Database Diagnostic Monitor* (ADDM) and *Automatic Workload Repository* (AWR).

ADDM is a self-diagnostic engine built into the database. ADDM will automatically monitor the database system and provide reports of any issues it uncovers. The reports can be viewed through the EM interface. AWR is the repository of system statistics used by ADDM to perform automatic system monitoring. The frequency of collections by AWR and the length of time they are stored is configurable by the Oracle Applications DBA. ADDM and AWR can also be used for performance tuning. Additional details regarding using ADDM and AWR for performance tuning are provided in Chapter 7 of this guide.

▶ *Note*   Contact your Oracle Sales Representative regarding licensing requirements for the Diagnostics Pack.

Additional Monitoring and Troubleshooting

This section covers some miscellaneous topics related to monitoring Oracle Applications. These items are important to provide a complete overview of the system.

Client Java Cache Location and Removal

Many client issues can be resolved by clearing the Java Cache on the client machine. This can be done through the Java link on the control panel. The main Java screen allows for the cache to be removed. The following steps will clear the cache:

1. Open *Control Panel.*
2. Select *Java* icon.
3. Select *General* tab.
4. In the *Temporary Internet Files* section select the *Settings...* button.
5. Click the *Delete Files...* button.
6. Check file options and select *OK.*

Monitoring Changes to the Environment

The Oracle Applications DBA should monitor the system for modifications to the environment. Examples of monitoring that should occur include changes to Applications profiles, invalid objects, and

Concurrent Manager. Additional details regarding these items are described in the following text.

Applications profile changes can have unexpected effects to the system. Problems associated with a user changing a profile at the site level can affect the entire application. Due to the potential issues caused by profile changes, any changes to the profile values should be tracked. Changes to profile values made within the Applications will track who changed the profile and when it was changed. The old values of the profiles are not tracked, so you should maintain a listing for your environment. Note that the OAM Dashboard will display profiles changed within the past 24 hours; however, you can automate monitoring through a script to check the fnd_profile_option_values table.

▶ *Tip*   If you change Oracle Applications profile values outside of the Applications be sure to use the Oracle API fnd_profile.

You should monitor for any changes to the number of invalid objects in the database. Objects may become invalidated by patches or system maintenance such as recreating objects. Also, if you have custom packages, they can become invalidated through internal patches developed by your organization. If new objects become invalidated, you can run the utlrp.sql script in $ORACLE_HOME/rdbms/admin directory on the database.

▶ *Tip*   If there are issues in the database, check for newly invalidated objects. If there are objects listed as invalid that were not showing up before, then run the $ORACLE_HOME/rdbms/admin/utlrp.sql script. Check the invalid list to see if the script made any changes.

Any changes to Concurrent Managers should be monitored. Changing the number of threads for a manager or the work shifts for a manager could result in issues for the application. Information about the Concurrent Managers can be found in the fnd_concurrent_queues table. Additional details regarding Concurrent Manager definitions were also provided in Chapter 2 of this guide.

Turning off Debugging Options

During any monitoring or troubleshooting activity it may be necessary to enable debugging or to increase the logging levels of the application. If debugging or logging has been turned on, then it needs to be turned off after troubleshooting has completed. Leaving debugging and logging levels enabled can cause performance issues on the application.

▶ *Tip*   When possible, perform debugging and logging in a test environment. Reserve production level debugging and logging for cases where the issues cannot be replicated in another environment. If necessary to debug in production, turn on the minimum levels of debugging or logging to lower the impact to production. Also, if debugging must be performed in production, be certain to perform production level debugging and logging during non-peak hours.

Network Monitoring

Monitoring and troubleshooting network issues can be done with client level commands or using an Applications form. This section will provide information regarding the following tools that are available for network monitoring and troubleshooting:

* Using ping and tracert, two very useful operating system commands for monitoring networking issues

* Performing a network trace from a Forms Session to detect network latency issues

Using ping and tracert for Network Monitoring

There are several operating system commands that can be used for troubleshooting network issues. From the client experiencing problems, issuing commands such as ping or tracert can provide valuable information.

The ping command will demonstrate whether the client has access to the node. Without access to the node, the user will be unable to access the Oracle Applications. Assuming that the Applications node for the deployment is vis.domain.com, the user must be able to access the address vis.domain.com. If access exists, the ping command should return the following:

C:\> ping vis.domain.com

Pinging vis.domain.com [192.168.20.1] with 32 bytes of data:

Reply from 192.168.20.1: bytes=32 time=39ms TTL=53
Reply from 192.168.20.1: bytes=32 time=41ms TTL=53
Reply from 192.168.20.1: bytes=32 time=38ms TTL=53
Reply from 192.168.20.1: bytes=32 time=54ms TTL=53

Ping statistics for 192.168.20.1:
    Packets: Sent = 4, Received = 4, Lost = 0 (0% loss),
Approximate round trip times in milli-seconds:
    Minimum = 38ms, Maximum = 54ms, Average = 43ms

Some useful troubleshooting information is provided with the results of the ping command. If the output indicates that packets are lost, there may be network issues for that client. Also, if the reply times out or takes an abnormally long time, there may be network issues. If the ping command returns the following output, there may be a problem with your Domain Name System (DNS):

C:\> ping vis.domain.com

Ping request could not find host vis.domain.com. Please check the name and try again.

If this error is experienced, you should contact a networking specialist in your organization to resolve the issue.

Another useful network command is tracert. This command will show the network path taken to connect to a particular domain. The information returned by tracert can provide useful information about connection time.

C:\>tracert www.oracle.com

Tracing route to a398.g.akamai.net [74.128.20.8]
over a maximum of 30 hops:

1   9 ms   7 ms   8 ms 74-138-208-1.dhcp.example.com [74.138.208.1]
2   7 ms   7 ms   15 ms 74-128-22-29.dhcp.example.com [74.128.22.29]
3   7 ms   7 ms   8 ms 74-128-20-8.dhcp.example.com [74.128.20.8]

Trace complete.

Performing a Network Test from the Application

Oracle Applications also provides a *Network Trace* form that the user may execute. This form is accessed by logging in to the Applications and choosing the *Application* → *Network Test* menu option. Click the *Run Test* button, and the form will return information about network latency and bandwidth. The number of iterations and trials can be modified for each execution of the test. A sample of the output is shown in Figure 6-6.

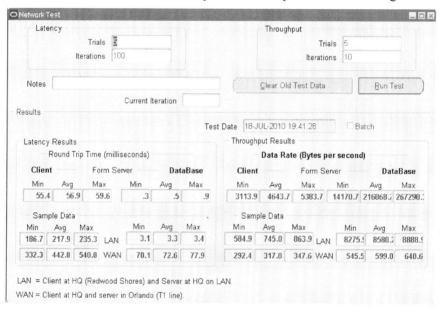

Figure 6-6. *Forms Network Test*

This information can be used by your company's or customer's networking team to determine whether networking bottlenecks exist.

Monitoring and Troubleshooting Best Practices

Monitoring and troubleshooting are very important skills for an Oracle Applications DBA. Effective monitoring can help to prevent problems from occurring, or prevent small problems from becoming big ones. When issues do arise, then the ability to quickly troubleshoot them will help to reduce impact to the system.

The most important thing to do in order to minimize off hours support issues is to proactively monitor your systems. Many situations that turn into big problems can be avoided through appropriate monitoring. For example, an archive directory that fills up can cause the database to hang. If you monitor for low available disk space on this directory, then you can prevent a problem from occurring.

It is important to document what metrics are set for monitoring the system. The settings should be regularly reviewed for relevance. Time should be taken to analyze the initial settings of metrics used for monitoring. The metrics should address specific issues. Over time, additional metrics may be added as new problems occur. Be sure to add the metrics to your documentation.

As issues are encountered, update monitoring steps to validate that the issue will not go uncaught again. By troubleshooting problems, you can often uncover new or better ways to monitor the system. The steps taken to troubleshoot problems can often be applied to create an automated monitoring job.

Monitoring can be automated through scripting or the use of monitoring features in a tool such as Oracle Enterprise Manager. It is best to use a tool that will allow you the ability to customize your monitoring as needed. No tool will have everything you need out of the box, so the ability to extend the tool to meet your needs is critical. Also, be sure to regularly test the monitoring processes to validate they are functioning. This includes monitoring the notification methods; for example, if a failure occurs but a message is not sent due to other problems with message delivery then your monitoring is not functioning.

Chapter 7

Performance Tuning

This chapter will focus on performance tuning techniques for many of the components of the Oracle E-Business Suite. In the course of reading this chapter, you will become familiar with various tools that will enable you to diagnose and fix performance degradation problems.

The two main sections of this chapter focus on the process and tools for performance tuning:

* **Overview of performance tuning methodology**: The Oracle Applications DBA must identify and document the cause of performance degradation, and then develop an action plan for implementing a solution. This section will outline the steps in this process.

* **Tools for resolving performance issues**: Some of the tools that can be used to identify performance issues were covered in Chapter 6. A review of these tools will be provided in this section. In addition to this, recommendations for configuration that will assist with performance optimization will be provided. Key performance tools for the database will be discussed, followed by a section for tracing sessions.

There are numerous books dedicated to the subject of performance tuning. This chapter is not meant to provide intricate details for in-depth performance tuning; however, it will provide an overview of the information required for identifying and resolving performance issues.

▶ *Note*   Tuning may also be performed on SQL statements and the networking and I/O components of Oracle Applications; however, an extensive discussion this type of tuning is beyond the scope of this guide.

Performance Tuning Process

Performance issues may occur on any of the tiers, infrastructure, or modules that make up the Oracle Applications environment. Because of the complexity of the application, it is necessary to gather information from the user community or other sources to determine which component of the Applications is experiencing the degradation in performance. This section provides you with a method for identifying and documenting performance issues and their resolution.

The first phase is to identify the cause of the degradation by collecting information to help you understand the underlying issue. The second phase is to develop an action plan in order to provide resolution.

Identifying Performance Issues

Traditional methodologies for performance tuning begin with tuning the Applications code and SQL. Since Oracle E-Business Suite is a packaged application, the first step in the traditional methodology is often difficult to implement. There are times when code performs so poorly that assistance from Oracle Support and Development is required to fix the underlying code. This situation will usually surface as a requirement while the Oracle Applications DBA works to identify the underlying performance issue.

To begin resolving performance problems, it is imperative that the nature of the degradation is understood. The strategy presented here for diagnosing the cause of performance degradation starts with general questions and proceeds to questions specific to different pieces of the application: the client tier, the network, a module of the application, and the entire application. It is advisable to document performance issues and the answers to these questions in order to facilitate resolution to the problem.

The Oracle Applications DBA may pose the following questions in order to collect the required information. If the answer to a question is no, proceed to the next question.

Question: Can the performance issue be systematically reproduced?

If the answer is yes: Document the process. Proceed to next question.

Question: Is the performance issue observed in only one instance?

If the answer is yes: Determine the difference between the instance where it performs poorly versus the instance where performance is normal. It is possible that the difference is a configuration parameter or a recently applied patch.

Question: Are all users of the Applications that are experiencing the performance degradation located within the same network segment?

If the answer is yes: The performance issue could be a networking issue. Suggest testing the module on a PC that is located on a different segment of the network. It may be necessary to involve the networking team to enable sniffer tracing on the network segment that is suspected to be performing poorly and to assist in identifying the cause of the underlying network performance problems.

Question: Is the performance degradation limited to a particular window of time?

If the answer is yes: The performance issue could be the result of a scheduled job on the database or server. This job may be causing resource contention. Check all scheduled activity at the application, database, and server level. Monitor the database and server during the time period of performance issues for high resource processes. If a resource-intensive job is found, reschedule it for a better time or acquire more resources to support the required processing.

Question: Is the entire application experiencing performance degradation?

If the answer is yes: Begin monitoring the database and server to identify the underlying performance issue. Tools for monitoring database and server performance are described later in this chapter. Additional methods for troubleshooting are outlined in Chapter 6 of this guide.

Question: Is the performance degradation limited to one module?

If the answer is yes: Ask the user community to provide the name of the module that is performing poorly. Then proceed to work with the user community to open an SR and generate a user trace to provide to Oracle Support. Additional details regarding generating trace files are provided in Chapter 6 of this guide. For this type of issue, it is best to try to reproduce the problem in a recently cloned environment. Gathering trace files is much easier in a non-production environment.

Question: Is the performance degradation limited to one user?

If the answer is yes: If only one user is experiencing performance degradation, the degradation is most likely isolated to the client. Suggest that the user experiencing the performance issue try the task on a different workstation. If the user successfully executes the application from a different PC, additional monitoring needs to take place on the user's workstation. It is possible that additional memory or CPU resources are required, or operating system or browser patching is required. Additional tips for diagnosing client issues are discussed later in this chapter.

This list of questions may be enhanced and revised to suit your environment. Update the questions regularly, and keep them in an easily accessible location. Be certain that the people providing the first line of support for Oracle Applications are familiar with the questions developed by your organization. If these questions have already been addressed when performance issues are brought to the Applications DBA, the time required to resolve the problem can be reduced.

Additional information regarding performance tuning may be found in *My Oracle Support Article ID 69565.1*. Using this article and the preceding sample questions, you may begin to develop your own template for performance tuning. The article is specific to the 11i version of Oracle E-Business Suite, but there is useful information that applies to release 12 as well.

Developing an Action Plan

When a performance problem is reported, the Oracle Applications DBA should be able to respond with an action plan for attempting to resolve the issue. Once the issue has been narrowed down to a possible cause, steps for resolving the issue should be outlined. Next, a more detailed tuning effort should take place, focusing on the possible source of problem. The tools discussed in the following section will assist you in determining the steps required for a more detailed tuning effort.

After a resolution to the problem has been identified, update the action plan with the steps taken to resolve the issue. This information can be provided to management and the user community for feedback during the tuning process. This document also becomes a tool for future tuning efforts. If the same problem is encountered again, a potential solution has already been documented.

Tools for Identifying and Resolving Performance Issues

Tools and methods for identifying and resolving performance issues may be categorized at the database, server, application tier, and user levels. The Oracle Applications DBA will need to be familiar with all of these tools. The tools available will vary, depending upon the versions of the database and Applications installed. The following topics will be discussed in this section:

* **Server tuning**: This section will review tools provided in Chapters 4 and 6 for monitoring server performance. The review will include how to use top, sar, vmstat, and ps to analyze performance related server data

* **Application tier tuning**: This section outlines how to analyze performance issues for application tier services. Included in this section are configuration guidelines for improving performance.

* **Database tier tuning**: Tools for tuning the Oracle11g database, including *Active Session History* (ASH), *Automatic Workload Repository* (AWR), and *Automatic Database Diagnostics Monitor* (ADDM), will be covered. In addition to this, an overview of Oracle's Enterprise Manager (EM) Grid Control's Diagnostics Pack will be covered.

* **User tuning**: This section will cover how to trace a user session and recommendations for best practices for managing user sessions.

* **Network latency**: This section will review the importance of monitoring network latency.

Server Tuning

Reviewing resource consumption on the server is typically a good starting point for identifying underlying performance degradation. Standard UNIX commands can be used to monitor server CPU and memory consumption. The commands were introduced in Chapter 4 of this guide. The following is a review of the commands as they apply to performance tuning.

Using top

The UNIX top command provides an overview of CPU and memory utilization. The statistics are refreshed every few seconds to provide near real time data. Statistics for CPU, memory, and swap space for the top command are shown in Tables 7-1 through 7-3.

Table 7-1. *CPU States as Displayed by top*

Column	Description
User	Percentage of CPU utilized by user.
System	Percentage of CPU utilized by the server.
Idle	Percentage of CPU idle time.

Table 7-2. *Memory as Displayed by top*

Column	Description
Av	Available memory.
Used	Used memory.
Free	Free memory.

Table 7-3. *Swap as Displayed by top*

Column	Description
Av	Available swap space.
Used	Used swap space.
Free	Free swap space.

Upon executing top, the CPU, memory, and swap statistics are displayed, followed by a list of active system processes. The process information displayed is very similar to what is displayed by the ps command, which will be described shortly in the *Using* ps section. To exit top, press q. An example of executing top is displayed in Figure 7-1.

```
top - 21:33:58 up 17 days, 13:26,  3 users,  load average: 4.20, 6.14, 3.60
Tasks: 366 total,   1 running, 365 sleeping,   0 stopped,   0 zombie
Cpu(s):  0.7%us,  0.3%sy,  0.0%ni, 98.8%id,  0.2%wa,  0.0%hi,  0.0%si,  0.0%st
Mem:   2051852k total,  1999312k used,    52540k free,     5968k buffers
Swap:  1930656k total,   962420k used,   968236k free,   557868k cached

  PID USER      PR  NI  VIRT  RES  SHR S %CPU %MEM    TIME+  COMMAND
 4434 vis       20   0  2628 1344  884 R    2  0.1  0:01.18 top
  988 root      20   0 49460  11m 2712 S    0  0.6 83:17.86 Xorg
 1690 vis       20   0 63804 4228 2456 S    0  0.2  8:25.26 compiz.real
 2931 vis       20   0 1161m 9560 8404 S    0  0.5  0:01.52 oracle
 3195 vis       20   0 1162m  48m  47m S    0  2.4  0:02.59 oracle
 3803 vis       20   0 1164m  31m  27m S    0  1.6  0:02.75 oracle
 3911 vis       20   0  536m  38m 3264 S    0  1.9  0:22.07 java
 3920 vis       20   0  539m  36m 3252 S    0  1.8  0:20.76 java
 3945 vis       20   0  542m  40m 3204 S    0  2.0  0:25.41 java
 4073 vis       20   0 1162m  48m  44m S    0  2.4  0:01.01 oracle
    1 root      20   0  2628  672  440 S    0  0.0  0:06.13 init
    2 root      15  -5     0    0    0 S    0  0.0  0:00.01 kthreadd
    3 root      RT  -5     0    0    0 S    0  0.0  0:00.06 migration/0
```

Figure 7-1. *Execution of top*

Using sar

System Activity Reporter (sar) has many different parameters that can be used. CPU utilization can be shown with the -u switch, for example, and memory swapping can be shown with the -w switch.

The sar command requires two arguments, the first being the time interval between samples, and the second being the number of samples to take. Table 7-4 lists relevant columns and descriptions of the data displayed by executing sar -u to capture CPU utilization.

Table 7-4. *Columns and Descriptions for the sar -u Command*

Column	Description
%user	Percentage of system utilized by users.
%system	Percentage of system utilized by the OS.
%iowait	Percentage waiting on I/O.
%idle	Percentage of server that is idle.

Figure 7-2 shows the output of the sar -u command, displaying CPU utilization with five samples in 10-second intervals.

```
$ sar -u 10 5

09:36:28 PM     CPU     %user    %nice  %system  %iowait   %steal    %idle
09:36:31 PM     all      0.50     0.00     0.41     3.31     0.00    95.78
09:36:34 PM     all      1.16     0.00     2.15     0.08     0.00    96.61
09:36:37 PM     all      1.29     0.00     0.81     3.14     0.00    94.77
09:36:40 PM     all      0.83     0.00     0.41     0.74     0.00    98.02
09:36:43 PM     all      0.83     0.00     0.17     2.73     0.00    96.27
Average:        all      0.92     0.00     0.79     2.01     0.00    96.28
```

Figure 7-2. *Executing sar -u*

Table 7-5 lists relevant columns and descriptions of the data displayed by executing sar -r to capture memory utilization.

Table 7-5. *Statistics Displayed by the sar -r Command*

Column	Description
kbmemfree	Free memory in KB.
kbmemused	Memory used in KB.
%memused	Percentage of memory used.
kbbuffers	Memory used as buffers by the kernel in KB.
kbcached	Memory used to cache data by the kernel in KB.
kbcommit	Estimated memory needed for current workload in KB.
%commit	Percentage of memory needed for current workload.

Figure 7-3 shows the output of the sar -r command, displaying server data for six samples with 5-second intervals between each sample.

```
$sar -r 5 6

09:38:46 PM kbmemfree kbmemused %memused kbbuffers  kbcached   kbcommit   %commit
09:38:49 PM     54156   1997696    97.36      8544    553936    4366768    109.65
09:38:52 PM     49684   2002168    97.58      8560    554036    4374020    109.83
09:38:55 PM     48940   2002912    97.61      8540    556800    4377204    109.91
09:38:58 PM     49312   2002540    97.60      8556    555320    4375948    109.88
09:39:01 PM     47708   2004144    97.67      8428    553608    4375884    109.88
09:39:04 PM     50560   2001292    97.54      8364    553112    4375428    109.87
Average:        50060   2001792    97.56      8499    554469    4374209    109.84
```

Figure 7-3. *Execution of sar -r*

Using vmstat

Another command that can be used to display UNIX performance statistics is vmstat. Common statistics displayed by vmstat are arranged in the categories shown in Table 7-6.

Table 7-6. *Categories for the vmstat Command*

Column	Description
procs	Information about processes.
memory	Memory Information about virtual and real memory.
swap	Information about page faults and paging activity.
io	Information about I/O.
system	Information about system interrupts and switches.
cpu	Information about percentage of CPU time.

Additional details for key vmstat columns in the different categories are shown in Table 7-7.

Table 7-7. *Key vmstat Statistics*

Column	Description
r	Run queue.
free	Amount of idle memory (KB).
si	Amount of memory swapped in from disk (KB/s).
so	Amount of memory swapped to disk (KB/s).
bi	Blocks sent to a device.
bo	Blocks received from a device.
us	User CPU time.
sy	System CPU time.
id	Idle CPU time.

Executing vmstat without any options will result in statistics being displayed since the last reboot, as shown in Figure 7-4.

```
$ vmstat
procs -----------memory---------- ---swap-- -----io---- -system-- ----cpu----
 r  b   swpd   free   buff  cache   si   so    bi    bo   in   cs us sy id wa
 0  0 973288  48924   7756 605916    3    1     1     6    6    2  4  1 95  0
```

Figure 7-4. *Server statistics displayed by vmstat*

The example of vmstat in Figure 7-5 displays five summaries at 3-second intervals, the first summary being the summary since boot up.

```
$ vmstat 3 5
procs -----------memory---------- ---swap-- -----io---- -system-- ----cpu----
 r  b   swpd   free   buff  cache   si   so    bi    bo   in   cs us sy id wa
 1  0 980768  55504   7940 587216    3    1     1     6    6    2  4  1 95  0
 0  0 980636  56116   7956 587040  176    0   176    27  333  704  1  0 98  1
 0  1 982484  51024   7952 590700  285  731   311   763  650 1069  5  3 85  7
 0  0 982452  55628   7976 586024   21    0    21    60  381  653  1  0 98  0
 0  0 982356  52528   7984 590100  129    0   132    17  338  722  2  0 97  1
```

Figure 7-5. *Summary of server statistics displayed by vmstat 3 5*

Using ps

The UNIX ps command is used to display active processes. This command can be sorted by any of the columns that are displayed by it. Sorting by the seventh column, which is the CPU column, is demonstrated in Figure 7-6. The columns displayed in the output in Figure 7-6 are process, process ID, parent process ID, CPU utilization of process, total execution time, controlling workstation, login time, and process owner.

```
$ ps -ef | sort -k7 | tail
vis      4045      1  0 21:28 ?        00:00:03 oracleVIS (LOCAL=NO)
vis      2945      1  0 21:20 ?        00:00:03 ora_mmon_VIS
vis      3729      1  0 21:25 ?        00:00:04 oracleVIS (LOCAL=NO)
vis      2931      1  0 21:20 ?        00:00:04 ora_dia0_VIS
vis      3195      1  0 21:23 ?        00:00:06 oracleVIS (LOCAL=NO)
vis      2941      1  0 21:20 ?        00:00:07 ora_smon_VIS
```

Figure 7-6. *Sorting processes by CPU with the ps command*

▶ *Note*   Your version of UNIX or Linux may impact the behavior of some of these commands; check results of the commands to validate they provide you the information you need.

Analyzing Server Performance Data

By using any of the UNIX commands described in the previous sections, key performance statistics for the server can be gathered. CPU usage, memory usage, and resource intensive processes should be furthered analyzed.

If the CPU is displaying small amounts of idle time, it is possible that Oracle processes are experiencing CPU contention. If CPU consumption cannot be associated with one process but rather is the sum of many processes, additional CPU resources may be required. Within vmstat, the number displayed for the run queue should be less than the total number of CPUs on the server.

If the top CPU consumer is an Oracle process, you should identify the source of the process. If it is on the application server, determine if it is a Forms, AS, or Concurrent Manager process. Review the log files for errors or use some of the monitoring tools previously discussed to determine the cause of the high activity. Sometimes it may be necessary to bounce the Forms or Apache Server or kill the process at the operating system level to remove a process that is spinning out of control. If the process is on the database server, drill down into the underlying activity in the database for the session that matches the UNIX process ID. This may be accomplished with EM Grid Control or by executing queries in the database. Use AWR or generate user traces to determine whether the database process needs to be tuned in order to reduce CPU utilization.

Memory swapping occurs if real memory is exhausted and its contents need to be swapped to disk. If there is a high amount of memory swapping, it is likely that Oracle is experiencing memory contention. It might be possible to decrease the amount of memory being consumed by the SGA or AS, but often memory contention is resolved by purchasing additional RAM for the server.

Application Tier Tuning

Common Applications components that require performance tuning attention include Web services, Forms services, and Concurrent Manager Processing. This section will cover tuning recommendations for each of these services.

Apache Tuning

The Apache Server runs on the server as httpd processes. You may retrieve a listing of the Apache processes on the server for the VIS instance by executing the following:

$UNIX>ps -ef | grep httpd| grep vis

When it comes to the Apache Server, be sure to set logging at the lowest level possible. Excessive logging and debugging may result in performance degradation. For standard operations, keep the log levels in the httpd.conf file set to warn. If the levels are changed for troubleshooting purposes, ensure that the levels are reset before resuming normal usage. The lowest logging levels in the httpd.conf and ssl.conf file are as follows:

LogLevel=warn
SSLLogLevel=warn

You may also update these settings using the Applications context file and running AutoConfig. Using the OAM interface, you would search for the apache_loglevel parameter. Typically, log level settings are implemented for a brief period of time and it is better to apply the settings directly to the configuration file instead of setting them via the Applications context file and executing AutoConfig.

JVM Tuning

Frequent garbage collection by the JVMs can have a significant impact of the performance of the Applications nodes. If the heap memory settings are too low, then the system can require more frequent garbage collections. If that is the case, increase the settings of Xms and Xmx to values higher than 512M. Review the total amount of memory available on the system before increasing the memory for the JVMs to ensure there is enough space.

The memory allocated to the JVMs can be managed within the Applications context file. The parameter to review for memory allocation is s_oacore_jvm_start_options. Also, review the number of JVMs that are started on each Applications node. The parameter that controls the number of Java processes that OPMN starts is s_oacore_nprocs. These parameters affect total memory consumption.

Improperly tuned memory settings may result in performance problems with web based applications. If log files or browser sessions report an "out of memory" error, the JVM most likely has hit a memory limitation.

The FND: View Object Max Fetch Size profile can be set to limit the number of rows an executed query returns to a user in an HTML application. You should set this profile to no greater than 200. If this number is increased, JVM memory can be exhausted. If the value of 200 is not great enough, you should set the profile at the application level for the Applications that require the ability to return more rows. This will reduce the overall impact of the parameter.

The recommendation is to limit the number of JVMs to 1 JVM per 2 CPUs on the Applications node. At most, the number of JVMs should not exceed the number of CPUs on the node. Each JVM can be expected to handle at most 100 users. Factor these numbers into the architecture of your system to ensure you have an adequate number of application servers and CPUs per server.

If the session timeout set by the ICX: Session Timeout profile is greater than 30 minutes, session memory usage may result in performance degradation. In conjunction with this, be sure to validate the AutoConfig parameters of s_sesstimeout and s_oc4j_sesstimeout. Be certain to set the session timeout to the lowest acceptable level for your user community.

JDK releases typically include performance enhancements; therefore, as with other components of the Applications tier, upgrading to the latest version of JDK available will help the performance of your system.

Forms Tuning

Forms sessions run on the server as frmweb processes. You can retrieve a listing of the Forms processes on the server for the VIS instance by executing the following command:

```
$UNIX>ps -ef | grep frmweb | grep –i vis
```

If an frmweb process is one of the top processes on a server, as determined by top, sar, or ps, you should try to link the Forms process to a database session. This can be done by viewing active Forms sessions in OAM as outlined in Chapter 6 of this guide. If there seems to be no valid reason for this session to be among the top sessions, then it might be necessary to kill the session or bounce the Web and Forms services.

Forms performance issues may arise when dead connections persist on the server, consuming server resources. Enabling Forms dead client detection by setting the FORMS_TIMEOUT parameter can eliminate dead connections. The value specified for the parameter is in minutes.

Another means of tuning Forms processes is to enable the Forms abnormal termination handler by enabling the FORMS_CATCHTERM parameter. Setting FORMS_CATCHTERM to 1 will cause Forms errors to dump output to the FORMS_PATH directory.

Both the FORMS_TIMEOUT and FORMS_CATCHTERM parameters can be set by modifying the context file and then running AutoConfig or by exporting them as environment variables and restarting the Forms Server. Key context file parameters for Forms tuning are shown in Table 7-8.

Table 7-8. *Parameters for Forms Tuning Sessions*

Context File Parameter	Environment Variable	Recommended Value
s_forms_time	FORMS_TIMEOUT	5
s_forms_catchterm	FORMS_CATCHTERM	1

Users of the Oracle E-Business Suite may also want the ability to cancel a Forms query. This may be achieved by setting the FND: Enable Cancel Query profile option to Yes at the site, application, responsibility, or user level. If you do not enable this profile option, the only method for canceling the query is to kill the Forms session. When this profile option is enabled, a cancel query dialog box will appear in order for the user to cancel the query.

While this seems like a good feature to offer your users, it comes at the expense of increasing client, middle tier, and database CPU usage. Be careful when enabling this feature. Since it can be controlled down to the user level, it is recommended that you grant this option only to certain users. If you decide to enable cancel query, the parameters shown in Table 7-9 may be used to tune its effects.

The FORMS_LOV_INITIAL environment variable can assist in reducing network traffic. Set it close to the maximum value in order to reduce network traffic. The FORMS_LOV_MINIMUM environment variable specifies how frequently polling occurs. The more frequent the polling, the more quickly the query will be cancelled. The FORMS_LOV_WEIGHT environment variable uses an equation to determine network latency in order to reduce the number of round trips.

These variables can be set in the context file for your Applications node and implemented with AutoConfig. Be certain to test the effects of setting these parameters before promoting them to your production environment.

Table 7-9. *Environment Variables Used to Tune the Cancel Query Feature*

Environment Variable	Value	Description
FORMS_LOV_INITIAL	1000–32000	Number of ms until the *Cancel Query* button appears.
FORMS_LOV_MINIMUM	1000–32000	Value in ms between polling of the client from the middle tier to check whether the query cancel dialog box should be displayed. Recommended setting is between 1000–5000.
FORMS_LOV_WEIGHT	0–32000	Value used to adjust the polling period based on network latency.

▶ *Tip*   The MAXBLOCKTIME value, set in the context file with s_forms_maxblocktime, must be larger than the maximum query polling interval. The default value is 5000ms. If MAXBLOCKTIME is not set greater than the query polling interval, this will result in excessive CPU usage, which will cause performance degradation.

Concurrent Manager Configuration Recommendations

Performance problems can be minimized through proper configuration of your environment. Server architecture is especially important for the nodes running the Concurrent Managers.

The Concurrent Manager nodes must have a high speed connection to the Database Node. Oracle used to recommend that the managers run on the same node as the database, but this is no longer the recommended configuration.

The Oracle Applications DBA should be familiar with the jobs scheduled through the Concurrent Manager. The number of jobs running at certain times and the number of threads defined for each manager can help determine the number of Concurrent Manager nodes required to support the application. When sizing the nodes, be sure to factor in the full requirements for each Concurrent Manager. If the number of threads required to handle business processing exceed the available CPU, then it may be necessary to enable Parallel Concurrent Processing in order to prevent performance issues.

Concurrent Manager Tuning

Performance problems on the Applications tier may also arise from contention with resource intensive Concurrent Manager requests. The solution for this issue could result in implementing architecture changes, performing regular maintenance on the Concurrent Manager tables, or tuning jobs.

As part of an overall strategy for concurrent processing, multiple Concurrent Managers should be defined to handle long running and short running requests. It may also be necessary to define module specific Concurrent Managers—for example, a long running Concurrent Manager for GL and a long running Concurrent Manager for AP. Much of this is dependent upon the scheduling requirements for your site.

The Oracle E-Business Suite's predefined Concurrent Manager is called the Standard Manager. The Standard Manager should be reserved for standard Oracle requests. In order to support a large volume of concurrent requests, it may also be necessary to implement Parallel Concurrent Processing by load balancing concurrent requests across multiple nodes.

▶ *Tip*   Schedule as many Concurrent Manager processes as possible during non-peak hours to reduce contention with the daily business processing.

Concurrent Manager performance problems could also result as a result of not routinely purging the concurrent request history. A symptom of this problem would be a low buffer cache hit ratio in the AWR report. Detailed information regarding purging this history is outlined in Chapter 4 of this guide. Keep a minimal amount of Concurrent Manager execution history in the system. Oracle recommends setting the purge to keep no more than 30 days of data online. If your environment generates an excessive amount of concurrent activity, you may consider limiting the history to less than 30 days. The requirements for retaining Concurrent Manager output are environment specific.

If performance problems are related to one particular job, focus on tuning that job. Make sure that users are scheduling the job with appropriate parameter values; failing to do so may cause the job to perform excessive processing. For Oracle seeded jobs, you should consider opening an SR. If statistics are up to date on the objects being queried by the job, the problem may be a known bug with the concurrent request. Oracle Support should be able to provide guidance for resolving the issue.

If performance problems are associated with a custom job, the Oracle Applications DBA and development team should work to tune the job. The user trace and SQL tuning information presented later in this chapter can assist with that tuning effort. A custom Concurrent Manager may be required to processes certain jobs. *My Oracle Support Article ID 170524.1* provides details for creating a custom Concurrent Manager.

If performance problems are associated with one particular manager, and there appears to be high CPU consumption on the Concurrent Processing Node, the ICM Sleep Time may be set to a value too low for your system. *My Oracle Support Article ID 178925.1* describes the process of altering the ICM Sleep Time setting.

Database Tier Tuning

The best tools for identifying database performance issues are *Automatic Workload Repository* (AWR) and *Automatic Database Diagnostic Monitoring* (ADDM), provided by Oracle since version 10*g*. It is possible to perform tuning tasks by querying the Oracle database dictionary, which contains performance related data, but such tasks are beyond the scope of this guide. We will rely on using the standard Oracle tools, such as *Automatic Workload Repository*, *Active Session History*, and *Automatic Database Diagnostic Monitoring* for collecting system performance data.

Using Automatic Workload Repository (AWR)

The *Automatic Workload Repository* (AWR) collects performance data automatically on a scheduled basis. The data collection is done with minimal overhead by utilizing the background process called *Manageability Monitor* (MMON), which is responsible for taking the snapshots of database performance statistics. Building this sort of performance diagnostic information into the database is part of Oracle's manageability infrastructure. In addition to database information, AWR gathers operating system statistics that can be seen in the V$OSSTAT view.

The default collection method used by MMON is to take snapshots every 60 minutes. This data is stored for seven days before it is automatically purged from the system. The collection data is stored in the SYS schema within the SYSAUX tablespace. Over 100 tables are created to store the AWR data, which can be accessed using the DBA_HIST_% views. Some of the more common views are listed in Table 7-10.

Table 7-10. *Common AWR Views*

View Name	Description
DBA_HIST_BASELINE	Information on the AWR baselines.
DBA_HIST_DATABASE_INSTANCE	Information on the database and instance.
DBA_HIST_SNAPSHOT	Information on AWR snapshots.
DBA_HIST_SQL_PLAN	Information on SQL execution plans.
DBA_HIST_WR_CONTROL	Information on the parameters set for AWR.

EM Grid Control provides a graphical interface for managing AWR as part of the Diagnostic Pack. Using EM Grid Control, the Oracle Applications DBA can easily manage the AWR settings and generate reports. This information can be accessed in the *Snapshots* link in the *Additional Monitoring* links section of the *Performance* tab in EM Grid Control.

The management of AWR may also be performed using the DBMS_WORKLOAD_REPOSITORY package. For example, to change the frequency of snapshots from one hour to two hours, and data retention from seven days to ten days, execute the following command using number of minutes for the two parameters:

```
SQL>exec dbms_workload_repository.modify_snapshot_settings ( -
>interval => 120, -
>retention => 14400)
```

To manually create a snapshot when the snapshot interval is not sufficient, use the following procedure:

```
SQL>exec dbms_workload_repository.create_snapshot()
```

Within AWR it is possible to create a baseline of snapshots, and in EM Grid Control this feature is called *Preserved Snapshot Sets*. This baseline may be created from snapshots taken during periods of normal database activity. If problems occur at a later date, a new baseline may be created, and these two baselines can be compared to identify performance problems. To create a baseline from snapshot_id 1 and snapshot_id 2, use the following command:

```
SQL>exec dbms_workload_repository.create_baseline( -
>start_snap_id => 1, -
>end_snap_id => 2, -
>baseline_name => 'Test')
```

The performance report is generated by running the awrrpt.sql script. This script requires two snapshots covering the time when the performance issue was experienced as input. Here is an example of executing the AWR performance report:

```
SQL>@$ORACLE_HOME/rdbms/admin/awrrpt.sql
```

The AWR report provides performance information that is categorized in sections. The report should be reviewed by a senior level Database Administrator. Additional details regarding AWR may be found in *My Oracle Support Article ID 884046.1* and *My Oracle Support Article ID 842884.1*. A high level overview of some of the sections of the AWR report are provided in Figures 7-7 through 7-12.

	Snap Id	Snap Time	Sessions	Cursors/Session
Begin Snap:	1043	30-Mar-10 12:00:22	24	1.7
End Snap:	1044	30-Mar-10 13:00:25	25	1.8
Elapsed:		60.05 (mins)		
DB Time:		0.48 (mins)		

Figure 7-7 *Beginning of the AWR Report*

After the display of the snap time, the report summary information is provided. The first section in the Report Summary is the Cache Sizes. Figure 7-8 displays the information in the AWR Report regarding Cache Sizes.

Report Summary

Cache Sizes

	Begin	End		
Buffer Cache:	584M	584M	Std Block Size:	8K
Shared Pool Size:	400M	400M	Log Buffer:	12,744K

Figure 7-8. *AWR Report: Cache Sizes*

The next section shows the Load Profile for the system during the report period as shown in Figure 7-9. This information can provide an at a glance view of activity in the system. This section is useful for comparing behavior during different time periods. For example, a time period with a higher value of physical reads per second may indicate that a large report is being run which is pulling data not normally in the buffer cache.

Load Profile

	Per Second	Per Transaction	Per Exec	Per Call
DB Time(s):	0.0	0.6	0.00	0.07
DB CPU(s):	0.0	0.5	0.00	0.06
Redo size:	544.3	39,222.6		
Logical reads:	757.8	54,608.3		
Block changes:	7.8	565.1		
Physical reads:	18.8	1,357.4		
Physical writes:	0.6	41.5		
User calls:	0.1	8.1		
Parses:	1.6	112.2		
Hard parses:	0.2	10.9		
W/A MB processed:	95,653.1	6,893,015.0		
Logons:	0.0	2.1		
Executes:	2.6	190.4		
Rollbacks:	0.0	0.2		
Transactions:	0.0			

Figure 7-9. *AWR Report: Load Profile*

The next sections show the memory usage in the instance as shown in Figure 7-10. These sections provide hit ratios for Buffer Cache and Shared Pool memory regions, which can be used to validate the SGA.

Instance Efficiency Percentages (Target 100%)

Buffer Nowait %	100.00	Redo NoWait %	100.00
Buffer Hit %	97.51	In-memory Sort %	100.00
Library Hit %	92.53	Soft Parse %	90.29
Execute to Parse %	41.06	Latch Hit %	100.00
Parse CPU to Parse Elapsd %:	0.01	% Non-Parse CPU	49.74

Shared Pool Statistics

	Begin	End
Memory Usage %	33.46	38.73
% SQL with executions>1	88.29	72.36
% Memory for SQL w/exec>1	84.84	54.69

Figure 7-10. *AWR Report: Instance memory statistics*

The next section shows the top five wait events in the database. This is a very importation section of the AWR report. The top events should be reviewed for any areas of improvement. If comparing reports from two different time periods, this is often the first place to look for differences. This list includes the percentage of time spent on each event. The effort in reviewing the top events should be spent on the events with the most area for improvement. Figure 7-11 displays an example of the Top 5 Timed Foreground Events.

Top 5 Timed Foreground Events

Event	Waits	Time(s)	Avg wait (ms)	% DB time	Wait Class
DB CPU		26		88.23	
db file sequential read	269	3	11	9.98	User I/O
log file sync	12	0	13	0.55	Commit
SQL*Net message to client	62	0	0	0.08	Network
db file scattered read	1	0	7	0.03	User I/O

Figure 7-11. *AWR Report: Top 5 Timed Foreground Events*

The next section of the report displayed is a section listing of the main AWR report. This shows the type of information included in the report. Often, reviewing SQL Statistics and Segment Statistics will be enough to identify areas for tuning. Depending upon behavior of the system, other areas of the report may need to be more closely reviewed. Figure 7-12 displays an example of the section listing for the main report.

The output may be manually analyzed by reviewing the details provided in the report. Starting with Oracle10g, the *Automatic Database Diagnostic Monitoring* (ADDM) can automatically analyze AWR information. The features of ADDM are explained in the next section.

Main Report

- Report Summary
- Wait Events Statistics
- SQL Statistics
- Instance Activity Statistics
- IO Stats
- Buffer Pool Statistics
- Advisory Statistics
- Wait Statistics
- Undo Statistics
- Latch Statistics
- Segment Statistics
- Dictionary Cache Statistics
- Library Cache Statistics
- Memory Statistics
- Streams Statistics
- Resource Limit Statistics
- init.ora Parameters

Figure 7-12. *AWR Report: Main Report*

Using Automatic Database Diagnostic Monitoring (ADDM)

The goal of the database manageability infrastructure is to provide a self-monitoring and self-tuning database. Rather than the DBA manually analyzing AWR and ASH data, Oracle provides the Automatic Database Diagnostic Monitor (ADDM) to automatically analyze the data collected by the monitoring tools. By following a set of tuning rules developed by Oracle experts, this program will create recommendations that will reduce overall time spent in database calls.

The ADDM analysis will list areas for improvement in its reports that are not necessarily critical. Keep in mind that the goal of tuning is to seek the areas where you can make the biggest improvement.

▶ *Tip*   Be careful when using any automatic analysis tool. The recommendations provided by the tool may not be appropriate for your system. Before implementing any recommendation from such a tool, be sure that you understand the reasoning for the change. Thoroughly test any such change before promoting the change to your production system.

As with AWR and ASH, which are also part of the Diagnostic Pack, EM Grid Control provides a rich, graphical interface to ADDM. EM Grid Control's interface to these tools provides the easiest method of interaction. However, you may still perform analysis and build reports manually as a database user with the ADVISOR privilege by using the Oracle provided DBMS_ADVISOR package. The $ORACLE_HOME/rdbms/admin/addmrpt.sql script will generate an ADDM report.

The method of executing this script is very similar to generating an AWR report. You will be prompted for a beginning and ending AWR snapshot to use for the analysis. If the database has been restarted during the time between the two snapshots, the analysis provided by ADDM will be invalid.

▶ **Note**   In order for ADDM to function, the STATISTICS_LEVEL initialization parameter must be set to either TYPICAL or ALL. A setting of BASIC will disable ADDM. Oracle recommends only setting this parameter to ALL when performing diagnostics on the system.

Information related to ADDM may be accessed in the DBA_ADVISOR_% views. Key ADDM views are listed in Table 7-11.

Table 7-11. *Common ADDM Views*

View Name	Description
DBA_ADVISOR_FINDINGS	Information on the findings of ADDM.
DBA_ADVISOR_LOG	Information on the current state of all tasks in the database.
DBA_ADVISOR_RATIONALE	Information on the rationale for all recommendations by ADDM.
DBA_ADVISOR_RECOMMENDATIONS	Information on the recommendations for all diagnostic tasks.
DBA_ADVISOR_TASKS	Information on the existing tasks in the database.

Using Active Session History (ASH)

A key element of Oracle's database manageability infrastructure is *Active Session History* (ASH). ASH is another component of the EM Diagnostic Pack. Oracle collects information every second on active database sessions and stores this information in memory within the System Global Area (SGA). By collecting this data, the *Automatic Database Diagnostics Monitor* (ADDM) process will be able to better identify issues related to data access by sessions. The MMON *Lite* (MMNL) background process is responsible for writing session data to memory. It assists the MMON process by flushing ASH data to AWR tables. MMNL assists with collecting performance data with minimal overhead to the system. The MMNL process will write the data from memory into tables every hour.

ASH data can be accessed through the V$ACTIVE_SESSION_HISTORY view for manual analysis. This view contains information about the database user, the module being run, SQL execution plans, wait events, CPU time used, and database objects being accessed. Given the frequency of samples from Oracle, this view will contain current data and it makes ASH useful for near real time analysis of your system. To view information collected by ASH for a specific duration, run the ashrpt.sql script in the $ORACLE_HOME/rdbms/admin directory on the Database Node. An excerpt of the report is shown in Figure 7-13. The format of the information provided is similar to the AWR report.

	Sample Time	Data Source
Analysis Begin Time	30-Mar-10 12:44:11	V$ACTIVE_SESSION_HISTORY
Analysis End Time	30-Mar-10 12:59:13	V$ACTIVE_SESSION_HISTORY
Elapsed Time	15.0 (mins)	
Sample Count	19	
Average Active Sessions	0.02	
Avg Active Session per CPU	0.01	
Report Target	None specified	

ASH Report

- Top Events
- Load Profile
- Top SQL
- Top PL/SQL
- Top Java
- Top Sessions
- Top Objects/Files/Latches
- Activity Over Time

Figure 7-13. *Information from ASH Report*

In addition to performing online analysis, the contents of the ASH buffer may be downloaded to a trace file. The process for doing this utilizes the ASHDUMP event:

SQL>alter session set events 'immediate trace name ashdump level 10';

This command will create a trace file in the database's trace directory. The file created will be a comma separated text file containing a structure similar to the V$ACTIVE_SESSION_HISTORY view. For analysis, this file may be loaded into the database using the SQL Loader utility. Utilizing ASHDUMP allows for offline analysis, which can be useful for analyzing the data from a hung system. Also, the dump file can be imported into a different system in case the target system becomes unavailable.

Analyzing the AWR Report

When reviewing the AWR report, you should focus on a few key items. These items will help to identify the most common types of performance issues. Other issues may require a more detailed analysis of the reports.

The *top five wait events* of the report will tell you where the most time is spent in the database. Look for opportunities to tune the top event in order to save the most time in the system.

The *Top SQL* section has useful information. The *Top SQL* is listed by *Elapsed Time*, *CPU Time*, *Logical and Physical Reads*, and *Executions*. Look carefully through these queries for anything usual. A short running query that has a high amount of executions can result in noticeable performance problems. A query with a high amount of logical reads may benefit from tuning.

The *Top Objects* section shows objects with the most physical and logical reads. This section helps to identify objects that might need more frequent statistic collections. It can also identify objects that could benefit from creating additional indexes or even implementing partitioning if you have that option.

There are many other useful sections in the report. Additional sections include memory advisors that identify hit ratios in the buffer cache and usage information for the shared pool and PGA. There are also important OS statistics collected as well as latch and detailed wait information in the database.

Analyzing SQL Statements in Oracle11g

Oracle provides some additional tools for analyzing SQL statements beyond generating trace files. These tools may be used for tuning custom code as well as identifying issues with Oracle provided code. These tools are part of the Database Tuning Pack with Oracle Enterprise Manager Grid Control.

SQL Tuning Advisor

Along with the automatic database analysis tools introduced in Oracle10g, there is a *SQL Tuning Advisor* (STA) whose purpose is to automate the SQL tuning process. The STA will analyze SQL statements for areas of improvement, looking for the same issues that the DBA would look for manually. Problems such as stale statistics, poor execution paths, and poorly structured SQL statements will be identified by the automatic analysis.

The report can be manually generated. This process is described in *My Oracle Support Article ID 262687.1*. The following is an example of creating a SQL Tuning Advisor report:

```
SQL>DECLARE
 2 my_sql_task varchar2(100);
 3 BEGIN
 4 my_sql_task := dbms_sqltune.create_tuning_task(
     sql_text=> 'select * from emp where emp_id=101',
     scope =>DBMS_SQLTUNE.scope_comprehensive,
     time_limit => 60,
     task_name => 'tune_emp',
     description => 'Task to tune a query on the EMP table');
 5 END;
 6 /

SQL>exec dbms_sqltune.execute_tuning_task (task_name => 'tune_emp')

SQL>select dbms_sqltune.report_tuning_task('tune_emp') from dual;
```

The output of the tuning report may include recommendations such as analyzing the emp table if the statistics are invalid.

▶ **Note**　　The user executing the report must be granted the ADVISOR privilege.

SQL Access Advisor

While STA is useful for tuning individual SQL statements, there is often a need to tune multiple queries. This tuning effort is possible through the use of the *SQL Access Advisor* (SAA). The SAA tool will analyze multiple statements and recommend the creation of objects such as indexes and materialized views to improve the overall performance of the queries. The group of queries to be tuned is called a SQL Tuning Set (STS).

Running SAA is a simple process if you use the EM Database Tuning Pack. A description of manually running the SAA is provided in *My Oracle Support Article ID 259188.1.*

Using EM Grid Control's Database Tuning Pack

The tuning process can be made quite a bit easier with the Database Tuning Pack . This pack contains some of the SQL tuning features previously covered, along with other SQL monitoring and object reorganizing tools.

The key features of the Database Tuning Pack include the following items: *SQL Tuning Advisor*, *Automatic SQL Tuning Advisor*, *Real Time SQL Monitoring, SQL Profiles, SQL Access Advisor, SQL Tuning Sets,* and *Object Reorganization Wizard.* These features serve to make the Oracle Applications DBA's job easier.

The Database Tuning Pack provides improvements in the ability to find and tune long running SQL statements with the *Real Time SQL Monitoring.* The *Object Reorganization Wizard* can improve system performance by rebuilding fragmented objects.

If you have purchased this pack, spend plenty of time reviewing these features in a test instance. When you have developed a comfort level with the features, you can use them to easily and quickly resolve performance issues.

Client Tuning

Tuning the client machines involves several key areas. This section will cover resources on the client machines as well as best practices for exiting sessions.

Resource Utilization

Inadequate resources on the workstation often cause performance degradation on the client. You should review client recommendations for the version of the Applications that is running in your company. Recommended client configuration for R12 can be found in *My Oracle*

Support Article ID 798258.1. Usually, upgrading memory will gain more benefit than upgrading CPUs.

To help manage memory requirements, it is a good idea to promote usage standards among Oracle EBS users. Minimize the number of other Applications running at the same time as the E-Business Suite. These other Applications will consume resources needed by the Forms sessions.

Minimize customizations to the user workstation. High resolution wallpaper, internet browser toolbars and plug-ins can all be consumers of resources that would be better spent servicing business applications.

Generating Trace Files

When performance tuning it can be helpful to generate trace files to review details of what is happening within the system during a given time. In order to not impact other areas of the system, any extra logging should be turned off as soon as possible. If issues can be reproduced in a test environment, then the trace files should be generated from that location. Additional details on generating trace files can be found in Chapter 6 of this guide.

My Oracle Support Article ID 357597.1 includes details on how to enable SQL tracing for web applications. This information can be reviewed by the Oracle Applications DBA or provided to Oracle Support if a Service Request has been logged for a performance issue.

Exiting Client Sessions Properly

When users are finished with their session, it is important for them to properly exit the application. This does not mean just closing their open window, but actually logging out of the application.

Sessions that remain open will eventually time out of the application. The system will have to spend some time freeing the resources used by client sessions. Any unexpected behavior on the application tier could result in memory leaks or runaway CPU consumption.

Another danger to leaving sessions open is that the open session could still have locks on objects in the database. Depending on the modules being used, these locks could result in blocking sessions for other forms sessions or for concurrent requests.

Using the Client System Analyzer

Performance issues on the client can be diagnosed using the Client System Analyzer tool provided by Oracle. The Client System Analyzer is executed from any form by navigating to the *Help* → *Diagnostics Menu* → *Client System Analyzer*. After selecting these menu options, the Client System Analyzer applet and a compatible Java Virtual Machine (JVM) will be downloaded. The Client System Analyzer is displayed in Figure 7-14.

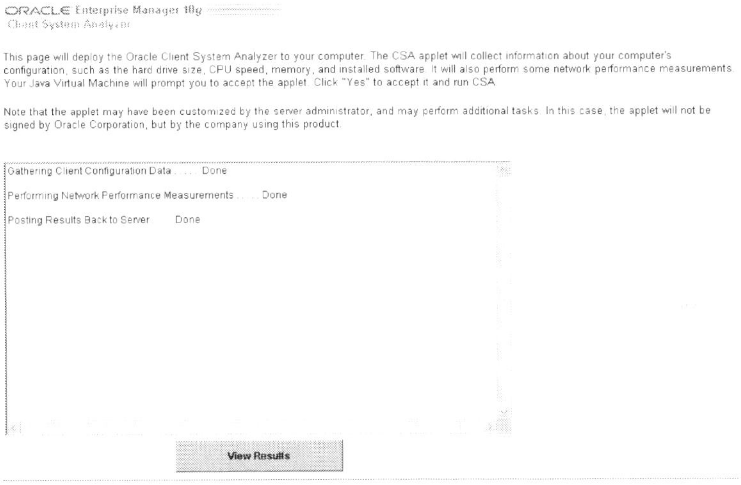

ORACLE Enterprise Manager 10g
Client System Analyzer

This page will deploy the Oracle Client System Analyzer to your computer. The CSA applet will collect information about your computer's configuration, such as the hard drive size, CPU speed, memory, and installed software. It will also perform some network performance measurements. Your Java Virtual Machine will prompt you to accept the applet. Click "Yes" to accept it and run CSA.

Note that the applet may have been customized by the server administrator, and may perform additional tasks. In this case, the applet will not be signed by Oracle Corporation, but by the company using this product.

Gathering Client Configuration Data . . . . Done

Performing Network Performance Measurements . . . . Done

Posting Results Back to Server   Done

View Results

Figure 7-14. *Client System Analyzer*

This tool will collect CPU, memory, operating system, and other relevant workstation information. To view the results of the analysis, click the *View Results* button.

Manually Analyzing the Client

If the Client System Analyzer is unavailable for your use, many of the steps can be performed manually. Being able to perform some basic analysis of the client machine will be useful as performance issues arise.

Some of the key areas where client systems may encounter resource constraints are memory and CPU usage, and data on this usage can be obtained for the client using *Windows Task Manager*. Pressing the *Ctrl*, *Alt*, and *Del* keys simultaneously will allow you to initiate the Windows Task Manager. Select the *Performance* tab to display CPU usage and memory usage charts, as shown in Figure 7-15. Note that the exact display may vary depending on the version of Windows used by the client.

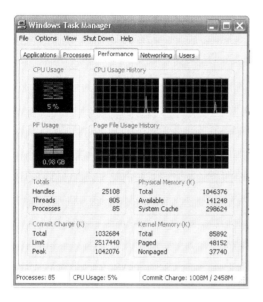

Figure 7-15. *The Performance tab of Windows Task Manager*

If either chart shows excessive usage, select the *Processes* tab to view running processes. This display can be sorted by the *CPU* or *Mem Usage* columns in order to identify resource intensive processes. For example, this investigation could show a virus scanning utility consuming high amounts of CPU that results in client level performance problems running Oracle Applications Forms.

Network Latency

Network performance issues can have a significant impact on the entire system. Detailed information on network tuning is out of scope for this book; however, some basic information will be reviewed.

A key metric to review with network performance tuning is network latency. Network latency is a measure of the communication speed between different nodes. The E-Business Suite Applications requires a lot of communication between the database and Applications nodes. Given this behavior, it is important to have a high speed connection between the nodes. Latency between the nodes should be less than 3ms.

The ping command can be used to measure latency. From an Applications node you can ping the Database Node to view latency. If the latency is high, engage your network team to help resolve the issue.

$UNIX>ping vis.domain.com

```
PING vis.domain.com (192.168.20.1) 56(84) bytes of data.
64 bytes from vis.domain.com (192.168.20.1): icmp_seq=1 ttl=64 time=0.125 ms
64 bytes from vis.domain.com (192.168.20.1): icmp_seq=2 ttl=64 time=0.117 ms
64 bytes from vis.domain.com (192.168.20.1): icmp_seq=3 ttl=64 time=0.132 ms

--- vis.domain.com ping statistics ---
3 packets transmitted, 3 received, 0% packet loss, time 1999ms
rtt min/avg/max/mdev = 0.117/0.124/0.132/0.014 ms
```

Oracle Application Server Web Cache can be used to bypass some of the network traffic. The features of caching and compression can help reduce this traffic. *My Oracle Support Article ID 380486.1* includes numerous details on installing and configuring Oracle Application Server Web Cache

Additional Tuning Considerations

There are additional Applications profiles that may affect the performance of the application. Some of these profiles affect the behavior of the application, while others are diagnostic and logging settings. For additional detail about profile options that impact Oracle Applications Framework, review *My Oracle Support Article ID 395445.1*. Some profile options to review are outlined in Table 7-12.

Table 7-12. *Additional Profile Options to Consider for Performance Tuning*

Profile	Recommended Value	Description
ICX: Match case view	checked or hidden	This profile option controls queries that would disable indexes with the upper clause in an advanced search. The default value of unchecked allows for poor performing queries due to unused indexes.

Table 7-12. *Continued*

Profile	Recommended Value	Description
FND: Diagnostics	No	This profile option controls whether users are able to turn on global diagnostics. This should be disabled for performance and security reasons.
FND: Debug Log Module	%	This profile may be used to set logging for a specific application. If FND: Debug Log Level is set to STATEMENT, you must set this profile to a specific module; otherwise logging will cause severe performance degradation.
FND: Debug Log Enabled	Yes	This profile can enable or disable debug logging. When set in conjunction with the FND: Debug Log Level profile, this profile controls if information is logged.
FND: Debug Log Level	UNEXPECTED	This profile will write errors that occur in the Applications in the log file. When set to UNEXPECTED, only errors that require administrator assistance to resolve will be logged. Other values for this profile include STATEMENT, PROCEDURE, EVENT, EXCEPTION, and ERROR. When set in conjunction with the FND: Debug Log Enabled profile, this profile controls the amount of information that is logged.

Performance Tuning Best Practices

For overall Applications health, it is important to stay current with patches and upgrades for the Technology Stack components. Often, patches and later versions of the Technology Stack include performance improvements, as well as additional configuration options. The Oracle Applications DBA should monitor and apply current releases for the ATG Product Family. Oracle provides *My Oracle Support Article ID 244040.1* which includes recommended patches to improve performance. You should make it a habit to periodically monitor this article for updates that will assist with improving performance of your environment.

Performance problems are often the result of preventative maintenance tasks not being performed. Key preventative maintenance tasks include generating statistics, recompiling invalid objects and regularly purging data. Make certain that all required preventative maintenance is properly executed.

The Oracle Applications DBA should work with the user community to identify commonly used modules. Document typical execution timings for the functionality of all commonly used modules. These timings should be reviewed and updated when patches specific to that module are applied to the application. This level of documentation will provide a baseline of performance expectations for the application. Capturing AWR baselines for key time periods will also assist with this effort.

Load testing is critical for the success of any application. Load tests provide an environment that will simulate production and determine whether additional resources are necessary in order to meet business requirements. Load tests should be implemented when upgrading, applying patches that change the underlying Technology Stack components, and implementing new functionality.

While resolving performance issues, it is often necessary to work with Oracle Support and Development. When doing so, provide all applicable reports (ASH, AWR, and/or trace files) in addition to other statistics that have been collected. Also, provide a detailed description of the performance degradation that is being experienced, including screen shots of the process if applicable. All of this information will assist Oracle in resolving the issue. Although rare, it may be necessary for Oracle to release a one-off performance patch for the issue being experienced. It is advisable to log an SR when the performance issue is first experienced in order to expedite resolution from Oracle if an underlying code change is required.

▓ Chapter 8 ▓

Resources

There are a variety of resources available to Oracle Applications DBAs that can be utilized to expand your knowledge and provide support for your day-to-day tasks as well as offer guidance for providing strategic initiatives. The resources that will be discussed in this chapter are as follows:

* **Oracle Support**: This section will look at *My Oracle Support*, Oracle Support's web site, and cover searching for information in *Knowledge Base* articles, reviewing product and operating system platform certification combinations, and the various aspects of Oracle Service Requests.

* **User communities and conferences**: This section will outline the key user groups and conferences for Oracle Applications DBAs.

* **Online resources**: This section will outline additional online resources of interest to Oracle Applications DBAs.

* **Books and periodicals**: This section will offer tips for finding additional printed materials covering topics of interest for the Oracle Applications DBA.

▶ *Tip*   Oracle rebranded and redeployed a new support site in 2009. Oracle's new support site is called *My Oracle Support*. It can be accessed by using the following URL: https://support.oracle.com. The former Oracle Support site was called MetaLink. Its URL was http://metalink.oracle.com. If you access the former URL, you will be redirected to the new URL and the new support site.

Working with Oracle Support

Managing the E-Business Suite includes interacting with Oracle Support. The main interface to Oracle Support is its web site which is called *My Oracle Support*. The *My Oracle Support* site is one of the most important resources for an Oracle Applications DBA. The site is Oracle's primary location for information about all Oracle product support, including the E-Business Suite.

On *My Oracle Support*, you can search Oracle's *Notes*, *Bulletins*, *Alerts*, *Bug Database*, and *User Forums*. *My Oracle Support* is also the site for managing Service Requests (SRs) and downloading patches for Oracle products. Your ability to use all the features available on *My Oracle Support* depends on the privileges that have been granted to your *My Oracle Support* account.

My Oracle Support

The most common use of *My Oracle Support* is as a technical repository. Searching *My Oracle Support* is the best starting point for finding information on a specific topic such as an error message or a general question. This section will cover basic searches, advanced searches, and tips for locating information on E-Business Suite, reviewing certification matrices, and downloading patches.

▶ *Tip*   *My Oracle Support* requires you install the Flash plug-in for your browser. If you do not want to use the features provided by the Flash plug-in, you can access a non-Flash version of *My Oracle Support* with the following URL: https://supporthtml.oracle.com.

Dashboard

Upon logging in to *My Oracle Support*, you will be presented with the *Dashboard* screen, as shown in Figure 8-1.

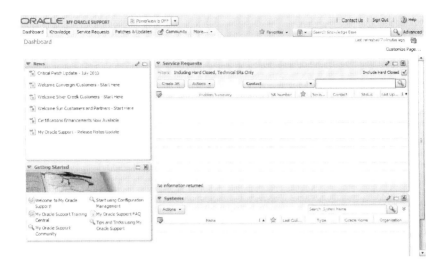

Figure 8-1. *An example of My Oracle Support's Dashboard*

The *Dashboard* is made up of several regions that display information and contain a wide range of functionality. While Oracle supplies a default set of regions, you can customize the page by changing which regions are displayed on the page. You can also customize many of the individual regions by modifying the layout or the number of rows displayed.

One of the default regions is the *Getting Started* region. This region provides information that is beneficial to the new user of *My Oracle Support*. Among other items located in the *Getting Started* region are details around using *Configuration Management*, tips for using *My Oracle Support* and links to *My Oracle Support Community* and *My Oracle Support Training Central*.

The *Dashboard* can be customized by clicking the *Customize Page* link at the top right of the page. After clicking *Customize Page*, a list of regions will be shown that can be placed on the page. To place a region on a page, simply drag the region from the list to a location on the page. Duplicate regions can be placed on the same page.

Many individual regions can be customized as well. A region with the table icon can have its display altered to show or hide specific columns and to group the data. In addition, the table icon can be used to save the region's information to the clipboard or a file.

Knowledge Home

The *Knowledge Home* provides multiple methods of accessing the *Knowledge Base*. Like the *Dashboard*, the *Knowledge Home* is a customizable page where the user can add or remove regions and modify some display attributes of the region. This is an excellent page from which to begin searching or browsing the *Knowledge Base*.

Browse Knowledge

The *Browse Knowledge* region allows you to browse through the *Knowledge Base*. If the desired product is known, you can type the name of the product in the search box. As an alternative, you can refine your browsing criteria by drilling down through the menu options. Of particular interest to the Oracle E-Business Suite administrator are the *Oracle Database Products* and *Oracle E-Business Suite* menu options. The following section will describe the key components of the *Browse Knowledge* region.

Knowledge Articles

The *Knowledge Articles* region has two tabs for browsing knowledge articles. In addition, customizing the region and specifying a specific product to which the articles must pertain can refine the listing of articles shown in this region. The tabs for this region are as follows:

* *Alerts*: This tab displays knowledge articles that may contain information of immediate importance to your systems.

* *Recently Updated*: This tab displays knowledge articles that have recently been updated.

Recent Activity

The *Recent Activity* region of the page displays information in which the user has expressed an interest. The region uses three tabs to communicate this information:

* *Recently Viewed*: This tab displays the most recent articles you have viewed. Links to the articles are displayed in the order they were viewed with the most recently viewed article being listed at the top.

* *Recent Searches*: This tab displays the most recent searches you have performed. The searches can be rerun from this tab by clicking on the search term. The searches are displayed in the order they were run with the most recent search being listed at the top.

* *Favorite Articles*: This tab displays articles that you have designated as being favorites. An article can be marked as a favorite by clicking the star icon at the top of the article. Favorites are listed in the order they were marked with the most recently marked being listed at the top.

In the Knowledge

The *In the Knowledge* region details new information that may be of interest to users of the *Knowledge Base*. You can view this region for information on subjects such as upcoming webcasts or new features of *My Oracle Support* that will assist you.

Search Knowledge Base

The *Search Knowledge Base* feature is immediately available upon connecting to *My Oracle Support*. To initiate a global search, type a search string in the text box located at the top right of the screen. Click the *search* icon to view the results. Sample output from a search for information about ORA-600 errors is shown in Figure 8-2.

Figure 8-2. *An example of My Oracle Support's basic search*

Advanced Searches

If the results returned from the *Search Knowledge Base* feature are insufficient, or you want to limit the result set, you can refine your search using two different methods. These methods are using the *Advanced Search* feature or using the *Refine Search* region of the results page.

The *Advanced Search* feature can be accessed by clicking the *Sources* icon to the left of your search and then selecting Advanced Search. Within the *Advanced Search* feature, you can customize your search to return a more focused result group. For example, if you want your search to include the *Knowledge Base Archives*, you could select that option in the source criteria. Other options found in the *Advanced Search* screen include a variety of text fields for refining the search parameters. The *Advanced Search* screen is displayed in Figure 8-3.

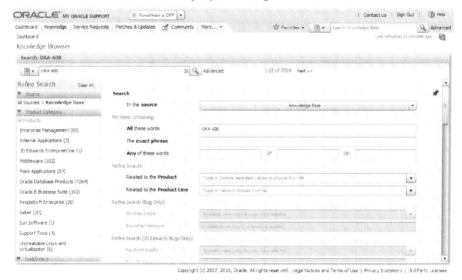

Figure 8-3. *The Advanced Search Screen from My Oracle Support*

In addition to the *Advanced Search* feature, you may also use the *Refine Search* region of your results page to limit your search. The *Refine Search* region is a collection of predefined filters that can be applied to an existing search. For example, after conducting a search, you could limit your results to just the Oracle E-Business Suite Product Category.

Certification Matrix

Information related to product availability and about certification for different platforms and versions can be obtained from the *Certification Matrix*. Selecting the *More* tab followed by selecting the *Certifications* link on *My Oracle Support* will allow you to access this feature.

Certification information may be searched by the criteria in the *Find Certification Information* region on the *Certification Information* page, as shown in Figure 8-4. Additional information regarding the certification matrix can be found in *My Oracle Support Article ID 763087.5*.

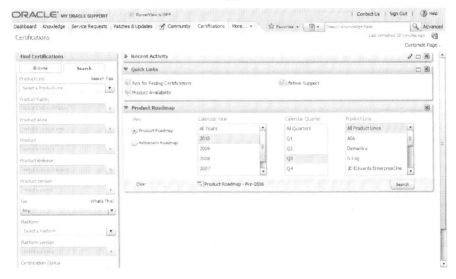

Figure 8-4. *The Find Certification Information region on My Oracle Support*

▶ *Tip*   Prior to performing any Technology Stack component upgrade, the certification matrix on *My Oracle Support* should be reviewed. Ensure that the versions for the products to be upgraded are certified for your operating system.

Locating and Downloading Patches

My Oracle Support is the source for downloading patches for the Oracle E-Business Suite components. The *Patch Search* region of the *Patches & Updates* tab is the most direct path to search for patches. There are three tabs in the *Patch Search* region:

* *Oracle, Siebel and Hyperion*: This tab allows you to search for patches using either the Patch ID when you know a specific patch number or an advanced search using Product or Family information.

* *Saved*: This tab shows you searches that you have saved and allows you to execute them again.

*   *Recent*: This tab shows you searches that you have recently performed and allows you to execute them again.

   The *Patching Quick Links* region has additional methods of locating patches for your environment. These methods include:

*   *Recommended R12 Patches*: This option will allow you to search for E-Business patches by Maintenance Release, Product or Product Family, Platform or Language, or Updated Date.

*   *Latest R12 Packs*: This option will take you to the latest patches available for the E-Business Suite.

*   *E-Business Suite* (Under *Software* and *Patch Sites*): This option will take you to an advanced screen that will allow you to search by the criteria shown in Figure 8-5.

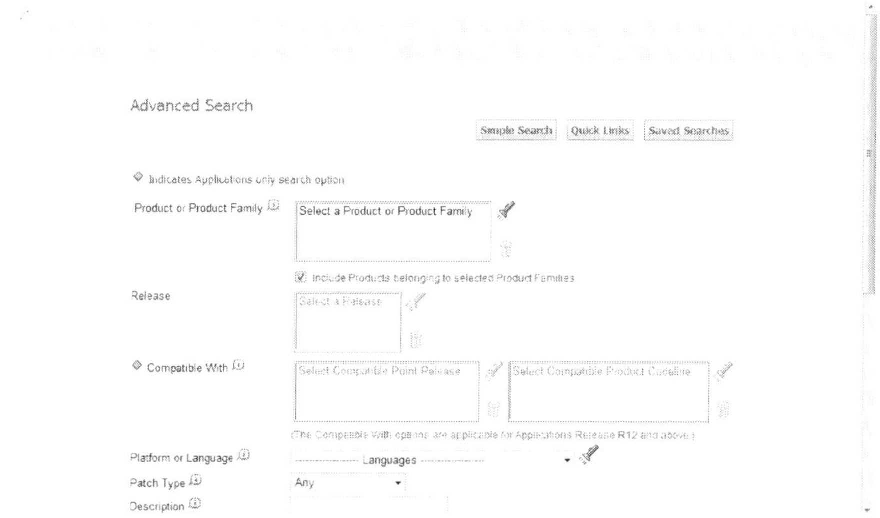

Figure 8-5. *The Advanced Search screen on My Oracle Support*

▶ *Tip*   Patches frequently become obsolete or are superseded. Information regarding obsolete or superseded patches is automatically displayed when you search for a patch. When researching which patches you should apply, you should consider replacing obsolete or superseded patches with their new patch replacement.

Oracle Support Service Requests

Management of the E-Business Suite may often require you to obtain assistance from Oracle Support. Due to the complexity of the applications, customers are frequently required to initiate Service Requests (SRs). The overall performance and availability of your Applications can be improved by effectively managing the SR process. This section will enhance your understanding of the SR process by outlining tips for opening and managing SRs.

Details for an SR

Prior to opening an SR, gather as much information as possible regarding your environment and the problem being experienced. At a minimum, you should have a one sentence description of the problem, and any applicable error codes and messages that are generated. Any additional information that you can provide will assist in expediting SR resolution. For example, you should consider running provided diagnostics utilities, generating trace files, or setting debugging levels to capture additional information for Oracle Support. The captured information can be uploaded to the SR when it is opened, or at any time after the SR is created. For ease of transmission, multiple files should be zipped prior to uploading to Oracle Support.

It is possible to have some of the information required for an SR filled in for you by using the *Configuration Manager*. The Configuration Manager is a program that runs inside your ORACLE_HOME which collects system configuration information and uploads that information to Oracle. This typically runs on a daily basis and sends only updated configuration information. When opening an SR, you will have the option to AutoFill information using a specific configuration which has been uploaded. You do this by selecting the *System/Configuration* radio button in the SR creation screen and selecting the desired configuration from the drop down list. Using Configuration Manager is beneficial as it eases the process of opening SRs. It prevents the possibility of posting inaccurate information in the SR and eliminates the need to post duplicate information for multiple SRs for the same environment. It also gives Oracle information about your environment that support may otherwise have to ask you to collect during the working of your SR, thereby reducing the time required for SR resolution.

Each registered *My Oracle Support* user is associated with at least one Customer Support Identifier (CSI). The CSI allows Oracle Support to track the customer's support and licensing information. Many organizations have multiple CSI numbers.

SR Severity Level

When an SR is created, it is assigned a severity level. Prior to opening an SR, you should determine the severity level the request should be assigned. This severity level will provide Oracle Support with a notion of the importance of the problem. The severity level of an SR may be modified throughout its life. An explanation of how to modify the severity level of an SR will be provided later in this section. The following describes the four severity levels (SEVs) for SRs:

* **Severity 1**: Complete loss of service for production or mission critical applications

* **Escalated Severity 2**: Partial loss of service that will be worked continuously during business hours

* **Severity 2**: Partial loss of service

* **Severity 3**: Minor loss of service

* **Severity 4**: No loss of service

When a Severity 1 SR is created, or when an existing SR has its severity level raised to Severity 1, the customer must provide contact information for primary and secondary contacts as well as a management contact. A business justification must also be provided for a Severity 1 SR. As such, Severity 1 SRs should be reserved for true emergencies. Severity 1 SRs require 24x7 attention and work from the customer as well as Oracle Support.

Creating an SR

In the *Service Requests* region on the *Dashboard* or *Service Requests* page there is a *Create SR* button which will begin the SR creation process. This button will open a page with a series of regions requesting information for the SR. As mentioned previously, you may AutoFill your configuration information at this point. You will also be required to enter a CSI number. If your company has multiple CSI numbers, be certain to associate the SR with the appropriate one. You may also save a profile with basic SR information such as Product, Platform and Database Version. SR profiles may be selected upon SR creation.

Subsequent regions will prompt you for a description of the problem as well as related configuration and log files. You can easily go back to previous regions by clicking on the appropriate region to change previously entered data. The SR can be tracked by the number it is assigned upon creation. SRs should be created as soon as it is determined that the issue cannot be resolved without the assistance of Oracle Support. Postponing the creation of an SR will only result in delaying resolution.

Managing an SR

This section will provide some guidance to efficiently working with Oracle Support once an SR has been created.

Searching SRs

If multiple Service Requests have been logged, it may be difficult to locate a particular SR created by yourself or another user. Finding a specific SR is often necessary if a user has asked for your assistance or if you need to find a problem resolution that is documented in a closed SR. To search for a specific SR, navigate to the Service Request region. SRs may be searched and sorted with the following options:

*   **Contact**: This will return all SRs created by a specific user. A partial string may be entered in the search box to match multiple users.

*   **Problem Summary**: This will return all SRs whose problem summary matches the string entered in the search box. A partial string may be entered to match multiple problem summaries.

*   **Severity**: This will return all SRs for the selected severity; the options are 1, 2, 3 or 4.

*   **SR Number**: This will return a specific SR.

After executing the search, the result list of SRs may be sorted by clicking on any of the column headings. The following column headings are displayed by default:

*   Problem Summary

*   SR Number

*   Favorite (Represented by star icon)

* Severity

* Contact

* Status

* Last Updated

Updating SRs

The status of the SR will determine whether you need to perform any actions. For example, if the status is set to Work in Progress, it is on Oracle Support to provide the next update. If the SR is at a status such as Customer Working, the customer is required to give an update.

Provide timely updates in order to expedite issue resolution. Typical customer requests include providing configuration, trace, or log files, running scripts, applying a patch, or modifying the configuration.

Escalating an SR

If you feel that your SR is not receiving appropriate attention, you can update it and request an updated action plan from the analyst. The next level of escalation would be to request that a duty manager contact you in order to discuss the SR.

The fastest and Oracle recommended way to escalate an SR is to phone in the request, and to follow the phone call up with a posting to the SR. If you only update the SR through the *My Oracle Support* web site, it could be a few days before your SR is reviewed and you are contacted. SRs should only be escalated if the issue is severe enough to warrant such action. Overusing or misusing escalation features does not provide any benefit to the customer. Working with Oracle Support, or any other organization's support staff, is a collaborative process. By providing timely and accurate updates, you help ensure that your issues are resolved as quickly as possible.

Escalating an SR does not raise the severity level of the SR. If you need to change the severity level, update the SR with a request to raise the severity level, or phone in a request. Raising the severity level of an SR may be necessary if there has been a major status change related to the SR subject, such as a project due date being altered. Additional details for effectively working with Oracle Support are outlined in *My Oracle Support Article ID 166650.1.*

Description of Codes Found in SRs

SRs are frequently updated with different status codes or bug codes. If development is involved in the Support process, bug codes are provided in the status of the SR.

A description of SR status codes can be found in the Table A-1 in the appendix in this guide and in *My Oracle Support Article ID 166650.1*. A description of the bug codes can be found in Table A-2 in the appendix in this guide and in *My Oracle Support Article ID 733245.5*.

Requesting an Oracle Support Web Conference

Service Requests that are not making sufficient progress towards resolution or are difficult to communicate in the context of the online SR may benefit from using Oracle Collaborative Support. This feature allows the analyst from Oracle to establish a web conference with you. By doing this, they are able to see your desktop while you reproduce an error. Oracle Collaborative Support may be initiated at the request of either Oracle or the customer.

Collaborative Support is also useful when the analyst has numerous troubleshooting steps that would require a great deal of communication and time to work through. The analyst can observe as the steps are performed and provide you with immediate feedback rather than waiting for SR updates.

Phoning Oracle Support

Due to the vast number of features available online, it is rare that Support is contacted by phone. However, in the event that this is required, the US number for contacting Oracle Support is 1-800-223-1711. For international numbers, please refer to the *Support* → *Global Support Contacts* menu on http://www.oracle.com. Have your SR number ready when you call. Calling Oracle Support is also recommended when escalating an SR or when a duty manager is requested for call back.

Closing an SR

Finally, when an SR has been resolved by the client or with the help of the analyst, you can close the SR by selecting the Close option from the *Actions* button on the SR detail screen. This will remove the SR from the list of active SRs, thereby allowing the analysts to work on other issues. When closing the SR, an optional input text box for entering resolution details will be displayed. It is beneficial for Support to know the steps that resolved the issue.

My Oracle Support Training Center

For additional information on getting the most out of *My Oracle Support*, you can visit the *My Oracle Support* Training Center. This is most easily accessed by clicking the *My Oracle Support* Training Center link in the Getting Started region of the Dashboard. The Training Center offers both live webcasts and recorded training on the use of *My Oracle Support*. Topics range from Dashboard customization to installing and utilizing the Configuration Manager.

User Communities and Conferences

There is an extensive user community for Oracle Applications and Oracle Technologies. You can use these resources as a source of information and assistance. Sometimes it is valuable to have feedback from people outside of Oracle.

User Groups

There are two major user groups for Oracle Applications and Oracle Technologies: the Oracle Applications Users Group (OAUG) and the Independent Oracle Users Group (IOUG). A description of the OAUG and IOUG is provided in the following section.

Oracle Applications Users Group

The OAUG was founded in 1990 with the stated mission of representing the interests of Oracle Applications users worldwide in securing the optimum use and ongoing development of the Oracle Applications products. Membership in the OAUG provides the Oracle Applications DBA with a wealth of information related to that role. In addition to the existing content found on the OAUG web site, http://www.oaug.org, there are numerous educational opportunities. The web site also contains details regarding membership dues.

The OAUG consists of numerous Special Interest Groups (SIGs) and Geographic User Groups (GEOs). The list of SIGs and GEOs is maintained on the OAUG web site. Review the list of SIGs for groups related to your interests. For Oracle Applications DBAs, the Database and

E-Business Applications Technology SIGs are good sources of technical Oracle E-Business Suite information. Other SIGs that might be applicable to your interests include product specific SIGs. Look for GEOs close to your location for opportunities to interact with regional colleagues.

SIGs and GEOs modify their scope frequently, so you should periodically review their availability. It is not a requirement to be a member of the OAUG in order to join a SIG or GEO. You may register as a SIG member on its web site. Many of the SIGs maintain list servers or discussion boards. Additional services provided by the SIGs can be found on their respective web sites.

Independent Oracle Users Group

The IOUG is a user group dedicated to technical users of Oracle Database. The focus of this user group includes education, networking, and advocacy. Unlike the OAUG, the IOUG is not focused on Oracle Applications. The IOUG contains many excellent services that the Oracle Applications DBA can utilize for Applications Technology Stack components.

As with the OAUG, there are many regional groups (RUGs) that provide excellent networking opportunities. These RUGs can be found from the main IOUG web site, http://www.ioug.org. In addition to the regional groups and other networking opportunities, the IOUG provides extensive technical reference material within its Technical Repository. Book reviews, monthly tips, and links to online resources are also available from the IOUG web site.

Conferences

Conferences are an excellent source of information for Oracle Applications DBAs. In addition to the sessions, there are numerous keynote addresses that provide insight into the future direction of the products. Of even more value is the opportunity to network with other professionals involved with the E-Business Suite.

COLLABORATE

The *COLLABORATE* conference is an Oracle User Group conference consisting of the OAUG, IOUG, and Quest International Users Group. These groups have combined their yearly conferences to better serve their user communities. The conference includes SIG sponsored meetings and sessions along with general sessions and key note addresses. The combined conference will cover a wide variety of material for Oracle Applications DBAs and functional users of the E-Business Suite.

Oracle OpenWorld

The *Oracle OpenWorld* (OOW) conference is the largest annual Oracle conference. OpenWorld includes topics related to Oracle Applications, Oracle middleware, and Oracle Databases, among other subjects.

OOW may be even better known for the numerous keynote sessions provided by the leaders of the technological community. These keynotes include a regular address from Larry Ellison on the future direction of the corporation. The conference also includes a demonstration area where the Oracle Applications DBA can see demos of Oracle products and vendor products that can assist in the management of Oracle systems.

Online Resources

This section will cover some of the additional web based resources available to the Oracle Applications DBA. This information can help you expand your skill sets.

Oracle Web Sites

Over time, the Oracle Applications DBA may become so accustomed to using the *My Oracle Support* site that the features available from Oracle's corporate site, the *Oracle Technology Network* (OTN) and other Oracle maintained web site are overlooked.

The main corporate site of Oracle Corporation, http://www.oracle.com, provides a wealth of information regarding Oracle products. The material is not limited to product information, but also includes customer case studies, market data, and corporate data. Additionally, web seminars, also called webinars, describing new products or new features of existing products are readily available.

Additional technical information can be obtained by accessing the OTN web site, http://www.oracle.com/technology. Membership to the OTN web site is free. The site is a great source for detailed information about products and features. From this site, users can download products and any required documentation for testing. OTN also provides numerous articles, sample code, and discussion forums, among other resources.

Another site maintained by Oracle is the *Oracle Learning Library*. The Oracle Learning Library provides Oracle by Example (OBE) tutorials and demos. Search utilities are available on the site to find specific examples of using Oracle products including the Oracle E-Business Suite. The Oracle Learning Library web site can be accessed with the following URL:

http://apex.oracle.com/pls/apex/f?p=OTNCR:1:0

Some Oracle employees have blogs which they use to communicate information concerning their area of expertise. One such blog that you should be aware of is written by Steven Chan, a Senior Director in the Oracle Applications Technology Group. Steven's blog can be found at http://blogs.oracle.com/stevenChan. A complete list of Oracle blogs may be found at http://wiki.oracle.com/page/List+of+Oracle-related+blogs.

The Oracle Applications Technology Group (ATG) publishes the ATG newsletter which can include tips, recommended reading and other useful information for the Oracle Applications DBA. To view past newsletters or to subscribe, go to *My Oracle Support Article ID 378287.1*.

Additional Community Resources

In addition to the well defined user groups and official Oracle web site, there is the broader Oracle community. A lot of useful information can be found through these resources. Using Yahoo, Google, or other web search engines, an Oracle Applications DBA can find additional information portals.

Many of the web sites that turn up in such searches are companies that post white papers or presentations on their main site. These may include consulting companies interested in providing such information as a means of advertising. Other results may be personal pages of Oracle professionals who are interested in sharing their knowledge with other users. Some consulting companies have regular newsletters that they release on a monthly or quarterly basis, and these newsletters often contain documentation, tips, and other information that you may find useful.

Another unofficial means of sharing information with like-minded professionals is through mailing lists, online forums, or newsgroups. Rather than opening a level 4 SR, an Oracle Applications DBA may post a message on a forum seeking responses to a question.

> ▶ **Caution**   Any information found through forums or personal web page searches should be treated with appropriate caution. Thoroughly test any scripts or commands that come from such sources. You should develop a full understanding of any actions recommended by these sources prior to testing.

Books and Periodicals

Even though there is a great deal of reference material online, there is no replacement for the portability and usability of a good book or magazine. Within the Oracle community, there is a large amount of literature available for Oracle Applications DBAs.

Books

An Oracle Applications DBA's library should not only include books related to Oracle but also books on other components of the Technology Stack. A good scripting book can be very useful for Oracle Applications DBAs with systems running on the Linux environment. The following is a list of recommended books for an Oracle Applications DBA:

* *Oracle PL/SQL Programming: Covers Versions Through Oracle Database 11g Release 2 (Animal Guide)* by Steven Feuerstein, Bill Pribyl

* *Oracle Essentials: Oracle Database 11g* by Rick Greenwald, Robert Stackowiak, Jonathan Stern

* *Expert Oracle Database 11g Administration (Expert's Voice in Oracle)* by Sam R. Alapati

* *Oracle Data Guard 11g Handbook* by Larry Carpenter

* *Unix for Oracle DBAs Pocket Reference* by Donald Burleson

Periodicals

There are several periodicals an Oracle Applications DBA would be wise to subscribe to. These magazines contain regular feature articles that provide insight into the latest trends for Oracle Applications and Oracle

Database technology, and they should be regular reading for the Oracle Applications DBA. These are some of the common magazines:

* *Oracle Magazine*: A free Oracle publication. Current and archived issues of *Oracle Magazine* can be accessed online. A free subscription may also be requested from this site.

* *Profit*: A free Oracle Applications publication. Current and archived issues of *Profit* can be accessed online. A subscription may also be requested online.

* *SELECT*: An IOUG publication provided to IOUG members.

* *OAUG Insight*: An OAUG publication provided to OAUG members.

▶ **Tip**   Access the following URL for current and archived issues of *Oracle Magazine* and *Profit* and to subscribe: http://www.oracle.com/oramag/index.html.

In addition to providing insight into product direction, these periodicals include several articles and regular columns that provide tips and techniques for managing Oracle Applications Technology Stack components.

Resources Best Practices

It is important for the Oracle Applications DBA to actively participate in the user community. This is not limited to reading articles and attending conferences and user group meetings, although those activities are strongly encouraged. The value of user communities is created by the participation of its members.

You should look for opportunities to share your knowledge with colleagues and peers. Everyone has unique experiences that can benefit other professionals. Look for areas where you can contribute to this community. Write articles for the periodicals that you read on a regular basis. Develop presentations for conferences or for user group meetings you attend. Contribute to technical forums and newsgroups when possible. Volunteer your time with user groups. These organizations will benefit greatly from your input—both groups need assistance from experienced and dedicated professionals like you.

Appendix

Table A-1. *Oracle Service Request Status Codes*

Status	Owner	SubStatus	Description	Use
Open	Support	New	Initial setting	Set by system when SR is created
Open	Support	Work in progress	Support update pending	Set when the next action will be by Support
Open	Customer	Customer Working	Customer update pending	Set when the next action will be by the Customer
Open	Support	Review update	Support review required	Set when the SR Owner should review an update to the SR (from the Customer, an internal resource, etc.)
Open	Development	Development working	Development update pending	Set when the next action will be by Development
Open	Support	Awaiting internal response	Internal Oracle update pending	Set when the next action will be by an internal resource other than the SR Owner

Table A-1. *Continued*

Status	Owner	SubStatus	Description	Use
Open	Customer	Solution offered	Customer confirmation required	Set when a potential solution is provided to the Customer and awaiting their feedback; the 'Solution Implement Date' field must be set as well - this is the customer provided date for their evaluation to complete
Open	Support	Close initiated	Service Request closure initiated by Auto-Close process.	Set by system when the Auto-Close process completes without customer response; next step by SR Owner is generally to execute the closure process for the SR (refer to Closing a Technical SR for further details)
Open	Customer	Close requested	Service Request closure initiated by Customer on My Oracle Support.	Set by system when the Customer requests the SR be closed; next step by SR Owner is generally to execute the closure process for the SR (refer to Closing a Technical SR for further details)
Open	Support	Auto-close	Service Request Auto-Close process initiated	Set when the Customer has stopped responding on an SR (refer to Closing a Technical SR for further details)

Table A-1. *Continued*

Status	Owner	SubStatus	Description	Use
Open	Support	Review defect	Support review required	Set by system when the defect has been updated in the source defect system (ICE/SAR only)
Closed	N/A	Resolved with solution	Customer confirmed solution or works as expected	Customer confirms the solution works as expected
Closed	N/A	Resolved with workaround	Customer confirmed workaround	Customer confirms the workaround is acceptable
Closed	N/A	Customer abandoned	No response from customer	Customer fails to respond and the SR is closed per our policy (refer to Closing a Technical SR for further details)
Closed	N/A	No fault found	Unable to determine problem	Unable to determine problem; Customer error or misunderstanding of functionality
Closed	N/A	Enhance-ment request	Product enhancement required	Enhancement request is filed
Closed	N/A	Duplicate	Duplicate Service Request	Close the duplicate SR and work continues in main SR
Closed	N/A	Not Entitled	Customer not entitled to support	For non-technical SRs only; Used by Global Customer Hub

Table A-1. *Continued*

Status	Owner	SubStatus	Description	Use
Closed	N/A	Defect pending	Used when a severity 3/4 defect is filed and we close the SR with customer agreement to monitor the defect.	Used when a severity 3/4 defect is filed and we close the SR with customer agreement to monitor the defect.

Table A-2. *Oracle Bug Codes*

Status	Description	Usage
10	Description phase	Used to file a bug without all the needed information (for instance, trace files from the customer), to inform Development that a bug will soon become Status 11.
11	Code bug (Response/Resolution)	Used to indicate that the bug is ready for Development, or to indicate that additional required information has been provided for a Status 30 bug.
12	To external (user group) review	Used to send an enhancement to Oracle User Group review.
13	Documentation bug (Response/Resolution)	Used to request documentation enhancement.
14	Bug Assigned to Solution Partner	Used to keep track of bugs which are fixed by third party companies.
15	To Internal (Oracle) Review	Used to send an enhancement to Oracle's product managers.

Table A-2. *Continued*

Status	Description	Usage
16	Support bug screening	Used by BDE to pre-sort well-formed bugs before development start fixing.
19	Approved for User Group Voting	Used to include the enhancement in the report for the User Group.
20	To Requestor, Need More Information	Used to request more information from the filer.
21	Cost Required, To Development	Used to request a product enhancement cost estimate from product managers.
22	Approved for Future Release	Used to send an enhancement to product managers for scheduling.
23	Scheduled for Future Release	Used to send an enhancement to Development to be included in a release.
30	More information required. To filer.	Used to request more information from the bug filer.
31	Could Not Reproduce. To Filer.	Used to notify filer that bug cannot be reproduced.
32	Not a Bug. To Filer	Used to notify filer that bug was not valid.
33	Suspended, Required information not available.	Used to notify filer that the work has been suspended until information is received.
35	To Filer for Review	Used to request verification of the bug fix from bug filer.
36	Duplicate Bug. To Filer.	Used to notify filer that the bug is a duplicate.

Table A-2. *Continued*

Status	Description	Usage
37	To Filer for Review/Merge required	Used to request verification of the bug fix from bug filer and to request that integration merge the fix into the base code.
39	Approved, waiting for codeline to open	Used to indicate that a backport has been approved and is waiting for codeline to open. When the codeline is opened, status will be changed to 40.
40	Waiting for the base bug fix	Used to show that bug is waiting for another bug to be fixed.
43	Product/Platform, to Filer	Used to indicate that the bug will not be fixed and that filer should approve by updating the bug to Status 83: Closed, Product/Platform .
44	Not Feasible to fix, to Filer	Used to indicate that the bug will not be fixed and that filer should approve by updating the bug to Status 84: Closed, Not Feasible to Fix. (Use only when the product or platform is near the end of its lifecycle or when the fix would require a major re-write).
45	Vendor OS Problem, to Filer	Used when an operating system problem is the cause of the bug, to indicate that, following verification, the bug filer should update to Status 95.

Table A-2. *Continued*

Status	Description	Usage
51	Support approved backport - to Development.	Used to approve a backport (GPU=B). This status is reserved for use by Worldwide Support only.
52	Pending approval by product line	Used to approve a backport and to indicate that a porter can begin to work on the bug. This status is reserved for use by porting managers.
53	Backport/Patchset Request Rejected	Used to notify filer that the request to backport this bug is rejected.
60	CM: Awaiting Promotion	Configuration Management: Used to indicate that the fix has been developed and is awaiting promotion to the TEST environment.
66	CM: Awaiting Deployment	Configuration Management: Used to indicate that the fix has been tested and is awaiting a patch or release.
70	Closed, data fix, cause - user error	Applications: Used when the user performed an illegal operation, such as directly updating data using plsql. This includes bad data being populated by custom code. This caused the data to be inconsistent and required that the data be fixed using a data fix script.

Table A-2. *Continued*

Status	Description	Usage
71	Closed, data fix, cause - data import	Applications: Used when bad data was imported into the system, either through automated batch load, or as the result of data conversion during the installation of the product. This caused the data to be inconsistent and required that the data be fixed using a data fix script.
72	Closed, data fix, cause - code error	Applications: Used when bad data was populated into the database due to an error in Oracle supported software. This caused the data to be inconsistent and required that the data be fixed using a data fix script.
73	Closed, data fix, cause - unknown	Applications: Used when bad data was found to exist in the customer's database, which required that the data be fixed using a data fix script. The root cause was never determined.
74	Closed, Verified by QA	Applications: Used to close bugs verified by Quality Assurance team.
80	Development to Q/A	Used to indicate that a fix is available, but the code has not passed Quality Assurance.
81	Q/A to Dev/Patch or Workaround Available	Used to indicate that a patch or workaround is available, but the code has not passed Quality Assurance.

Table A-2. *Continued*

Status	Description	Usage
82	Q/A to Enhancement Evaluation	Used to indicate that a product enhancement has been implemented, but the code has not passed Quality Assurance.
83	Closed, Product/Platform	Used to close a bug that was not fixed because of product or platform obsolescence.
84	Closed, not feasible to fix	Used to close a bug that was not fixed because the fix was not feasible.
87	Fix verified/Merge Required	Used to indicate that the fix has been verified, but the code has not passed Quality Assurance, and to request that integration merge the fix into the base code.
89	Q/A to Technical Writing	Used to indicate that a documentation bug has been fixed, and is available for technical review.
90	Closed, Verified by Filer	Used to close a bug that has been fixed and verified .
91	Closed, Could Not Reproduce	Used to close a bug that development could not reproduce.
92	Closed, Not a Bug	Used to close a bug that was not a bug.
93	Closed, Not Verified by Filer	Used to close a bug that could not be verified by the bug filer.
94	Closed, Duplicate Enhancement	Used to close a bug that is a duplicate enhancement

Table A-2. *Continued*

Status	Description	Usage
95	Closed, Vendor OS Problem	Used to close a bug that is a vendor OS problem
96	Closed, Duplicate Bug	Used to close a bug that is a duplicate bug
97	Suggestion Rejected	Used to indicate that a suggestion has been rejected.
98	Suggestion Implemented	Used to indicate that a suggestion has been implemented.
99	Closed, Documentation Bug Fixed	Used to close a documentation bug.

Table A-3. *My Oracle Support Article IDs and Titles Ordered by Page Referenced in this Guide*

Article ID	Article Title	Page(s)
389422.1	Recommended Browsers for Oracle E-Business Suite Release 12	3
393931.1	Deploying Sun JRE (Native Plug-in) for Windows Clients in Oracle E-Business Suite Release 12	3, 176
384241.1	Using Forms Socket Mode with Oracle E-Business Suite Release 12	5
380489.1	Using Load-Balancers with Oracle E-Business Suite Release 12	9, 28
384248.1	Sharing The Application Tier File System in Oracle E-Business Suite Release 12	10, 162
380490.1	Oracle E-Business Suite R12 Configuration in a DMZ	13

Table A-3. *Continued*

Article ID	Article Title	Page(s)
380486.1	Installing and Configuring Web Cache 10g and Oracle E-Business Suite 12	13, 233
376700.1	Enabling SSL in Release 12	13
269293.1	Oracle Applications Tablespace Model FAQs	34
396009.1	Database Initialization Parameters for Oracle Applications Release 12	36, 175
174605.1	bde_chk_cbo.sql - EBS initialization parameters - Healthcheck	40
406982.1	Cloning Oracle Applications Release 12 with Rapid Clone	80, 81, 83
760772.1	Cloning Oracle Application 11i /R12 with Rapid Clone - Database (9i/10g/11g) Using Hot Backup on Open Database	81
459932.1	How To Set A Different "Test Email Address" For The Workflow Notification Without Connecting To OAM	83
215268.1	Implementing and Using the JSP Precompiler	97
437260.1	How to Change Applications R12 Passwords using Applications Schema Password Change Utility (FNDCPASS)?	102
601736.1	Utility /Script To Check The Techstack Component Versions (Forms, Http Server, JDK, Framework, Database, etc)	107, 111
368252.1	EBPERF FAQ - Collecting Statistics with Oracle Apps 11i	126
156968.1	coe_stats.sql - Automates CBO Stats Gathering using FND_STATS and Table sizes	128

Table A-3. *Continued*

Article ID	Article Title	Page(s)
144806.1	A Detailed Approach To Purging Oracle Workflow Runtime Data	131
846628.1	Interesting links about Applications Management Pack and Applications Change Management Pack for E-Business Suite	137, 191
459156.1	Oracle Applications Patching FAQ for Release 12	141, 149
145837.1	Latest Oracle HRMS Legislative Data Patch Available (HR Global / hrglobal)	159
856035.1	Oracle HRMS Support Newsletter July 2009	160
140511.1	How to Install HRMS Legislative Data Using Data Installer and hrglobal.drv	160
393861.1	Globalization Guide for Oracle Applications Release 12	162
252422.1	Requesting Translation Synchronization Patches	162
139684.1	Oracle Applications Current Patchset Comparison Utility - patchsets.sh	169, 170
454811.1	Upgrading to the Latest OracleAS 10g 10.1.3.x Patch Set in Oracle E-Business Suite Release 12	172
437878.1	Upgrading OracleAS 10g Forms and Reports in Oracle E-Business Suite Release 12	172
854428.1	Patch Set Updates for Oracle Products	175
418664.1	Overview of Using Java with Oracle E-Business Suite Release 12	176

Table A-3. *Continued*

Article ID	Article Title	Page(s)
209768.1	Database, FMW, EM Grid Control, and OCS Software Error Correction Support Policy	176
438652.1	R12: Forms Runtime Diagnostics (FRD), Tracing And Logging For Forms In Oracle Applications	184
224270.1	Trace Analyzer TRCANLZR - Interpreting Raw SQL Traces with Binds and/or Waits generated by EVENT 10046	187
453527.1	How To Trace a Concurrent Request And Generate TKPROF File	189
69565.1	A Holistic Approach to Performance Tuning Oracle Applications Systems	206
170524.1	How to Create a Custom Concurrent Manager	219
178925.1	How to change the sleep time for a Concurrent Manager	219
884046.1	Understand each field of AWR	221
842884.1	How To Understand AWR Report / Statspack Report	221
262687.1	How to use the Sql Tuning Advisor	228
259188.1	Oracle10g: Using SQLAccess Advisor (DBMS_ADVISOR) with the Automatic Workload Repository	229
798258.1	Oracle Applications Release Notes, Release 12.1.1	230
357597.1	How To Generate A SQL Trace In OA Framework For Oracle Applications	230
395445.1	Oracle Application Framework Profile Options Release 12	233

Table A-3. *Continued*

Article ID	Article Title	Page(s)
244040.1	Oracle E-Business Suite Recommended Performance Patches	235
763087.5	Tips for Finding Certifications	243
166650.1	Working Effectively With Global Customer Support	248, 249
733245.5	Service Requests	249
378287.1	Oracle ATG Newsletters Archive	253

Table A-4. *Listing of all Figures in this Guide*

Figure Caption	Page
Figure 1-1. Oracle Applications: A Basic, Three tier Physical Architecture	6
Figure 1-2. Oracle Applications: An Advanced Multi-node Physical Architecture	15
Figure 2-1. Concurrent Manager Definition Screen	30
Figure 2-2. <APPS_BASE> Application Tier Filesystem Layout	32
Figure 2-3. <INST_TOP_BASE> Application Tier Filesystem Layout	32
Figure 2-4. <APPS_BASE> Database Tier Filesystem Layout	35
Figure 2-5. Using OAM to edit the Applications context file	46
Figure 2-6. Example output from the AutoConfig Search Utility	48
Figure 2-7. Example output from an AutoConfig Check Config Report	53
Figure 2-8. Example output from an AutoConfig Performance Profile Report	55

Table A-4. *Continued*

Figure Caption	Page
Figure 2-9. OAM screen for adding custom parameters	57
Figure 3-1. Display of rapidwiz help option	64
Figure 3-2. Rapid Install: Installing the Database Technology Stack	66
Figure 3-3. Database Technology Stack Install: RDBMS Inputs Page	67
Figure 3-4. Database Technology Stack Install: Setup Verification Install Screen	67
Figure 3-5. Rapid Install: Installing the Applications Technology Stack	68
Figure 3-6. Applications Technology Stack Install: Enter the Applications Context File	69
Figure 3-7. Applications Technology Install: Define New Oracle Home Locations	69
Figure 3-8. Setup Verification Install Screen: Click Next to Continue the Applications Technology Installation	70
Figure 3-9. Oracle Applications Release 12.1.1 Rapid Install Wizard	71
Figure 3-10. Select Wizard Operation	71
Figure 3-11. Configuration Choice	72
Figure 3-12. Global System Settings	73
Figure 3-13. Database Node Configuration	74
Figure 3-14. Primary Applications Node Configuration	74
Figure 3-15. Primary Applications Node Configuration: Edit Services	75
Figure 3-16. Primary Applications Node Configuration: Edit Paths	75
Figure 3-17. Node Information: Add Server button	76

Table A-4. *Continued*

Figure Caption	Page
Figure 3-18. Rapid Install: System Checks Screen	77
Figure 3-19. Rapid Install: Validate System Configuration	77
Figure 4-1. Usage options for opmnctl	90
Figure 4-2. Status output for opmnctl	91
Figure 4-3. AD Administration Main Menu	92
Figure 4-4. OAM: Edit parameters	99
Figure 4-5. Modify configuration parameters for JSP recompliation	99
Figure 4-6. License Manager Home Page: License and Reports	101
Figure 4-7. Resetting an Applications user's password with the Define User functionality	103
Figure 4-8. About Page: Used to determine Technology Component Versions	107
Figure 4-9. Forms About dialog box showing Forms version information	109
Figure 4-10. Results of executing select statement against v$version	111
Figure 4-11. Results of executing select statement against dba_registry	111
Figure 5-1. Readme file for patch 9204440	143
Figure 5-2. Sample patch documentation spreadsheet	145
Figure 5-3. The Oracle Patch Application Assistant (PAA) Main Menu	146
Figure 5-4. AD Controller Main Menu	155
Figure 5-5. The DataInstall Main Menu	160
Figure 5-6. The DataInstall legislative data submenu	161
Figure 5-7. OAM Simple Search screen for patches	164
Figure 5-8. OAM Advanced Search screen for patches	165

Table A-4. *Continued*

Figure Caption	Page
Figure 5-9. Results from the Timing Reports	166
Figure 5-10. Patch Wizard Tasks menu	166
Figure 5-11. Scheduling options for patch analysis	167
Figure 5-12. Register Flagged Files menu	168
Figure 5-13. File History menu	169
Figure 5-14. Output from the patchsets.sh script	170
Figure 6-1. Using adapcctl.sh to display the HTTP Server status	183
Figure 6-2. Generating trace files for OA HTML Applications	185
Figure 6-3. Generating trace files for Forms	186
Figure 6-4. The Administer Concurrent Managers screen	188
Figure 6-5. Oracle Diagnostic Tests screen	191
Figure 6-6. Forms Network Test	200
Figure 7-1. Execution of top	209
Figure 7-2. Executing sar –u	210
Figure 7-3. Execution of sar –r	210
Figure 7-4. Server statistics displayed by vmstat	212
Figure 7-5. Summary of server statistics displayed by vmstat 3 5	212
Figure 7-6. Sorting processes by CPU with the ps command	212
Figure 7-7 Beginning of the AWR Report	221
Figure 7-8. AWR Report: Cache Sizes	221
Figure 7-9. AWR Report: Load Profile	222
Figure 7-10. AWR Report: Instance memory statistics	222
Figure 7-11. AWR Report: Top 5 Timed Foreground Events	223
Figure 7-12. AWR Report: Main Report	224
Figure 7-13. Information from ASH Report	226
Figure 7-14. Client System Analyzer	231

Table A-4. *Continued*

Figure Caption	Page
Figure 7-15. The Performance tab of Windows Task Manager	232
Figure 8-1. An example of My Oracle Support's Dashboard	239
Figure 8-2. An example of My Oracle Support's basic search	241
Figure 8-3. The Advanced Search Screen from My Oracle Support	242
Figure 8-4. The Find Certification Information region on My Oracle Support	243
Figure 8-5. The Advanced Search screen on My Oracle Support	244

Table A-5. *Listing of all Tables in this Guide*

Table Caption	Page
Table 2-1. Key Parameters in the DBC File	26
Table 2-2. Key Parameters in the httpd.conf File	27
Table 2-3. Key Parameters in the appsweb.cfg File	28
Table 2-4. Key Parameters in the CONTEXT_NAME.env File	31
Table 2-5. OATM Tablespaces	34
Table 2-6. Common Oracle Database Initialization Parameters for R12	37
Table 2-7. Recommended Settings for Oracle11gR1 and 11gR2 Database Initialization Parameters for R12	39
Table 2-8. Example Port Numbering Scheme	42
Table 2-9. Profile Options Available for Applications Password Security	58
Table 4-1. Database Tier Component Startup and Shutdown scripts	87
Table 4-2. Applications Component Startup and Shutdown Scripts	88

Table A-5. *Continued*

Table Caption	Page
Table 4-3. AD Administration Main Menu and Sub Menus	93
Table 4-4. Description and Values for <optional_args> with adrelink.sh	95
Table 4-5. [COMMAND] Parameter Options for ojspCompile.pl	98
Table 4-6. [ARGS] Parameter Options for ojspCompile.pl	98
Table 4-7. Parameters to use when executing Perl scripts with ADPERLPRG	108
Table 4-8. Parameters for chown	115
Table 4-9. Parameters for chmod	116
Table 4-10. Parameters for chmod	117
Table 4-11. Parameters for the tar Command	120
Table 4-12. Parameters for the lprm Command	124
Table 4-13. List of commonly used user related UNIX commands	125
Table 4-14. List of commonly used server related UNIX commands	125
Table 4-15. Location and description of Oracle Applications log files	133
Table 4-16. Layout of entries in crontab	136
Table 5-1. Commonly Used adpatch Options	149
Table 5-2. admrgpch Options	158
Table 7-1. CPU States as Displayed by top	208
Table 7-2. Memory as Displayed by top	208
Table 7-3. Swap as Displayed by top	208
Table 7-4. Columns and Descriptions for the sar -u Command	209
Table 7-5. Statistics Displayed by the sar -r Command	210
Table 7-6. Categories for the vmstat Command	211
Table 7-7. Key vmstat Statistics	211

Table A-5. *Continued*

Table Caption	Page
Table 7-8. Parameters for Forms Tuning Sessions	216
Table 7-9. Environment Variables Used to Tune the Cancel Query Feature	217
Table 7-10. Common AWR Views	220
Table 7-11. Common ADDM Views	225
Table 7-12. Additional Profile Options to Consider for Performance Tuning	233
Table A-1. Oracle Service Request Codes	257
Table A-2. Oracle Bug Codes	260
Table A-3. My Oracle Support Article IDs and Titles Ordered by Page Referenced in this Guide	266
Table A-4. Listing of all Figures in this Guide	270
Table A-5. Listing of all Tables in this Guide	274

Index

A

AD administration (adadmin), 91-96, 129, 148, 153
  log files, 92
  menu options, 92
AD Control (adctrl), 153-156
AD Merge utility (admrgpch), 157, 162
AD Patch or AutoPatch (adpatch)
  test mode, 152
  options, 149-150, 161
AD Relink (adrelink.sh), 95-96
AD Splicer (adsplice), to add products, 100
ADCRI, 195
ADDM, Automatic Database Diagnostic Monitoring, 195, 207, 219, 223-226
adident, using command, 105-106
admin scripts, execution of, 50, 87-89, 112-113, 183, 187
ADR, Automatic Diagnostic Repository, 11g diagnostic features, 195
APPL_TOP
  Unified, 1, 7, 9, 10
  Unified, definition of, 9
Application Tier, 3
Applications Context File, definition of, 18, 44
Applications Management Pack (AMP), 137, 179, 189, 191-192
Applications Tier Filesystem
  APPL_TOP, 9- 10, 17, 19-22, 32, 78, 88, 91, 92, 95, 108, 134, 145, 151, 153, 156, 162-164

APPS_BASE, 17, 19-25, 31-35, 79, 86-87
  ENV Files, 19, 25
  INST_TOP, 32, 50, 56
  PRODUCT_TOP, 21, 51, 54
ASH, Active Session History, 207, 219, 224-227, 235
AutoConfig
  adding customizations with OAM, 57
  backup files, location of, 52
  context files, 44
  customizing Applications configuration with, 55, 57
  executing, 48
  log files, location of, 52
  parallel execution, 51
  Performance Profiler, 54
  reviewing changes upon execution, 53
  Template Files for customization configuration, 18, 47, 55-56
  search utility, 47
  using, 47, 54
AWR, Automatic Workload Repository, 195, 207, 219

B

bde_chk_cbo.sql, usage for checking Database Initialization parameters, 40

Best Practices
    Architecture, 14
    Configuration, 60
    Installation and Cloning, 83
    Monitoring and Troubleshooting, 200
    Patching and Upgrading, 176
    Performance Tuning, 235
    Resources, 255
    Toolkit, 138

C

chmod, using command, 116
chown, using command, 114
Cloning
    details, 80
    post steps, 82
coe_stats.sql, for gathering database statistics, 128, 267
component,start/stop, 86-88, 130
Concurrent Manager
    monitoring, 187
    tuning, 218
    Work shifts, 29
Concurrent Processing
    defnition, 5
configuration files, location of, 23, 27, 31
context file, description, 44
CPU states, as displayed by UNIX top command, 208
CPU utilization, as displayed by UNIX sar command, 209-210
CPUs, Critical Patch Updates, 139, 140
crontab, usage for scheduling jobs, 86, 126, 129, 133, 135-136

D

database
    alert log, 39, 192, 195
    Listener log, 193
database
    initialization parameters, 18, 33, 36, 39-40, 150, 175

bde_chk_cbo.sql, checking, 40
    recommendations, 33, 36
    how to set, 36
Database Connection File(DBC), 25
database context file, definition of, 18, 45
Database Technology Stack, 33, 35
database, blocking sessions, 194, 230
database, removing sessions, 124
database,tuning, 219
DataInstall Java utility, hrglobal, 160
debugging, disabling, 198
df, using command, 119
Distributed AD, 11, 162
du, using command, 119

E

EM Grid Control
    Diagnostic Pack, 195,220,225,226
    Applications Management Pack, 137, 179, 189, 191, 192, 268
Enterprise Manager Grid Control, 126, 135, 137, 174, 179, 191, 195, 207, 213, 220, 225, 228-229
environment files, 19
External Web Servers for internet access, 12, 13

F

find, using command, 118
flexfields, recompiling, 93
FND_STATS package, 126-29
FNDCPASS, utility for changing application passwords, 102, 104
Forms Server, 2, 13, 28, 88-89, 216
Forms Services
    configuration of, 26
    definition, 4

G

Grid Control usage, 126, 135, 137, 174, 179, 191, 195, 207, 213, 220, 225, 228- 229

H

hrglobal
DataInstall Java utility, 160
hrglobal.drv, driver for legislative data, 151, 160
httpd.conf file, 27, 214

I

Installations, types of, 63, 65, 70-71,
installing, Oracle Applications Release 12, 70
invalid objects, compiling, 129
ipcs, using command, 121-123

J

Java cache, removing, 196
Java Development Kit (JDK), 139, 171, 173, 175-177, 215
Java Runtime Environment (JRE), 176
JSP, JavaServer Pages, 2, 97-99, 149
recompiling automatically, 98
recompiling manually, 97

L

legislative patches, for HR Payroll customers, 151, 159-161
load balancing Web and Forms, 8
log files
adadmin, location of, 92
Applications, location of, 133
AutoConfig, location of, 52
Database, location of, 192
Patching, location of, 153
Rapid Clone, location of, 82
Rapid Install, location of, 63, 78

rotating, 132
LOG_HOME
logfiles, centralized location of, 23
logrotate, using, 132-133
lprm, using command, 123, 124
lpstat, for controlling print jobs on UNIX, 123-124, 182

M

Maintenance Mode, enabling and disabling, 93, 148
Memory segments, finding and removing, 121-123
Mixed Platform Architecture, 1, 8, 11, 12, 15
Monitoring
Concurrent Manager, 187
database, 192
environment changes, 196
network, 198
server, 180
using OAM for, 190

N

netstat, using command, 44
network monitoring, 198-199
NLS Patches, 161

O

OC4J, Forms, oacore, oafm, 4
ojspCompile.pl, 97-98
opatch, patching utility for database and web servers, 130, 134, 172-174
OPMN, managing and monitoring components, 90-91
Oracle Application Manager (OAM)
editing context files, 46
for patching, 163
usages, 46, 55, 190
Oracle Application Server Web Cache, 1, 8, 13-14, 233
Oracle Applications Diagnostics Tool, 190

Oracle Applications Manager (OAM)
    using to monitor, 190
Oracle Applications Tablespace
    Model (OATM), 18, 33-34
Oracle Diagnostic Tests, 191
Oracle HTTP Server, configuration of,
    20, 27-28, 56, 184, 214
Oracle Patch Application Assistant,
    146-147, 272
OPMN, Oracle Process Manager, 4,
    24, 90
oralnst.loc file, managing, 174-175

P

Passwords
    changing APPS, 104
    changing Oracle user, 104
Patch Set Updates (PSU), 174-175
Patching
    Applications Patches, types of, 139
    Applications, 140, 151, 157-158, 162
    Best Practices, 176
    codeline, 141
    CPUs, 139-40
    database, 172
    hrglobal, 151, 159-161
    Log Files, 153
    maintenance mode, 93, 141, 147-
        149, 151
    NLS, 161
    OAM Features, 141
    Oracle Application Server, 172
    preparing to, 141
    reports, 141, 163, 165
    Technology Stack Components,
        139
patchsets.sh, patch comparison utility,
    141, 169, 170-171
performance tools, 207
Performance Tuning
    Apache, 214
    Concurrent Manager, 218
    Forms, 215-216
    JVM, 214
ping, using command, 121, 198
port
    checking port availibility, 44

numbering convention, 42
    using port pools, 41
Preventative Maintenance
    Applications patching cleanup, 134
    gathering statistics, 126-129
    purging and archiving data, 131
    purging concurrent requests, 130-
        131
    purging workflow history, 131
    recompiling invalid objects, 129
    removing $APPTMP content, 135
    removing opatch footprint, 134
    removing pre-upgrade binaries, 135
    rotating or removing logfiles, 132-
        134
    stopping/restartng Oracle HTTP
        Server, 130
print jobs, finding and removing, 123-
    124, 182
Profile values, monitoring application,
    82, 197
ps, using command, 208, 212
PSU – Patch Set Updates, 174-175,
purging data, 131

R

RAC - Oracle Real Application
    Clusters, 1, 7, 11
rapidwiz, Rapid Install
    install utility, 64-65, 68, 70, 78-79
    log files, location of, 63, 78
recompiling invalid objects, 197
recompiling JavaServer Pages, 86, 97
regenerating Forms, Libraries and
    Menus, 96
relinking application executables, 95-
    96

S

sar, using command, 209
scheduling tools, 86, 126, 129, 133, 135-
    136
Secure Sockets Layer (SSL)
    encryption, 8, 13

security
database password, 59
semaphores
finding and removing, 121-122
server availability, 121
server performance monitoring, 211
Service Level Agreement (SLA), 15
Service Request (SR), creating and
managing, 246
Shared Application Tier Filesystem,
definition of, 10, 31
spfile, 36
SQL Access Advisor, 228-229
SQL Tuning Advisor, 228-229
SQL Tuning Set, 229
Standard Manager, Concurrent
Manager, 5, 29, 218
start/stop scripts, 86-88, 130
statistics
gathering manually, 126-129
gathering with Concurrent
Requests, 128
STATISTICS_LEVEL, initialization
parameter, 225
support
My Oracle Support, 238
Oracle Collaborative Support, 249
System Activity Report (sar), using
command, 209
System Global Area (SGA), 226

T

Tablespace, Oracle Application
Tablespace Model (OATM), 18, 33-
34
tar, using command, 119
Tech Stack
Database, installation of, 65-66
for Applications, 68
for Database, 33, 38, 65-67, 78, 86-
87, 110, 112, 173
for Java, 4, 10, 19, 23-24, 27-28, 31,
56, 65, 68-69, 78, 90, 108, 115,
119, 132-133, 172, 184
for Tools, 24, 27, 29, 65, 68, 78, 88,
119, 133, 172, 184

installation of, 4, 10, 17, 19-24, 31,
68-69, 162, 172
template files for customized
configuration, 18, 47, 55-56
tkprof, using command to analyze
trace files, 186-187
top, using command, 208
trace files
concurrent requests, 189
generating for Forms, 185
generating for OA HTML, 184-185
tracert, using command, 198-199
trcanlzr - Trace Analyzer, 186-187
Tuning
Apache, 214
Concurrent Manager, 218
Database, 219
Forms, 215-216, 276
JVM, 214

U

Upgrading
database, 175
JDK, 176
Oracle Application Server, 172
Sun JRE Plug-in, 176
uptime, using command, 121
user tuning, Client System Analyzer,
230- 231

V

Versions
database, 110, 246
Applications component, 106-107
Forms, 109
HTTP Server, 108
Java class, 109
vmstat, using command, 121, 181, 207,
211-213

W

Web Node
as a component of E-Business
Suite, 3, 8, 9, 108

Web Server
  as a component of E-Business
    Suite, 12, 14, 89
Web Services
  configuration of, 26
  definition of, 4

Workflow history
  Purging, 130-131

X

X Windows, usage, 113

60675531R00171

Made in the USA
Lexington, KY
15 February 2017